# THE Q B

# THE QB

## THE MAKING OF MODERN QUARTERBACKS

BRUCE FELDMAN

CROWN ARCHETYPE
NEW YORK

Published in the United States by Crown Archetype, an imprint of the Crown Publishing Group, a division of Random House LLC, a Penguin Random House Company, New York. www.crownpublishing.com

Crown Archetype and colophon is a registered trademark of Random House LLC.

Library of Congress Cataloging-in-Publication Data

Feldman, Bruce.
  The QB : the making of modern quarterbacks / Bruce Feldman.
    pages cm
1. Quarterbacks (Football)—History.  I. Title.
GV951.3.F45 2014
796.332'25—dc23
                          2014027734

ISBN        978-0-553-41845-3
eBook ISBN 978-0-553-41846-0

Printed in the United States of America

Jacket design by Michael Nagin
Jacket photography by Hunter Martin/Getty Images

10 9 8 7 6 5 4 3 2 1

First Edition

*To Christie, Ben, and Riley*

# Contents

Prologue    ix

1: Tomorrow We Change the Game    1

2: Magic Men    29

3: The Pageant World for Boys    51

4: DQ    67

5: The QB Whisperer from Dime City    98

6: The Mad Scientist    116

7: QB Heaven    145

8: Manningland    172

9: Off Script    184

10: Grad School    212

11: The Comeback Route    242

12: The Draft    266

Epilogue    289

Acknowledgments    295

Index    297

## _ _ _ _ _Prologue

**I came up with the** idea for this book while listening to Trent Dilfer talk about quarterbacks during the 2013 NFL Draft. Dilfer wasn't simply analyzing the QBs; he was romanticizing their performances and detailing what they were responsible for, beyond merely sizing up who they were. More than anything, though, he was decoding and deciphering what a quarterback actually must do in ways I'd never heard anyone speak about football.

Everything in football, of course, operates through the quarterback, now more than ever in a game that went warp speed in the twentieth century, long after it lapped baseball in popularity and meaning in American society. Therefore, there is no position in all of sports that is quite like the quarterback. Not even close. Quarterback is not only sports' most complex position but the most important to a team's success, too. It's also the hardest to evaluate.

The riddle of that, however, was easy to demonstrate through the years: College and NFL teams repeatedly failed at a stunning rate in their evaluations of the QBs they selected, and it cost them millions of dollars in the process. In the twenty NFL Drafts prior to 2013, fifty quarterbacks were selected in the first round, and about 40 percent of them proved to be busts, while only six of those fifty ever started—

and won—a Super Bowl. The level of futility and development in the college game was equally eye-opening. The 2010 recruiting class was a reminder of that: Of the 31 QBs ranked as blue-chippers deemed four- or five-star prospects by the online recruiting analysts only four (13 percent) won starting jobs, while 22 bolted to try and play somewhere else (71 percent).

An entire industry had sprung up in the 2000s to nurture quarterbacks in an attempt to cash in on sports' ultimate lottery. For a while, private coaching was kind of a sketchy subculture in football. Former-UCLA-coach-turned-Pac-12-Network-analyst Rick Neuheisel told me it was "interesting to see how all these guys [private coaches] became gurus," and that it looked "greasy," but he also marveled at what an exploding arena it was.

"I have half a mind to jump in[to] it myself," he said, "but I don't wanna be one of those guys that is chasing these dads." Those "dads" he refers to are the fathers of the young QBs vying for elevated star status in the online recruiting world and for spots in the Elite 11 camp on the Nike campus in Oregon. The overweening fathers often muck up the process even more, though Steve Clarkson, the godfather of the now-booming private-coaching business, has made a cottage industry of courting the dads.

I knew that Dilfer, as the "head coach" of Elite 11, had become a part of that world. He had essentially been beta testing his research via Elite 11 the previous two years while programming the next generation of QBs through his TV show. What I didn't know was just how much more involved he was about to get.

He said he hadn't made one penny off his dive into the private-QB-coaching business. Never charged a parent anything for all the private coaching sessions he did on the side. In fact, he told me he'd probably lost about $250,000 the previous year on the QB-training business, if you factored in the money he'd paid out to his coaches for their expenses and the public-speaking opportunities he'd passed up.

When Dilfer and I first spoke about my book idea a couple of days after the draft, he explained that he was about to launch a new high-tech venture that he vowed would "change the game," starting at the grassroots level. In reality, the business—fueled by his connections, commentary, and ESPN bandwidth—would permeate football at its highest level, too; TDFB ["A Holistic Coaching Ecosystem That Unites Coaches & Expands Their Influence"] would take hold from the top of the game and work its way down as much as it would the other way around. It sounded intriguing. The game had already changed, but how, exactly, would Dilfer's new QB-training-and-evaluation model work? What would make it so different from what already was out there? How distinct would his version of QB Heaven be from the Mannings' version that Archie and his boys put on every summer down in Louisiana? What were the nuances that determined whether a quarterback shined or sank on game day? More specifically, what, exactly, was it that made Aaron Rodgers, a guy who had zero college scholarship offers out of high school, into a future Hall of Famer, or made Peyton Manning so unique? Better yet, why did so many lifelong football recruiters keep screwing up their evaluations of these guys? And, back to Neuheisel's point, what does a quarterback guru actually *do*?

Dilfer's presence in "this space," as he often calls it, was unlike that of the other football veterans in the private-QB-coaching business. He was already entrenched in the elite NFL culture, and through his TV work and his personal relationships with the big-name players and coaches, he had already established a new, multidimensional football lingo that had become a part of how they spoke. Common "Dilferisms" are "throwing the receiver open" or "playing off platform." Arm strength became the more qualified "arm talent," because arm strength merely spoke to how hard a guy could throw the ball, not whether he was also adept at feathering a pass over a linebacker and in front of a defensive back, too. A quarterback wasn't just "accurate" anymore. Instead, there were five different variations of accuracy, ranging from the basic "rhythm accuracy" to the more nuanced "second-reaction accuracy." By the time, I pitched the idea for *The QB*, I realized how so many of the key figures in the quarterbacking world were actually interconnected by one person or another. In Dilfer's vernacular these were the mapmakers of a very unique genre. Among them were a group of men, who, like Dilfer, were haunted by personal failures and shortcomings. They were the marketing whiz, the mad scientist, the QB Whisperer, the brain guy, the magic men, and the Mannings. At the core of it all was the debate whether elite QBs were a product of more nature than nurture.

For my recruiting book, *Meat Market,* I had a chance to go behind the scenes for a real inside-perspective at how the recruiting process actually works in big-time college football. With this book, I figured I would have a similar opportunity to explore the world of the QB in a way it had never been shown before by telling it through Dilfer, the tortured former Super Bowl–winning quarterback; one of his protégés, George Whitfield; and through Whitfield's protégé, Johnny Manziel, who had become the hottest commodity in football. The book would have exclusive access to all three, so the reader would be alongside Johnny Football, whether that meant he was in Dime City with Whitfield, assisting Dilfer's Elite 11 crew in Oregon mentoring high school quarterbacks ranked a lot higher than he ever was, or hunkered down in College Station with his Texas A&M coaches as he took the next steps in his development after becoming the first freshman to ever be awarded the Heisman Trophy.

Manziel had blossomed under the tutelage of Whitfield and the coaches at Texas A&M, who managed to polish the undersize quarterback's raw skills without bogging him down with so much that it'd hamstrung his rare improvisational wizardry. Such a balance can be tricky, where nature and nurture often collide. Exactly how does the twenty-year-old thrive in this setting, much less survive? It was a question that often bewildered his own coaches, but it got at some of the same vexing issues that had been tripping up NFL brass for decades.

As it turned out, the book would unfold in what proved to be the most significant year in QB development in the sport's history. Five-foot-ten-inch Russell Wilson became the shortest QB to lead his team to a Super Bowl title, forcing the NFL establishment to reexamine its own prejudice against shorter quarterbacks. And then, Manziel became the first sub-six-foot QB to get drafted in the first round (or even in the top two rounds) by an NFL team in sixty years. Another freshman QB, Jameis Winston—an Elite 11 product—won the Heisman and led Florida State to the national title. It was also a year in which

Whitfield, "the QB Whisperer," became a bonafide TV presence after ESPN hired him to become a regular on its high-wattage Saturday series *College GameDay,* and was the year that Tom House—the professorial biomechanics guy who saved Drew Brees's career—finally leapt into the quarterback development business by debuting his 3DQB brand after claiming he "fixed" Tim Tebow, and was the year when Steve Clarkson, the marketing whiz and the de facto godfather of the private QB coach business, was profiled by *60 Minutes* and the *New Yorker,* and appeared on *The Colbert Report,* ironically as a sub for Whitfield, who had to start up his NFL draft camp. Such was the reach of this new business.

# THE QB

# 1.

# TOMORROW WE CHANGE THE GAME

MAY 31, 2013.

One by one they each gazed up at—and then hurried past—the eight-foot-tall bronze statue of Woody Hayes, posed leaning slightly forward with his hands on his hips, standing in front of the Ohio State athletic center bearing his name. Few of the two dozen QB gurus arriving from all over the country for a 6:00 p.m. Friday meeting stopped to check out the Buckeyes' seven Heisman Trophies positioned in the lobby. Inside the 53,000-square-foot complex, past the trophy cases and all the framed mantras, they made a beeline for the Buckeyes' team room, where the far-flung coaches were assembling.

The room is part theater, part classroom. It is where Urban Meyer meets with his players. The Ohio State coach had handed over the Buckeyes' facilities for the weekend's Elite 11 Super Regional event—part of what's become the *American Idol* of quarterbacking. Starting with the high school Class of 2000, the Elite 11 "campetition" has produced, among other future first-round draft picks, Tim Tebow, Matthew Stafford, and Andrew Luck.

The evening's first speaker was Steve Stenstrom, a dark-haired, slender Stanford grad with the air of an aspiring senator. Few of the men seated around the room knew it, but the forty-one-year-old

Stenstrom, not John Elway or Andrew Luck, had been Stanford's all-time leading passer. Stenstrom had bounced around the NFL, playing for five teams in six seasons. For the past decade, he's headed a Christian outreach program for coaches and pro athletes.

Stenstrom thanked everyone for being on time, and then he expanded on his background. He has a wife. Four kids. He coaches his son's Pop Warner football team. He was brought there to Ohio State to be a part of the event by his friend Trent Dilfer, another former NFL quarterback. At Stanford, he had the privilege of playing for the legendary Bill Walsh. The ultimate coach, he said. But more than that, an innovator.

"Innovators change the landscape for the rest of us," Stenstrom told the room. "I love—*luuuuuve*—spending time with innovators. I just get excited being around them, because they're doing something on the cutting edge. They just see things differently. They're just wired that way, and they're being who they're supposed to be."

Stenstrom had grown close to Dilfer over the past few years, he said, from their weekly breakfasts together (both former NFL quarterbacks had retired to Northern California). Stenstrom compared the journeyman ex–NFL QB to the sainted Walsh.

"Trent's helping innovate the quarterback landscape for all of us," Stenstrom said. "And, in the context of this room, there's some pretty exciting stuff happening around the quarterback space."

As Stenstrom continued, it was apparent that in a room packed with former quarterbacks—ranging from career NFL backups to small-college starters—the night would be long on hope and hyperbole. The imagery all around the Ohio State athletic center reflected a similar, relentlessly positive, chest-up spirit. The signage on the wall right above the podium promoted a formula of sorts: BELIEVE> EXPECT>ATTITUDE>BEHAVIOR = PERFORMANCE.

Stenstrom's intro lasted seven minutes, but before he called up Dilfer to the podium, he left the group with a prediction.

"I believe in life there are three different kinds of days," he said. "Mundane days. Memorable days. And milestone days.

" 'Mundane' are most of our days. You've gotta go through the mundane to get to the memorable and the milestone days. Days, weeks later, you have no idea what you did on a mundane day. The memorable days are the ones you usually have to plan for and script a little bit, where you try to create a memory. But every once in a while, milestones happen. Those are the days, you're talking about 'em five, ten years down the road. I love when I get a sense that there might be a milestone day unfolding."

Stenstrom walked back to his seat to applause as his buddy took the front of the room.

The 6′4″, 250-pound Dilfer, with his shaved head and goatee, looked more like a middle linebacker than an old quarterback. His narrow eyes, often appearing to be squinting, to be sizing you up, ratcheted up his intense presence. He'd ended his fourteen-year NFL career and transitioned immediately into the broadcast booth, where he had emerged as a bigger star on TV than he ever was in the NFL—much the way that many of the best coaches weren't necessarily the best players. Dilfer knew enough to know what he hadn't known back when he was a player. He had become consumed by the successes and failings of the quarterback world.

More so than any other position in football and in all of pro sports, quarterback is an identity. Guys play first base or power forward. You don't *play* quarterback. You *are* a quarterback. The key element of being a quarterback is external, and that, too, is a big reason TV producers love Trent Dilfer. His blunt demeanor was honed by two decades spent trying to command rooms bubbling over with testosterone and cluttered with other alpha males. Rooms like the one we were in.

"What started as an idea is going to culminate tomorrow," Dilfer began matter-of-factly. "I promise you, what Steve said is true. Tomorrow will be a milestone day. Tomorrow," he continued as his voice rose, "the landscape of youth development and evaluation in the quarterback space changes forever. 'Cause once you do something like we're going to do tomorrow with the group of people in this room, you can't ever go back. Once you taste something so good, you don't want the thing that was good before the great thing.

"There's a couple of different conversations that we'll have tonight, but from my perspective, it's all one topic: It's getting the most from the least and the best from the best, because that's my passion."

Dilfer had been the front man for Elite 11 for almost three years. But he was more than just the on-air face of a reality TV show on ESPN. His vision for where "the quarterback space" could go was different from what any of his bosses could've imagined when they asked him to be involved two and a half years earlier.

The Elite 11 was created in 1999 by a former wide receiver at Cal as a nationwide search to find—and mentor—the best high school quarterbacks in the senior class. Andy Bark, the founder of the media company Student Sports, Inc., came up with the idea after observing a huge disparity in the quarterbacks who showed up for the football camps that SSI ran nationwide. Many top prospects were sons of former big-time quarterbacks or coaches, or had been coached by private tutors from the time they were toddlers. Bark's goal was to help the guys who might fall through the cracks. The man Trent Dilfer replaced as the Elite 11's lead instructor was sixty-something-year-old Bob Johnson, a crotchety, Orange County, California–based high school coach who had developed his former NFLer son, Rob Johnson, as well as Carson Palmer, Mark Sanchez, and two other QBs who made it to the NFL, Jordan Palmer and Steve Stenstrom. For a decade, Johnson's primary focus with the young quarterbacks had been leading on-field drills. Dilfer, though, would be much more invested in the process. There would be more film study, more technique, an NFL-based playbook to learn, and anything Dilfer or his associates could conjure up to test the quarterbacks' competitive souls. He even added a "high-performance psychology" coach who had trained six gold medalists in the 2012 Summer Olympic Games.

Dilfer was brought on when ESPN turned the Elite 11 into a reality TV show in 2011. *Elite 11*—for the first time in the thirteen-year history of the camp—would no longer mean only landing an invitation to Southern California. Instead, twenty-four quarterbacks were brought out to Pepperdine University to compete in front of ESPN's TV cameras and Dilfer's glare. Tears were shed—by Dilfer, who often would get choked up addressing his quarterbacks. Since then, *Elite 11* has tweaked its format (in 2013, eighteen quarterbacks were picked to compete on the reality show, and they were doing so in Beaverton, Oregon, home of the posh Nike campus) and has grown in scope and drama.

The show is a cross between *The Real World* and *Hard Knocks,* only starring seventeen-year-old jocks. College coaches privately try to pick Dilfer and his staff's brains for intel on kids they're recruiting.

"When Andy asked me to take this thing over, it was already best-in-class," Dilfer told the QB coaches. "There's no doubt, the Elite 11 [camp] was best-in-class, but it had to be best-in-class *and* a TV show, and that's not easy. It could not lose its authenticity. There's people in this room who, two months into it, thought I was off my rocker, and I know who you are. They said, 'You're gonna get us all fired. It's crazy, what you're trying to do.' But I kept pushing the envelope. I knew the player wanted more. I knew the coach wanted more. I knew the audience wanted more.

"What's happened over time is, what started as a camp has now become a cult. We're making a change with the kids, and to me, that's good. I settled for 'good' as a player. I was just good. Never great.

"Good," Dilfer repeated, with a tinge of disgust.

"I am *not* going to settle for good with this. We're going to be great. It is going to be great. We're gonna take it to the community. At some point this is going to be a thirteen-week series. At some point this is going to be the second-biggest amateur sporting event in the country next to the Olympics. That's where we're going, but to do that, you have to start building internally."

Over the past few years, while he's traveled the country working with young QBs, Dilfer and his staff also have been scouting private quarterback coaches.

Several of the men seated around the room were former NFL backups who had noted the "quarterback guru" boom and decided to put up their own shingles.

It was a niche business that had become a cottage industry catering to wealthy parents hoping that, with the right tutoring (at some $200 an hour), their sons could be the next Tom Brady. Or at least earn a $200,000 scholarship and be BMOC.

The guy sitting right in front of Dilfer in the middle of the first

row, twenty-seven-year-old Hunter Cantwell, spent three seasons in
the NFL before being cut in 2011. Just ten feet from him was George
Whitfield Jr., a San Diego man who once tightened up Cantwell's
mechanics and has since groomed everyone from Ben Roethlisberger
to Cam Newton to Andrew Luck and been labeled by *Sports Illustrated* as "the Quarterback Whisperer." From Ohio, Whitfield would
fly down to Texas to work with his newest star protégé, Texas A&M's
Johnny Manziel, the 2012 Heisman Trophy winner. Behind Whitfield was Craig Nall, a Dallas-based coach who'd spent five seasons as
Brett Favre's understudy with the Green Bay Packers.

Dilfer's idea: to unify those coaches into his system, which was
geared toward showing a quarterback a lot more than just how to
throw a tight spiral.

The QB-guru biz has been around for decades. Dilfer, though,
was the first guy who ever tried to franchise it. And he had the ca-
chet, the resources, and the platform of *Elite 11*—and ESPN—to try
to make it happen. His vision would become a reality in a little more
than twelve hours. Its name: TDFB.

Billed as a "holistic coaching ecosystem that unites coaches &
expands their influence," TDFB's rollout was doubling as Elite 11's
Super Regional at Ohio State. In addition to all the QB coaches in
the room were: longtime NFL coach Norv Turner and his son, Scott,
a wide receivers coach with the Cleveland Browns; the creators of
eCoachSports, a video-analysis software system that conferences via
camera, player, and tutor; the creator of Axon Sports, a high-tech,
brain-training system geared to help quarterbacks process coverages
faster; and Axon's performance specialist, Joe Germaine, a former
Buckeye and NFL QB who was the 1997 Rose Bowl MVP.

"Tomorrow's gonna be epic," Dilfer said. "It's gonna be epic, because at the end of the day, the person who benefits the most is the kid.

"I don't know if all of you totally get this. QB isn't just the most
important position in sports, but, ultimately, it's also the most influential position in sports. What the dude with the ball does affects the
lady in the office across the hall. It affects everybody. We're talking
about influencing the next generation of influencers. Tomorrow, we
change the game."

• • •

THE COACHES WEREN'T THE only ones who had traveled long distances with big aspirations for the weekend at Ohio State. Brandon Harris and his family had driven almost a thousand miles from their home in Bossier City, Louisiana, to get to Columbus. Football experts in the Bayou State regarded Harris, at the time a 6′3″, 180-pound junior at Parkway High School, as the most gifted QB prospect Louisiana had produced in more than a decade. The Internet recruiting analysts from Rivals.com, ESPN, and 247Sports each regarded Harris as one of the top five quarterbacks in the Class of 2014.

Two months earlier, Harris had gone to the Elite 11 regional at the Dallas Cowboys practice facility and, by his own admission, struggled. The drills he was put through by the Elite 11 staff were new to him, he said. Harris graded his performance as a C. Harris, though, was optimistic that that weekend he'd earn a spot to the nationally televised Elite 11 finals.

Harris acknowledged that the status of being anointed "an Elite 11 Quarterback," given its history and exposure—and the fact that so many fans, especially on Twitter, gauge your worth by it—mattered to him. Truth be told, such things—such as whether a kid is ranked as a "five-star" or a "two-star"—are a big deal to most high schoolers, even if some are reluctant to admit it. Then again, the number of one's Twitter followers often has meaning to people twice Harris's age.

Regardless, Harris wasn't lacking for college scholarship offers. LSU, Texas A&M, and Ohio State were among the powerhouses in pursuit. The home-state Tigers waited until after they observed Harris throw during spring practice before offering him.

"[LSU offensive coordinator and former NFL coach] Cam Cameron told me afterward that he's been out to see four quarterbacks now, and I was the best of the group," Harris had told reporters earlier in the spring. "He thinks I've got big-time NFL potential."

Harris had arrived a day early in Columbus for an "unofficial" Ohio State visit. He was hosted by Urban Meyer and Buckeyes offensive coordinator Tom Herman.

"Coach Meyer said he really wants me to be the quarterback at Ohio State," said Harris.

Turned out, Meyer wouldn't be the only big-time college head coach Harris saw on the trip to Ohio State. LSU head coach Les Miles and his assistant, Cam Cameron, made the trek to Columbus for Elite 11, too. Even though college coaches are not allowed by NCAA rules to attend any such camps, both Tigers coaches were in the clear, since their sons, Manny (Miles) and Danny (Cameron), a pair of high school sophomores in Baton Rouge, also were taking part in the Elite 11.

The Elite 11 staff was curious to see how Brandon Harris performed. There were no doubts about his arm strength or his athleticism, although the staff wanted to see more polish on his passing skills instead of his being a "one-pitch pitcher," relying on his fastball.

"The big concern with him is about his mental makeup," said one of the coaches. "When we saw him in Dallas, he kept telling people how he'd never really been coached before. Like, he was using the same excuse, the same crutch, on people. He sounded rehearsed. You wonder if he's the guy who makes excuses when the chips are all on the table and things aren't going right. You wonder how he'd carry a locker room. Will kids see right through him?"

The critique, the kind you might hear an NFL scout offering his bosses while sizing up a college prospect, underscored how much the Elite 11 process had changed under Trent Dilfer. Before he took over, the selection process was largely reduced to rounding up the kids with the most recruiting buzz. Dilfer incorporated "war room" settings as part of the Elite 11 and its reality show, where the head coach (Dilfer) and his staff debated the merits of each QB. This can be a tricky proposition, given how many different schemes high school teams use and the wide variance in the level of the competition they play against. Or how good the coaching these kids have had.

THE LIST OF QUARTERBACKS who auditioned for the Elite 11 and didn't make it over the past decade is as impressive as the group that did. Robert Griffin III, Colin Kaepernick, and Johnny Manziel all tried out for it but didn't get selected—although Dilfer and his staff factor in anyone who went through an Elite 11 workout as part of their history. The Elite 11's pedigree that Dilfer rattled off is heady stuff: 71 percent of the NFL's quarterbacks in 2012 came through the Elite 11 process, including six of the past seven Heisman Trophy winners and five of the last seven number one overall picks in the NFL draft.

After a forty-five-minute dinner break, members of the TDFB brass addressed the room and threw more staggering numbers at the QB coaches. However, this data didn't relate to the past but more toward the opportunity in front of the folks in attendance.

Stenstrom returned to the podium to hammer home the TDFB landscape. One of the slides he put up on a big screen read, "Across all sports, coaching is a $5.9-*billion* industry," a stat that drew a few "oohs" from the room. He also noted that "75 percent" of coaches below the high school level coach because of availability, not ability.

"That is staggering," he said. "They're not bringing expertise. You guys can tell 'em how to coach. You can get them ready and school 'em up."

Taylor Holiday, a former minor league baseball player, was handling the marketing side of TDFB and the Elite 11. "We're gonna generate five million impressions in the next forty-eight hours," he said, throwing out a projection that seemed unwieldy for a group of private contractors, many of whom didn't even have websites. Still . . . "generate . . . five million . . . forty-eight hours." Sounded big.

Rick Hempel, an old IBMer, said he'd sold a golf-simulator company he'd built for $100 million. His new company, eCoach, was a TDFB partner. Hempel had seen the potential for his new venture after sending his fourteen-year-old son to a football camp. The week had cost Hempel $695. His kid loved it, but the downside: there was no follow-up with the instructors.

"A lot of business opportunities [have] been left on the table," he told the coaches. "Now you can *tether* to them."

Aside from Trent Dilfer, the speaker who did the best job of captivating the crowd was Jason Sada, the president of Axon Sports, a company billing itself as "the leader in athletic brain training." Sada's example of a person driving the same route so often, their mind seems to slip into autopilot mode to the point where they barely recall the act of driving, resonated with many of the coaches. Sada later evoked author Malcolm Gladwell's ten-thousand-hour rule. In Gladwell's *New York Times* best seller *Outliers,* he wrote that ten thousand hours of practice in your dedicated field is sufficient to be at your peak, citing the Beatles and Bill Gates as examples for his "Ten thousand hours is the magic number for greatness" claim.

Operating off a similar principle, Sada and his colleague Joe Germaine, the former star Ohio State Buckeyes QB from the mid-'90s, showed the coaches a large video screen that flashed defensive alignments and coverages for a quarterback to identify and diagnose in rapid-fire sequencing.

"You can get ten thousand reps without subjecting your body to wear and tear," Germaine said, adding that many top NFL quarterbacks had trained on Axon Sports products at their headquarters in Arizona.

"Guys," Dilfer said, "this is really, really cool stuff right here."

What wasn't offered over the course of the four-plus-hour meeting were some other sobering stats about the quarterback world: that in the twenty NFL Drafts prior to 2013, fifty quarterbacks had been selected in the first round, and about 40 percent of them proved to be busts, while only six of those fifty ever started—and won—a Super Bowl: Joe Flacco, Aaron Rodgers, Ben Roethlisberger, Eli Manning, Peyton Manning, and Trent Dilfer. Or that since 1990, there'd been twenty-seven QBs selected among the top five picks of the draft, and only six of those quarterbacks made it to more than two Pro Bowls.

His Super Bowl ring notwithstanding, Dilfer was haunted by stats of quarterbacking futility. He spoke a lot about being on a "journey" that had begun late in his playing career, in 2006, his thirteenth year in the NFL—seven years after he won a Super Bowl with the Baltimore Ravens. He'd looked at Brett Favre and kept asking himself, "Why did he end up great, and I ended up average?"

Dilfer, despite being 6'5", 225 pounds in high school, probably wouldn't have gotten a sniff from the Elite 11 people if it were around in his day. Or at least he wouldn't have in its earlier format. Dilfer played in an option offense in Northern California, where he only threw about ten passes a game. Oregon and Colorado State wanted him as a tight end, but the coaches at Fresno State were intrigued by his arm and his athleticism.

Dilfer blossomed at Fresno, leading the nation in passing efficiency in his junior season. He opted to leave early for the NFL and was selected number six overall in the 1994 draft by the Tampa Bay Buccaneers. He made it to one Pro Bowl, in 1997, but ended his career having thrown more interceptions (129) than touchdowns (113).

"I was so disappointed in my career," Dilfer told the coaches. "You get late in your career, and you go, 'Man, I wish I would've done it differently.' And, a lot of the 'Man, I wish I would've done it differently' circled back to knowledge. In 2006, I said I'm gonna go on this journey to figure out all this stuff that I don't know, from the X's and O's side but especially the developmental side."

Dilfer came to the conclusion that many of the shortcomings of NFL quarterbacks, including his own, were rooted in a perspective that was flawed from the inside, where people, QBs included, got hung up on the wrong things. The young players and the young fans were growing up with a truly false perception of what made great quarterbacks great and how to appreciate very good quarterback play when they saw it, he told me days before heading to Ohio State. "I know this because I bought into it for the first half of my career."

Dilfer tried to hammer home that point to his new protégés in Columbus.

"It's the most influential position in sports and probably the most poorly evaluated position, too," he said. "People dumb it down by using height, weight, arm strength, and a forty. That is how the majority of America has dumbed down the evaluation of the quarterback position. Well, everybody in this room who's played knows your soul has more to do with your success than your arm strength. Your ability to '*chunk*' and process large amounts of information in real time is probably more important than how quick your feet are. How about your ability to walk into a room and everybody in there feels your presence? How about when you're 1–4, and you're getting booed out of the stadium—I've had binoculars thrown at me as I've walked out of the stadium—how do you handle those situations? To me, those things are bigger than a lot of stuff that we've dumbed down the evaluation of the quarterback to.

"To me, it's QBA—Quarterbacking Architecture. We're going to build better quarterbacks, so it'd better start with their soul. The essence of who that person is—their competitive disposition."

Dilfer described himself as a onetime "high-ceiling" guy who had all-world talent, but he said that by the time he was about thirty years old, he'd been reduced to a "game manager." Or, worse still, a guy who played *to not* make a mistake, instead of making a play.

"The QB position had been minimized by many of my coaches," he said, "and my aggressiveness and intuitive feel for the position had been stripped away by years of 'Don't screw it up,' negative-reinforcement coaching."

Dilfer has often said he believes in "nurture" over "nature." Maybe that goes back to the optimistic bent he derived from being a quarterback all his life. That doesn't mean he buys that anyone can be developed, even with the best coaching, to become the next Aaron Rodgers, but he's convinced his group will create better QBs and better people. It's part of what he's getting at when he signs off on all his e-mails to his TDFB disciples with the tag "Coaching beyond the X's and O's." That's why every coach who becomes part of TDFB, even if they were an NFL starter, has to get certified by Trent Dilfer.

"The accreditation process isn't so we can put a stamp on you," Dilfer told the coaches. "It's to give you tools. There's a lot of opportunities to make a lot of money and have a lot of influence. This is a thirteen-year study. And when I say I've geeked out on quarterbacks, it's kinda pathetic. This is, at three o'clock in the morning, watching Tom Brady's, Aaron Rodgers's, and Philip Rivers's fourth step on a five-step rhythm drop and trying to find a commonality. This is going into the mental side of the game and spending hours and hours with the greatest human-performance coaches in the world. Reading books. Studying the mind. Studying the soul. All built around the quarterback."

One of the biggest criticisms of the private-QB-coach business is that most of the drills the players work on don't translate to the game on the field. That's a pet peeve of Dilfer's, too.

"I don't want any driving-range quarterbacks," he said. "I don't want grass basketball. Nothing pisses me off more than when one of our critics says we're making them good 'camp quarterbacks.' That's why every one of those stations has been thought out for hours about how it's transferable to a gamelike situation.

"Everybody in this room is good enough to pick some slappo off the street and teach him how to take a five[-step drop] and throw a hook. We can throw square-outs out the yin-yang. That's easy. It's hard to create environments that are transferrable to real football. That's what we're gonna do."

Dilfer said he had "home-schooled" himself on the nuances of elite quarterbacking by studying every Hall of Famer who had been inducted since the Class of 1983, a range that stretched from Joe Namath to Dan Marino to John Elway to Steve Young. His focus was to pull out any commonalities he could find. He realized that the Hall was full of slow-footed guys and guys who didn't have elite arms. The one thing every quarterback *had* was the knack for creating space and somehow extending the play.

"You have to have that, 'cause Norv [Turner] can only dial up the perfect play on rhythm so many times," he said. "At some point, you have to play beyond the X's and O's. Those are the athletic traits we want to identify as evaluators and train as coaches."

The bulk of quarterback training to date had entailed the science of repetition, Dilfer maintained. "We've had a community of guys who have gotten really good at being bad," he said. "I was one of them. I was never really on balance. I was one of the first guys to learn the high right elbow—the 'shelf.' Tight trap.

"You can get good at being bad if you rep it enough. Why not get good at being good? I'm not claiming that I know it all, by any stretch of the imagination. There's a lot of effective ways you can train a quarterback."

Being on balance is paramount for a quarterback, Dilfer's research showed. He looked for the most common posture that creates balance. What he found really opened his eyes. He realized that a wider base with evenly distributed weight was consistent in all of the players he studied. He also learned that the upper body posture and ball carriage had a pivotal role in creating the optimum passing platform, which was totally contradictory to what he—and most QB's—had been taught.

"Watch the elbows of every one of these elite NFL quarterbacks as they carry the ball. The elbows are actually pointing more down than out, and the ball is resting against the body, not away from it. Every one. There is not an exception. Why? Because raising the ball away from your chest or pointing your elbows out locks your trap. If your trap is engaged and locked, it adds tension to your forearm, and that adds tension to your hand. If you have tension in your hand, you can't consistently spin the ball.

"I lived it, guys. Elbows pointing down relaxes your traps, forearms, and grip, and also unlocks your lower half. Elbows out and the ball pushed up creates tension in the traps and tension in the upper half locks the body up—both lower and upper body. That decreases speed and functionality and makes it so much more difficult to spin the ball naturally and get more velocity!"

As Dilfer worked his clicker, slowing down video of Aaron Rodgers, Drew Brees, and other active NFL star QBs to reinforce his points, chins dropped around the room, and pens jotted down notes into binders. Dilfer tapped the Pause button at the beginning of a Denver Broncos highlight.

"Look at the base," he said. "When Peyton Manning came out [of college], he was notorious for being narrow in his base. He was on his toes and very narrow. He's on the Mount Rushmore of quarterbacks, and in his fifteenth year, his biggest point of emphasis was getting wider, because he's bought into the biomechanics that wider is better."

From a shot of the 6'5" Manning, one of the tallest quarterbacks in the NFL, the tape moved on to a Seattle Seahawks game and the shortest QB in the league.

"Russell Wilson is 5'10¾". You'd think he would want to play tall.

"We don't play tall in the pocket.

"We play strong in the pocket.

"On the top of his drop, he's probably 5'7", but he understands that's how he needs to play to maximize energy in his body."

Whether it was Rodgers, Brees, Manning, or Wilson, Dilfer showed clip after clip of quarterbacks making throws with all their cleats in the ground.

"We don't play on our toes," he said. "The guys who generate the most ball speed are the ones who generate the most ground force."

Many of the beliefs Trent Dilfer now holds are contrary to what he and most other quarterbacks were taught. He now believes the essential aspect of a quarterback's being able to fire a tight spiral comes from the player's wrist load. He credits former-Major-League-pitcher-turned-biomechanics-whiz Tom House for helping reshape his perspective, his lexicon, and for opening his eyes to the science of throwing.

"I never understood this until I started studying about how you load the ball as it goes back," Dilfer said. "It's amazing how consistent it is, and when you look at guys who struggle with accuracy, they don't do this. 'Opposite-equals' is a position that every great passer gets to. And when the hands separate, you have elbow-wrist association where your opposite wrists are at equal height. Every great quarterback gets there. It happens on foot strike. With the great golfers, their bodies are moving at the same speed as their core, and all that energy is being transferred out to the ball. Whether it's tennis, throwing a football, [or] hitting a golf ball, you have to be matched up.

"There's elbow-wrist association, and the new term is 'opposite-equal-foot-strike.' It's important to understand this."

He flipped through play after play before pressing Pause on the moment before the ball was unloaded. "Here's Matt Ryan, elbow-wrist . . . Drew Brees, elbow-wrist . . . Aaron Rodgers, elbow-wrist. It doesn't change. Every dude gets in[to] that position."

Another phrase Dilfer harped on was "hip-shoulder disassociation."

"I'm probably the only guy in this room—and the only guy on the planet—who believes that this [motioning to his shoulders] is more important than this [motioning to his legs]. Don't get me wrong.

I think you should train your feet up the yin-yang. But I think this," Dilfer said, motioning to his upper body, "tells this [motioning to his lower body] what to do.

"We've built a bunch of quarterbacks who need perfect environments. They can go back and crow-hop into a hook. They can do it in a camp setting beautifully. But then in the game, the quarterback goes back, and the guard gets beat[en]."

COACH: Well, the hook's wide open.
QB: Yeah, but, Coach, I had to step to my left.
COACH: So?

"I believe you train from the waist up," Dilfer continued, "and the waist down will follow. And the reason I came to this conclusion is all of this geeking out, watching film, and seeing that the best dudes in the league, their feet aren't right the majority of the time. A lot of times they don't have to be."

Aaron Rodgers, the Green Bay Packers star who didn't have a single scholarship offer when he came out of high school, was featured more than any other quarterback in Dilfer's tutorial. Rodgers's penchant for being able to deftly zing passes into narrow spaces while throwing against his body or seemingly out of position from his body's alignment left many of the coaches in awe. On one play, which was used as a prime example of his "hip-shoulder disassociation" premise, Dilfer paused the tape before polling the coaches on where they expected the ball to be thrown, given Rodgers's contorted posture. Most noted the positioning of his lower body and assumed the QB was throwing to his left. Instead, the ball zipped to the right—an unlikely direction, given his body angle.

"Wow," sighed one of the coaches as he marveled at what the Pro Bowler did.

"Oh, and, by the way, I don't wanna hear the argument," Dilfer said, "that *this guy* [Rodgers] is just more talented than the rest. I worked out with him for two straight years in the middle of my career, when I was still pretty damn talented. He was good—not great. He was fiercely competitive, though, and he wanted to be the best and was willing to learn anything. So, his body developed, and he thought outside the box in terms of his development. He watched number four [Brett Favre] closely and pushed his body and his mechanics to the limits, and now he is a made man. *This guy* is the perfect example of what can happen when you never stop developing. You're not what you were when you came out of college, or at least you don't have to be."

The night's entire presentation lasted almost four hours, an hour more than Dilfer had envisioned and about two more than the other guys had expected. A few of the coaches later admitted they thought that the forty-five-minute *intro* prior to dinner was what they had come for, not a whole evening's dissertation. Before the crew dispersed to check out the local bar scene, Dilfer closed with another pep talk.

"I miss the team," Dilfer said, and he started getting choked up. "You miss climbing the mountains. You miss failing. You miss the rawness of every day being a battle. We built TDFB using Elite 11 as a launching point, and [we used] all the cool stuff you saw tonight to build a team.

"I'm done with turf wars! I'm done with you guys worrying about a client here and a client there. It's bigger than that! I'm giving you Calvin Johnson as your receiver, Walter Jones as your left tackle, and Peyton Manning as your quarterback. I'll give you every tool you could possibly have to be successful, but it's gonna be a team. And when you're a team, it's team above self. Do you want to be part of this, and you'd be foolish not to—that's the perspective. My expectations will be exceedingly high. I'm giving you the tools. Let's go kill it. It starts tomorrow."

EVERYBODY IN RECRUITING LIES. The college coaches. The high school coaches. The kids do, too. It's an odd game of liar's poker that often plays out online with thousands of fans watching it unfold. Trent Dilfer had been lied to, also, he told the hundreds of parents his staff rounded up a half hour before the Saturday workout started. (Dilfer's eldest daughter, Maddie, was a high school volleyball star being recruited by college coaches. She committed to play volleyball at Notre Dame.) Dilfer made two promises to the parents about their young quarterbacks.

"First, he will leave here better than when he showed up, and second, we will tell you the truth," Dilfer said. "We won't lie to you."

One hundred and six quarterbacks from thirty-one states had signed in. Thirty-one QB coaches—"thirty-one of the best quarterback coaches in the world," Dilfer said, pausing a few breaths to let that math sink in. "One of those coaches is gonna know your kid intimately," Dilfer added. "These guys aren't making any money. Thirty-one guys here, and all they get is their travel paid for. I know you've made a great investment. So have we. It's kid-centric.

"I gotta get to eighteen quarterbacks. I have thirteen spots left. Maybe four, five, or six will come from this group. The goal for you guys and your kid is to get better today with more tools in the tool kit.

"We're looking for 'Dude Qualities.' Who's the 'Dude'? We're looking for the 'Dude.'"

Most of Dilfer's comments for the twenty minutes of his intro talk to the parents met with nodding or smiling or laughing. "Who's the Dude?," though, left them looking puzzled. He ran through all of TDFB's new features, even the forty-foot trailer parked outside "with some really ugly bald guy [himself] on it."

"It's groundbreaking. We're changing the game today [with] eCoach. Off-line is the traditional model for coaching: fields, classrooms. We're changing it for a new brand of coach. You'll have access to these guys three[hundred and]-sixty-five [days a year]. Virtually. The eCoachSports model is to connect the kid to the coach in a virtual relationship. We can do video motion analysis. We're opening our book to you and saying, 'Take it!' We're opening it to college coaches and saying, 'Take it!' Axon Sports is here, too. They're a worldwide leader in cognitive training. I could only throw so many square-outs, but I could sit in a lab and look at a fifty-inch screen and go through the same rep and have it applicable to the field. Get to the finals, and they'll have five days of working in an Axon lab. The edge of uncomfortable is where you find greatness."

Before the "campetition" started, Dilfer introduced two of his coaches: George Whitfield, "the biggest rock star in the quarterback-development space," and Jordan Palmer, an active NFL QB who had been around the Elite 11 so many years, he actually began as a preteen ball boy. Ninety minutes earlier, in a neon yellow long-sleeved shirt, Palmer was working up a sweat, going through many of the same drills the high schoolers would do. Craig Nall, the former Green Bay Packers backup—with a GoPro mini cam rigged to his shoulder— shouted encouragement, as did a handful of the other TDFB coaches, while the twenty-nine-year-old kept his quarterbacking skills sharp. In five days Palmer—the younger, less heralded brother of 2003 Heisman Trophy–winner Carson Palmer—had an audition with the Chicago Bears in hopes of getting an invitation to their training camp.

Palmer got a close-up on the life of a blue-chip quarterback from observing how his big brother handled everything. He also had the perspective of being the guy passed over for many of the other hyped QB prodigies. He never got invited to the Elite 11. At least not as a camper. He was a ball boy, a receiver, and even when he was in college as the starter at UTEP, he was a counselor. Palmer without hesitation can rattle off the names of all the Elite 11 QBs who got invited the year he didn't. He can also tell you how far each of them got in football. (Six of them never even threw one NFL pass, and only one of the eleven quarterbacks he was passed over for, career backup Drew Stanton, has had as long a pro career as Palmer.) Some of the other TDFB staffers joked that Jordan Palmer seemed as if he could be Trent Dilfer's kid brother as much as Carson Palmer's.

The younger Palmer's message to the parents took on a more nuanced tone.

"I think the worst thing your kids can do and you guys can do is put importance on the stars," Palmer said, referencing the online recruiting analysts' evaluation scale, ranging from elite college prospects—"five-stars"—to mediocre—"one-star."

"The biggest problem that you get as an athlete is not about where you came from or if you come from a single-parent home; it's about growing up with a sense of entitlement. 'I can't believe these people are making me wait in line. Don't they know who I am?' You start drilling that into their head, and endorsing that—it's the worst thing that you can do. Best thing my dad ever said to me was, 'Don't tell me. Show me.' "

Palmer reinforced that message with a story about his famous brother. On the day the elder Palmer signed his $126-million contract, Jordan and the rest of the family were in his house waiting to celebrate. "We had the champagne ready, and then he gets up and leaves. He went back into his office to study the playbook. I said, 'Hang on, you can't take one night off?' He said, 'No, I gotta go earn it.' "

NERVES OFTEN ARE THE toughest competition for young QBs. There are no helmets or pads at the Elite 11. No scoreboards, either. Just a lot of eyeballs watching, and for dozens of teenage boys looking to either make a rep or uphold one, that can be as unnerving as any high school game they'll play in. Making matters worse, the wind in Columbus was crackling. That only prompted the young quarterbacks to try to fire the ball that much harder.

Brandon Harris was one of the few quarterbacks who didn't seem the least bit bothered by the wind. His tight spiral knifed through, whereas the other QBs in his group—all kids with major college offers—sprayed tail-draggers all over the field. Harris's athleticism was eye-catching. So was his lack of fundamentals. At one point, after observing Harris wheel around, swinging the ball in one arm while pirouetting past two guys swatting at him with big black pads, Palmer called him over to show him some ball security measures— namely, to keep two hands on the ball in those situations. Harris nodded and made the correction on his next rep. Over to the side, the Louisiana native had drawn an audience. Even though their sons were in groups fifty yards away, Les Miles and Cam Cameron had wandered over to take a look at Brandon Harris and his group.

Harris, though, hadn't yet been awarded a golden Elite 11 ticket to the season-end event on the Nike campus in Oregon. Instead, De-Shone Kizer, an honor student from Toledo, Ohio, got an invite with all the QBs gathered around Dilfer.

"I'm not concerned that I didn't get picked yet," Harris said twenty minutes after the announcement. "I'm pretty sure I'm gonna get invited. I worked hard. I came out here and got better, and that's the only deal that I was focused on today.

"Trent and the staff know talent when they see it. They gave out one to DeShone. He had a great day, honestly. Trent's got six more. I can name you about fifteen guys off the top of my head who were good out here today. They grade off different things. Maybe DeShone did better things after a bad throw or something like that. Give him all the credit. If I get invited, great. If I don't, it's not gonna make me or break me. It's not gonna make it to where a school's gonna say, 'Hey, we're not gonna take you because you didn't get invited [to the Elite 11]. They don't care about that stuff. Not bashing a camp. It's just about you getting better and trying to get all this stuff together, and I know that's what Trent and the [others] are trying to work on."

Asked if he'd ever had any private coaching, Harris shook his head.

"None," he said, smiling. "I don't know about these other guys, but I haven't at all." Despite what the Elite 11 coaches had said about the matter, he seemed proud to admit it. As if the fact alluded to the idea that he had more "upside," to borrow the clichéd scouting buzzword, more room to develop, than did other young QBs who had spent hundreds of hours being groomed. Harris pointed out that he also played basketball and ran track. "Four by two, four by one, and four by four," he added, rattling off the names of the sprinting events he competed in for his high school.

"It's just natural. That's the deal with being raw. I wasn't a starting quarterback till I got to eighth grade. A lot of these guys probably grew up playing quarterback in T-League. I didn't."

There would be a handful of other quarterbacks invited to the Elite 11 later in the evening. Dilfer had scheduled a "war room" back at the Hilton Garden Inn, where he and his staff would discuss the merits of all their candidates. George Whitfield, one of Brandon Harris's bigger supporters among the staff, would not be able to participate in the war room. Whitfield had to leave Columbus to get to Texas, where he'd be training his prized pupil, Texas A&M phenom Johnny Manziel, and three other college QBs.

• • •

THE WAR ROOM FELT like one big poker club. There was bickering, posturing, tasteless jokes, and overcooked Italian food. At the core, it was just a bunch of guys talking about something they truly loved—football. Actually, it went deeper than that. It was guys giving their opinions about various aspects of the game and debating their own insights. This was a chance to show Trent Dilfer and their peers what they knew. A dozen TDFB coaches sat around the hotel meeting room. Dilfer was flanked by Yogi Roth and Brian Stumpf, a former wide receiver at Cal and longtime Elite 11 staffer. Also around the rectangular table were Matt James, another former college wideout and longtime Elite 11 coach; Jordan Palmer; and Joey Roberts, Dilfer's baby-faced protégé who also works for ESPN and was the Elite 11's general manager. Lining a wall was another group of guys balancing paper plates full of food on their laps—the TDFB coaches, who were told they wouldn't be part of the vote on which QBs got picked for the remaining slots in the Elite 11 but were free to offer opinions. In truth, such conversations often would reveal as much about the coaches as it would the high school quarterbacks.

Over the years, the Elite 11 staff based a lot of their invites off the high school tapes they evaluated. The footage still mattered a great deal to the TDFB guys, but in-person evaluation and "feel" seemed to count even more to Dilfer.

Before most of the coaches had even put the first forkful of food into their mouths, Palmer had already established the tone for the evening. He detailed a recent conversation he'd had with a highly touted "four-star" quarterback prospect's high school coach. The kid was a player whom most in the football recruiting world outside that room figured would be a lock to make the Elite 11.

"I was honest with 'em," Palmer said. "I told 'em the two biggest things he has to work on are coachability and likability."

It was a blunt assessment. It was basically, "Here's the problem with your kid. He's an asshole."

Palmer said the kid later followed up by saying, "I heard [you] guys thought I was a dick." Palmer said the young QB got the message, but he wondered if he really *got* it. Players have to want to play for the QB. Want to be around him. It's one thing to have an air of confidence. It's another to be unbearable. Maybe the kid would mature. The Dilfer group has had two vivid examples of high school quarterbacks who were deemed elite talents by the Internet recruiting folks and got invites to the Elite 11, and Dilfer couldn't stand either kid. Both felt entitled. Both were so caught up in their own Internet reputations that they came across as insufferable, and both—one a year ago, the other two years ago—recoiled when faced with competition in the Elite 11 setting—the biggest red flag in Dilfer's world.

Will Grier sounded like the opposite. The lanky 6′3″ quarterback from North Carolina once threw for 837 yards and 10 touchdowns in a 104–80 game at Charlotte's Davidson Day School. He was the son of a football coach who once was (former NFL QB) Jeff Blake's backup at East Carolina. On the day Grier worked out for the Elite 11 coaches at a Nike training camp in Charlotte in March, it was a sloppy, forty-degree afternoon with twenty-mile-per-hour gusts of wind.

"Those were probably the worst conditions we've had in thirteen years," Brian Stumpf said. "And he didn't flinch an inch or blink an eye."

None of the QBs in North Carolina had looked very sharp trying to grip and throw a wet, heavy ball into howling winds. Paul Troth, a Dilfer protégé at TDFB seated behind Stumpf, chimed in. The onetime East Carolina QB and Elite 11 alum (Class of 2000) was from the same area as Grier.

"I worked him out," Troth said of Grier, "and he told me, 'I'll throw a watermelon, Coach. It don't matter.'"

"I think he's got crazy confidence," Palmer said. "The good kinda confidence."

Translation: Will Grier was getting an invite to the Elite 11.

Within the first fifteen minutes of the night, it became apparent that the "intangibles" were vital to Dilfer's group. Another candidate Dilfer was quick to move on was Stephen Collier, a 6′3″ Georgia product. "He's got Dude Qualities," Dilfer said. "I think he's got a lot more in the tank than he's shown."

Dilfer's blessing triggered a well of support for Collier, a prospect who'd received only modest praise from the online recruiting analysts. Palmer said he had the ability to "dominate" at the college level. Roberts even noted that Collier was a 4.3 student.

Collier was invited, too.

Palmer, an aspiring broadcaster, was a quote machine.

On one dual-threat quarterback from the Eastern Seaboard: "I love that kid . . . he's gonna be a really good safety."

On undersized Arizona QB Luke Rubenzer: "I think he hates the fact that he's 5'11" so much that he loves it."

On an imposing Midwestern quarterback with scholarship offers from most of the Big Ten: "I think he's a mental midget, and he's probably gonna end up as a defensive end."

On the hardscrabble background of Manny Wilkins, a skinny 6'2" QB who'd bounced from Texas to Colorado to the Bay Area after his father died from a drug addiction five years earlier and whose mom battled her own problem with addiction: "I grew up wealthy in Orange County, and at some point you're at a serious disadvantage to the guys who have an edge. He's already had to overcome so much. I'm standing on the table for Manny."

"Standing on the table" is coach-speak for lobbying for a player or a recruit.

After almost ninety minutes, Dilfer's process had whittled the candidates to eighteen QBs for the final seven spots at the Elite 11.

"OK, MJ, stand on the table for someone," Dilfer said to James, the oldest coach in the room.

James brought up Sean White, a 6'1", shaggy-haired QB from Fort Lauderdale, who, unlike many of the kids under consideration for the Elite 11, hadn't committed to a college program yet. White had been one of the most determined quarterbacks, having come to two Elite 11 events in Atlanta and Columbus and also stayed for the Nike training camps the following day. White had not been anointed by the online recruiting experts as a highly ranked guy, and he didn't have a bunch of big-name schools that had offered him scholarships, but he had shined on the summer 7-on-7 circuit while leading the powerful South Florida Express squad, a team loaded with elite players.

"I think it helped a lot, because going against the best in practice all the time and competing with them really makes you better,"

White said. "That's why I think South Florida kids do so well in college—they are used to the competition level, because they already saw it in high school down [t]here." White had been practicing with his Express teammates weekly from February until June, with some time off in May, when his high school team—the University School Suns—had its spring practice sessions.

"Besides [Arizona quarterback] Kyle Allen, Sean's the most consistent passer we have had," said James. "His steps are on time. He throws it nice. He looks a lot like [unheralded-recruit-turned-Cincinnati Bengals-starter] Andy [Dalton] but better."

That comment triggered other comparisons. In the evaluation game, people love comparisons. Everyone good must look at least a little like someone else. There's a measure of security of opinion in that. Stumpf remarks that Kentucky QB commitment Drew Barker "is probably what Ben Roethlisberger looked like in high school. Drew's a chest-bumper. He's a leader."

Dilfer turned to Yogi Roth, seated to his left, and asked whom he'd like to fight for. Roth mentioned Brad Kaaya from the Los Angeles area.

DILFER: I think his tape is really good. He's 6′4″, 220, a good athlete, and he can play.
ROTH: I can project him in the NFL.
DILFER: I think he's a serious Dude.

Roth then invoked the name of another, taller QB who was one of the more talked-about prospects in the online recruiting world. "I don't know that he's a Dude."

Brandon Harris was a hyped quarterback prospect, but the group seemed skeptical of his Dude capabilities. The coaches all were high on his arm "talent"—"He definitely has a hose."

Dilfer said Harris was "twitchy," which might not sound like a compliment, but in the 2013 scouting vernacular, it was. The term was a nod toward an athlete being amped up with fast-twitch muscle fibers that are often discussed in regard to an elite sprinter, jumper, or someone with rare, essential explosiveness. Still, the group didn't have a great read on Harris. And perhaps the only TDFB staffer who'd be willing to stand on the table for Brandon Harris was George Whit-field and he was en route to go see Johnny Manziel.

Throughout the night, the TDFB group also took to Twitter to share the drama in real time, not just with the hopeful young quarterbacks but also with the diehard recruiting fans who live down this widening rabbit hole. Many of the "recruitniks" root for a certain QB to get invited because it'll reflect better if their favorite college team is involved. It's a twisted version of fantasy sports for others who are looking for validation of their own evaluation skills when it comes to sizing up a seventeen-year-old prospect. Taylor Holiday, Palmer's old high school buddy, who was handling the social media aspect for TDFB, was recording and tweeting out videos every time a coach notified the latest Elite 11 invitee. Dilfer and the coaches often sounded giddier about the breaking news than did the kid on the other end of the phone. Palmer reached one kid (Jacob Park) while he was working at an Italian restaurant chain. Another TDFB coach broke the news to Manny Wilkins while he was in the middle of playing *Call of Duty*.

At one point, Dilfer sent out a tweet from his TDFB account with a picture of a poster board listing the seventeen names of the QBs remaining in consideration for the final six available spots and added, "It's getting gnarly."

One of the names listed in the photo was Darius Wade. A 6'1", 185-pound left-hander from Middletown, Delaware, Wade was verbally committed to play football at Boston College and would become the first Delaware high school football prospect to sign with a Division I program in some forty years.

"He plays in Delaware," said Palmer. "We can't hold that against him. He had twenty-seven TDs and just one pick all season. He hasn't been exposed to much coaching or much competition up there. I think his learning curve is as much as anybody's. But he's a guy who is going to walk into the room, and you're gonna feel his presence."

Palmer added that Wade, in his mind, was a more talented version of another kid who was selected to the Elite 11 a year ago who ended up signing on with one of the biggest football programs in the nation.

"Darius told me at breakfast that he wants to be an architect, if that means anything," former Green Bay Packers backup QB Craig Nall said from the back of the room.

It didn't. Well, maybe it did a little, since it hinted at the kid's maturity. And, as Dilfer said, everything mattered.

"Everybody's gonna rally around Darius at Boston College," predicted Palmer.

Another one of the names listed from Dilfer's tweet was Cade Aspay, a 6'1", 180-pounder from Southern California. "Cade can 'tempo' the throws with the best of 'em," said Joey Roberts, also a Southern California guy. "He plays the ukulele, too."

"He's got tiny knees," interjected one of the TDFB coaches, alluding to Aspay's small frame. "But I think he's super-talented."

At issue: How did Aspay compare with Sean White, the 6'1" quarterback from Fort Lauderdale? "Cade's film is better, but Sean plays better people," said Dilfer, who wasn't ready to decide which QB got the next invite.

After five hours of deliberation, there were still four golden tickets remaining. Dilfer tweeted: "4 golden tickets left and we only know one way to figure this out. #MidnightMadness"

Actually, Dilfer had already figured out one of the spots he was filling. It was going to Luke Rubenzer, the 5'11"-ish QB from Arizona whom Dilfer had compared to Johnny Manziel and Russell Wilson. Even though Rubenzer was barely a blip on the online recruiting radar and had just one scholarship offer from a BCS program (Cal), his game tape and spunky personality had made Dilfer a believer. Rubenzer's private quarterback coach Dennis Gile, who also worked with fellow Elite 11 QB Kyle Allen, was a Dilfer TDFB protégé sitting nervously in the back of the room. Rather than just call Rubenzer with the good news, Dilfer wanted to pull a little prank he hoped would go viral for Elite 11 and TDFB.

Dilfer had Gile call Rubenzer at 12:30 a.m. at his hotel down the street in Columbus. Get out of bed. Get your cleats and your ball. We need to see more. Time for a midnight workout at a field across the street from the hotel.

After a long night of deliberations on other QBs, Dilfer and his coaches called Rubenzer under the guise of needing to see him make some more throws . . . at 12:30 in the morning. The headlights from five SUVs parked in front of a small muddy lot provided the light. "In the pressure chamber, you showed a little puckering," Dilfer told Rubenzer.

Dilfer had Rubenzer stretch his legs and told his colleagues holding flip cams to focus on Luke's feet as he fired a few warm-up passes to one of the TDFB coaches standing twenty yards out into the darkness. Just when the kid figured his workout would officially begin, Dilfer let the kid in on the joke as the rest of the TDFB crew howled. The little quarterback sighed in relief before getting a bear hug. Rubenzer got his invite to the Elite 11—or QB Heaven, as Dilfer calls it.

## _ _ _ _2.
# MAGIC MEN

In recruiting circles, there is a caveat that veteran scouts cling to when dealing with high school football coaches who rave about one of their own kids: How do they know what a "great" one actually is if they've never had one before?

Tom Rossley knew something about greatness. In fact, after what Rossley had been through in his football career, he was as qualified to sift through the murk of the quarterback world, with its booms and busts, as anyone. Rossley spent five decades in big-time football. He'd coached greatness. He'd recruited greatness. Once, back in the mid-'60s, as a wispy 6'4″ nineteen-year-old, he even had to give up his dream of playing quarterback due to the presence of greatness. Rossley was a redshirt freshman at the University of Cincinnati battling for the starting QB job with a true freshman. The coaches opted for the other kid, who was bigger and had a more powerful arm. They asked Rossley to move to wide receiver. As a senior, Rossley caught 80 passes for 1,072 yards in 1968. The guy who got the quarterback job, Greg Cook, went on to be selected by the Cincinnati Bengals with the fifth overall pick in the 1969 NFL Draft.

"I still think I was better than him, but that's beside the point,"

Rossley said with a chuckle two years after retiring from a career in coaching. "In my heart, I was always a quarterback."

Rossley went to camp with the Philadelphia Eagles as a free-agent receiver before being released.

"I was about to go to the Bengals, and we were in Vietnam, but they couldn't guarantee me that I'd get into a reserve unit, so I took a teaching job and started coaching in my high school," Rossley said. Two years later, he was a graduate assistant at the University of Arkansas for head coach Frank Broyles on a staff where Joe Gibbs was the offensive line coach and Raymond Berry was the wide receivers coach.

"I just fell in love with coaching," Rossley said.

Cook was the Bengals' opening-day starter as a rookie. The 6'4", 220-pounder even sparked Cincinnati—3–11 the previous year—to wins in its first two games in 1969. Then, in Week Three against the Kansas City Chiefs, Cook was sacked by Jim Lynch, who landed on the quarterback's throwing shoulder. Cook was shaken up but continued playing. He attempted another pass before leaving the game. Doctors didn't diagnose it at the time, but Cook had shredded his rotator cuff. In spite of that, Cook returned to action at mid-season after sitting out three games. He took cortisone shots and played though the pain, he later told *Sports Illustrated*. He still managed to lead the AFL and NFL in yards per attempt (9.4) and yards per completion (17.5), as well as in passer rating (88.3). He was voted Rookie of the Year by UPI.

Cook's torn rotator cuff, though, only got worse. He re-tore it playing basketball when he got hung up on the rim one day before he actually was ready to start throwing again, Rossley said. Cook's biceps also had become partially detached—another injury that had yet to be diagnosed and wouldn't be until Cook's rotator-cuff surgery. He would undergo three operations and would not play again till attempting a comeback four years later. He completed one pass in 1973 for the Chiefs, and that was the end of his NFL career.

Cook's name has wafted into football lore in a Bunyanesque manner, the way some star-crossed playground legends are discussed by NBA greats. Bill Walsh, the iconic NFL mastermind who was an assistant with the Bengals during Cook's rookie season, once told NFL Films that Cook could've become "the greatest NFL quarterback of all time." Cook's impact on the game is a poignant one. Without the use of Cook's prodigious arm strength and downfield passing acumen, Walsh rethought the Bengals offense to cater to his new QB, Virgil Carter's, talents. Walsh's new scheme employed rollouts and an underneath passing attack, becoming the framework of what would later be known as the West Coast Offense that won the San Francisco 49ers a fistful of Super Bowl rings.

"Greg Cook was a big strong guy who had good feet and could really zip the ball—a real rope-thrower," Rossley said. "The ball came out so quick. He was more of a drive-the-ball-down-the-field guy. I likened him to Terry Bradshaw, although I didn't think Bradshaw was as good as Greg Cook."

Meanwhile, Rossley's coaching career meandered from small colleges (Holy Cross) to small Division I programs (he had two different stints at Rice) and his alma mater. Rossley also coached in four different professional leagues—the NFL, the CFL, the AFL (the Arena Football League), and the now-defunct USFL. At age fifty-four, he landed a job with the Green Bay Packers, where he inherited the most remarkable quarterback he'd ever been around—Brett Lorenzo Favre.

Rossley had spent one season as the Atlanta Falcons quarterbacks coach in 1990. The organization was scouting QBs for the draft. Favre was tempting. He played at Southern Miss, which was the only program that had offered Favre a scholarship—and USM was basically living on the margins of big-time college football. Southern Miss had recruited Favre as a defensive back, but he pushed them to give him a chance to play QB. It didn't take him long to generate some buzz in the scouting community. The guy who began his freshman season as the Golden Eagles' seventh-string quarterback won the starting job by the third game of the year, when he led them on a come-from-behind victory over Tulane despite having spent the pre-game hungover and vomiting during warm-ups. In his junior year, Favre carried USM to an upset of number six Florida State.

The summer before his senior season, Favre lost control of his car, flipping it three times before he crashed into a tree. The wreck left him with a broken vertebra and a concussion, and thirty inches of his intestine had to be removed during emergency surgery. In spite of that, six weeks later, Favre still sparked Southern Miss to a 27–24 victory on the road against number thirteen Alabama.

The Falcons needed a young quarterback. Jerry Glanville, Atlanta's colorful head coach, drafted Favre in the second round with the thirty-third pick overall. Rossley, though, wouldn't be around to coach him. A few months before the 1991 NFL Draft, he left the organization to become the head coach at SMU. The Mustangs were emerging from the wreckage of the NCAA's "Death Penalty." Rossley lasted five seasons trying to rebuild the SMU program before being fired. His record: 15–48–3.

Rossley returned to the NFL as a position coach with the Chiefs and then the Chicago Bears before Packers head coach Mike Sherman hired him to be the team's offensive coordinator, where he'd finally get to work with Favre.

Favre had just turned thirty. He'd already been a three-time NFL MVP and led the Packers to a Super Bowl. He and Rossley bonded instantly. Favre always had stories.

"He told me the first time he worked out for an NFL team," said Rossley, "he got there late. They had him run a forty. He got to the end and went down on his hands and knees and started throwing up, because he'd been out drinking the night before. The coach said, 'Jeez, what did you drink last night?' "

Favre also had plenty of stories about his curious relationship with Jerry Glanville.

"He could really do a good Jerry imitation," said Rossley. "Jerry didn't call him by his name. He called him 'M'ssippi.' And every stadium they walked into, he'd say, 'M'ssippi, come over here. M'ssippi, let's see if you can throw this ball out of the stadium . . .' 'M'ssippi, let's see if you can throw this ball into the upper deck.' Every stadium it was a challenge. Brett has the strongest arm I've ever seen, and the strongest arm that's probably ever been in the NFL. He's amazing. It's God-given, and he's a little bit wild.

"When I first got there, I was doing footwork drills with Favre.

I'd say, 'Brett, your footwork is horseshit. We've gotta do some foot-work drills.' And he'd laugh at me. He would go through every drill, but he'd still play his way when it came to the games. He'd jump up and kick his feet or hop step after a throw. Matt Hasselbeck was our backup. He'd give them names, such as, 'that was the Missis-sippi Sidekick.' But I really think, when you watch it, that's one of the reasons he never had a knee injury or a hip injury, because his cleats were almost never in the ground. I remember watching Byron Leftwich when he came out of college, and he had such a long stride, and his feet were constantly in the ground, and thinking that he was gonna get hurt before long. One of the big reasons Brett was so great is because he's so competitive, and he has that field sense. He never had a knee injury in all that time because nobody ever got a clean shot at him. He could spin out of a sack or evade a guy coming from the blind side, and I'd say, 'Brett, how'd you see that guy?' He'd say, 'I didn't. I don't know how I knew he was there. I just knew.' It's a sense of where the players are on the field, and when he scrambles, he knows where guys are, and he can throw on the run and put it on him with accuracy."

Favre's freewheeling style, which some football people categorize as a "gunslinger," was akin to Magic Johnson's on a fast break, com-plete with everything from off-balance flings to cross-body chucks to sidearm and even slung-from-the-hip flick passes. In general, it was a mishmash of stuff coaches had spent a lifetime preaching against. Favre was fearless. It was as if doubt or caution or any element of self-preservation never crept into his mind, because his rampant gusts of self-confidence always overrode it. "More than anything, he played free," said Gil Haskell, another former Packers assistant.

Working with Favre proved to be an education for the coach in his mid-fifties. Favre did things Rossley had never seen pulled off. Things that you wouldn't, couldn't, ever coach a quarterback to do. In the presence of this, Rossley became convinced that truly great quarterbacks were born more than made. But surely they could also be screwed up if you messed with them too much—as Favre playfully reminded him often.

"Brett used to say, 'Well, I'm gonna play well this week *if* I can overcome my coaching.' And it kinda makes sense. He was being light with me, but he was telling me, 'Don't overcoach me.' "

Rossley's experience with Favre—and that's what it often felt like as a coach: you *experienced* Brett Favre—was the complete opposite of his time working in Chicago with another NFL quarterback he'd had a few years earlier. That guy, unlike Favre, was a first-rounder—the second overall pick of the 1993 NFL draft—and came from a big-time college program.

"Beautiful" is how Rossley described Notre Dame product Rick Mirer. "Pro-perfect-looking quarterback and could throw it great, but when you'd get him on the field, he was in a cloud. He didn't compete. He just couldn't see the field."

Mirer lasted one season with the Bears, throwing 0 touchdown passes and 6 interceptions before being released. After Rossley started working in Green Bay with Favre, the coach knew exactly what Mirer was missing.

Magic.

To get ready for the draft, Rossley and his coaching protégé in Green Bay, Darrell Bevell, a former standout quarterback at Wisconsin (and a coach who would later rise up the NFL ranks to become a top offensive coordinator with the Seattle Seahawks), compiled a list of characteristics they wanted in a Packers QB.

They debated what should be the number one component:

*Is it feet?*
*Arm strength?*
*Accuracy?*
*Height?*
*Is it body type?*

"We had twelve to fifteen different things," said Rossley. "But the number one thing for me that we'd put at the very top: magic. Just magic. I'd learned. You can't wow me with height and being pretty in drills. You gotta wow me when you're competing."

Whenever Rossley evaluated QBs, he wanted to see how they did in tight games with their teams trailing. Better still would be if those situations took place on the road. He also looked at how they handled themselves on third downs. Anyone can make plays or complete passes on first and ten.

It was a decade later before Rossley would be wowed again by another quarterback. This happened years after Mike Sherman, Rossley, and the rest of the Packers staff had gotten fired in Green Bay. The coach was in his mid-sixties and working for Sherman as Texas A&M's quarterbacks coach. Rossley was evaluating tapes of high school juniors. He was fascinated by the play-making wizardry of an undersized, wiry, white kid with an uncanny knack for knowing where everyone—especially defenders—were. Even if the kid couldn't see them. Around the Texas Hill Country, everyone had been buzzing about "Johnny Football."

"The tape was phenomenal," said Rossley. "It just went on and on and on."

"Johnny Football" a.k.a. Johnny Manziel accounted for 53 touchdowns and 4,400 yards running and passing as a junior at Tivy High in Kerrville, Texas (population: 23,000). The kid made dazzling scrambles and dizzying moves to evade would-be tacklers on one highlight that led into another for what seemed like an hour as the veteran coach marveled at what he was seeing. There were plays on the tape where coaches broke out a stopwatch to time that Manziel scrambled around behind the line of scrimmage for an unfathomable seventeen seconds, frustrating helpless defenders from sideline to sideline. Manziel looked like a one-man team, and according to college recruiters who scouted the area, he essentially was. Against mighty Steele High from Cibolo, Texas—a bigger program with more-touted prospects led by the nation's top running back recruit Malcolm Brown—Manziel ran for over 100 yards and passed for 319 more yards, amassing 5 TDs to lead the Fighting Antlers to a come-from-behind 38–34 upset as the QB outshined Brown's 329 rushing yards.

Still, for all Manziel's preternatural gifts, he lacked size, and he seemed a curious fit for the system Texas A&M ran. Like most programs that had run a pro-style system, A&M wanted a prototype 6'4", 220-pound guy behind center. The team's starting quarterback,

Ryan Tannehill, was that size. The QB Tannehill followed, Jerrod Johnson, was 6'5", 250 pounds. The Aggies' QB recruiting board had a couple of other bigger guys ranked above Manziel—Brett Hundley, a 6'3", 210-pound, mobile quarterback from Arizona; and Zach Mettenberger, a 6'5", 235-pound, strong-armed pocket passer who had begun at the University of Georgia but had gotten into some trouble off the field and had resurrected his career at a Kansas junior college. Mike Sherman, a career offensive line coach who had spent the previous decade in the NFL, was skeptical about how Manziel's unhinged game might translate to the college level. Rossley had his doubts about Manziel, too.

"I wasn't sure that he could stay in the pocket and plant his foot and make a throw, because everything with him was scramble and on-the-run and a makeup play."

In the spring evaluation period, the month-long stretch when college coaches are permitted to visit high schools, watch film, observe practice, and speak with coaches and counselors (but not the recruits themselves), Rossley drove to Kerrville. By NCAA rules, he wasn't allowed to have a conversation with Manziel, but he could eyeball the kid. The first thing Rossley noticed, and studied, was Manziel's hands. The kid might have had a scrawny frame with narrow shoulders and little meat on his bones, but he had freakishly big mitts. Seeing that also reminded Rossley of Favre.

"That was one of the first things we looked at when we evaluated quarterbacks in Green Bay—how big their hands were—because of how Brett was and how well he could play in cold weather," said Rossley. "That's such a key with handling the ball, controlling the ball, and with the snap coming out. The size of a quarterback's hands is even more important than his height. Brett Favre had huge hands, and so did Johnny. I could tell when I watched him grip and throw the ball. When I saw that, and then saw how he could zip the ball with velocity—his release was quick, and he was accurate—that was it for me."

Favre's hands were measured by the NFL years ago (from thumb tip to pinkie tip) at 10⅜ inches. For comparison's sake, Tony Romo's hand was measured at 8.88 inches. Anything bigger than 9½ is considered large for an NFL QB prospect. Most personnel people expect hand size to correlate with body size, but that's not always the case. Favre has abnormally big hands, as does 6′0″ Drew Brees (10¼ inches) and as does budding Seattle Seahawks star Russell Wilson, who stands, according to the NFL, at 5′10⅝″ yet has 10¼-inch hands, which were among the biggest the league had measured in a half decade for the hundreds of QBs who have passed through the NFL combine.

Rossley was sold on Manziel before making the four-hour drive back to College Station. His head coach, Mike Sherman, was not. Sherman's reputation was for evaluating offensive linemen. In his 2010 recruiting class, Sherman signed three linemen who developed into stars: Luke Joeckel, who ended up as the second overall pick in the 2013 NFL Draft; Jake Matthews, who ended up as the sixth overall pick in the 2014 draft; and Cedric Ogbuehi, who got feedback from the NFL College Advisory Committee, which came back with all first-round grades, yet the 6′5″, 300-pounder opted to return for his senior season at A&M in 2014 in hopes of becoming a top-five pick in the 2015 draft. Another signee from that class, Jarvis Harrison, ranked by online recruiting analysts as a "two-star" prospect, became a three-year starter on the line. In all, Sherman signed six offensive linemen in that crop, which will go down as one of the best line classes in college football history. (The other two guys barely cracked the Aggies' depth chart.)

When it comes to recruiting quarterbacks, college coaches have to be more selective. After all, you can only play one at a time. Plus, egos often get bruised. Sherman always reminded his staff that you can't afford to miss on a quarterback, because if you pick the wrong guy, your program is in trouble. Sherman only needed to look a few hours down the road to Texas. Longtime coach Mack Brown targeted the wrong QBs in back-to-back classes, turning off a few local quarterbacks whom he only saw as college defensive backs, at best, and they ended up stars in other places, while UT plummeted from the Top 25 rankings. That growing list of Longhorn misses included

Baylor's Robert Griffin III (from Copperas Cove, Texas); Stanford's Andrew Luck (from Houston), Arizona's Nick Foles (from Austin), and A&M's own Ryan Tannehill (from Big Spring, Texas). Johnny Manziel grew up dreaming of being a Longhorn, too. He spoke of bleeding Burnt Orange. His high school coach said that even if Brown had only offered Manziel a scholarship to Texas to play defensive back, the kid would've jumped at it. Brown, though, was skeptical of Manziel's size and whether he could stand in the pocket and throw the ball well enough and never offered him a scholarship. A handful of smaller colleges—Tulsa, Louisiana Tech, and Rice among them— told Manziel they'd love to have him as their quarterback.

But it was the programs he wanted the most—Texas and TCU— that weren't believers. That hurt Manziel. Scarred him. But three years later, he would concede—just as Jordan Palmer asserted about the short high school quarterback who idolized Johnny Football— that he hated being doubted so much that he actually loved it. It *worked* for him.

"He wasn't very tall, and I thought, 'Maybe some people would get hung up on his height; hopefully they will,' but not all of them did," said then–Louisiana Tech coach Sonny Dykes. "I thought he was 'a three-play guy,' where you just go, 'Whoa!' and watch for three plays and realize he's got something special. He ran around and threw it good enough. He just made so many plays with his feet, keeping plays alive."

Manziel's personality had a mischievous edge to it, as well. Just as Favre had, the young Texan could become his own worst enemy. Manziel came from a wealthy family with deep ties in oil and real estate. He often carried himself off the field as if the rules didn't apply to him, and on the football field he sure played as if they didn't, either, which, truth be told, is what made him special. But his coaches loved him, and so did his teammates, because they respected his heart as much as his talent. And, when it comes to football, veteran scouts will tell you, heart is a talent. During their homecoming game against Uvalde High School, Tivy was winning in a blowout. Manziel concocted a plan to get seldom-used teammate 5'5", 120-pound Robert Martinez to score a touchdown.

"Johnny was about to score a touchdown, but instead he slides down near the goal line and calls a time-out," said Mark Smith, Tivy High's coach. " 'Coach, we want Robert Martinez to score a touchdown. Put him in at running back.' "

"But he's not a running back," Smith told Manziel.

"Don't worry," Manziel replied. "I'll get him into the end zone."

Manziel literally dragged Martinez into the end zone.

During the summer before his senior year at Tivy, Manziel and his family traveled out west in hopes of increasing his options—and his profile. Their first stop was the University of Oregon's camp. Ducks head coach Chip Kelly said he was enamored with Manziel the first time he watched his highlight tape. "It's one of the most impressive highlight tapes I've ever seen," Kelly said. "I get that no one looks bad on a highlight tape, but usually a highlight tape is three or four minutes. His tape went on and on and on and on. You couldn't believe it. There's one sequence that is still vivid in my mind. He took a quarterback draw and went, like, 90 yards for a TD. But there was a hold, so they brought the play back. They literally called the exact same play, and he took it 95 yards for a touchdown. You're just shaking your head, going, one guy can't make this many big plays."

In Eugene, Manziel wowed Kelly and his staff. So much so that Manziel was named MVP of the camp after the way the Texan thrived in what Kelly described as a hodgepodge 7-on-7 setup during their team camp.

"You could tell that he had a real good understanding and had a real good football mind," Kelly said, adding that the direction in that setting was not very detailed. "You're holding up a card. 'Here are your routes. Go throw.' I just wanna see guys react. Do they just get fixed in on one receiver? Can they just take a look at a basic concept and deliver the ball where it should be delivered based on how the defense is playing? He excelled at it."

Kelly loved the fact that Manziel was a great all-around athlete—nearly a scratch golfer and such a good baseball prospect that the Ducks' baseball staff was intrigued with him, too. Kelly knew that Manziel's size might turn off some college coaches, but he'd had success with shorter quarterbacks before—provided they had big hands.

"I learned about the hand-size thing a long time ago from [long-time Boston College head coach] Jack Bicknell Sr., because he had Doug Flutie," Kelly said. "That was a big thing he talked about. You can take a smaller quarterback, but does he have small hands? Well, we saw Johnny's got big hands in terms of being able to handle the ball. I liked his motion, how he delivered it, and, obviously, athletically, he was special."

Manziel and his family's next stop was the Stanford camp, but before the Cardinal could make any pitch to the quarterback, Kelly called him. "We want you here at Oregon. This offense is tailor-made for you," Kelly told Manziel, who was drawn to the Ducks' potent system but also the "cool" factor of UO's cutting-edge look.

Manziel committed to Oregon over the phone. He was actually the Ducks' second QB to commit to play for Oregon in a month. Strong-armed Floridian Jerrard Randall had accepted a scholarship offer two weeks earlier. Then a couple of days after Manziel committed, yet another unheralded QB prospect, Marcus Mariota, a tall, slender Hawaiian with only one other college scholarship offer (Memphis), who took part in the same camp Manziel did, also told Kelly he was going to be a Duck.

"Give Oregon credit," said Texas A&M director of football operations Gary Reynolds, a former longtime NFL administrator. "They pulled the trigger on Johnny at camp. We were missing on him. Texas was missing on him. A lot of folks down here were missing on him. The thing with Johnny is, he didn't really shine at camp, because in camp you can't tackle him or even try to tackle him."

But Reynolds said that didn't stop Rossley from trying to sell Sherman on the shorter QB.

"There is no one else," Rossley said in a meeting after the Aggies camp. "*This* is the kid."

Of course, verbal commitments, especially ones made months before February's "National Signing Day," are not binding. That's why you'll sometimes hear about recruits talking about being "70 percent committed." College coaches also factor distance and local ties into the recruiting process. Most recruiters often feel compelled to extend a scholarship offer just to "get in the boat" with a recruit rather than be seen by the kid as skeptics. Those coaches also know they can find a way out of these nonbinding offers later in the process. But get hitched to a local kid, and that coach runs the risk of alienating local high school coaches. Finding out Manziel had committed to a school that was a thirty-three-hour drive from Kerrville, Texas, didn't deter Rossley.

"I worked his mom and dad real hard," he said. "I kept telling them, 'You don't want him going way out to Oregon. He's a Texas high school legend. Let's keep the legend in Texas.'"

Rossley believed he had bonded with Michelle Manziel the first time she met the coach. She came prepared to pitch her son's talent, armed with his highlight tape and all his stats. "Oh, we don't need those," Rossley told her. "I've already seen him play. We want him."

"She had gone to Texas and so many places and tried to get people to look at him, and they wouldn't," Rossley recalled of a spring visit. "The only thing I couldn't give them at that point was that he had to be face-to-face with Coach Sherman. Sherman had to offer him that scholarship. It took a while till we finally offered him, and in the meantime he committed to Oregon. But I kept recruiting him and got him to come over to a few games. The third home game he came to that we played in September, he had an A&M shirt on. I knew we had him."

MANZIEL ARRIVED IN COLLEGE Station and was fourth-team on the depth chart, behind starter Ryan Tannehill, a future first-rounder. Within the first month of the season, Manziel's uncanny knack for evading tacklers and wriggling out of trouble at practice convinced Rossley that his fourth-stringer was actually A&M's best Plan B.

"I told Johnny, 'If something serious happens to Ryan, we're gonna break that redshirt, and you're gonna have to play and finish the year for us,'" Rossley said. "And he was agreeable to that. He impressed me every day in practice. He was a great practice player, a great competitor, and was accurate and had a strong arm. The players all loved him and loved to be around him. Same as Favre, who was the life of the locker room."

Fresno State coach Tim DeRuyter, the former A&M defensive coordinator, said he got an idea of just how special Manziel was at mid-season that year. Manziel was the Aggies' scout-team quarterback facing DeRuyter's first-string defense as A&M prepped for Baylor and its speedy dual-threat QB Robert Griffin III. DeRuyter, after watching Manziel run for about 800 yards against his defense during the week, ripped into his players. He was convinced they had to be jakin' it. But on game day, the Aggies beat Baylor by 4 touchdowns and held RGIII to 15 rushing yards on 12 carries.

"After the game," DeRuyter said, "a couple of defensive guys came up to me and said, 'I'm tellin' ya, Coach, Manziel's a lot harder to tackle than RGIII was.' "

That win over number twenty Baylor was one of the last Sherman and the Aggies would have in 2011. A&M lost four of its final five regular-season games, including against archrival Texas at home on a last-second field goal. Sherman, Rossley, and the A&M staff were fired. Kevin Sumlin was hired from the University of Houston, bringing his hurry-up spread offense run by his thirty-three-year-old offensive coordinator Kliff Kingsbury, himself a onetime backup to Tom Brady with the Patriots.

Kingsbury grew up in New Braunfels, Texas, about an hour from Manziel's hometown. Kingsbury had heard about the local legend Johnny Football. He loved the kid's film. Kingsbury got a peek at his freakish athleticism playing basketball with some teammates, where the six-footer with the abnormally big hands was throwing down 360° dunks. The young coach told his friends that Manziel reminded him of a taller, more athletic version of Doug Flutie.

Manziel, though, struggled adapting to the new offense. Manziel toyed with the idea of quitting football and playing for the Aggies' baseball team.

George Whitfield had never heard of Johnny Manziel in the spring of 2011 when the Texan's mother called up the Southern California–based quarterback coach. As connected as Whitfield had become in the football world, he'd never been one to keep tabs on the recruiting sites.

"Honestly, if there's some high school kid breaking records an hour north of here, I probably wouldn't know it," Whitfield admitted.

Manziel's mother had heard about the work the self-described "Quarterback Builder" had done with Ben Roethlisberger and Cam Newton. Most observers saw Manziel, ranked as the thirty-ninth-best QB prospect in the country in his recruiting class by ESPN, as a long shot to win the A&M starting job.

Whitfield surfed around the Internet and found some high school footage of Manziel. The Aggie came out a week after A&M completed spring football. The week of training cost the Manziels $1,500, plus airfare and hotel.

In San Diego, Whitfield was already set to work with a high-profile quarterback prospect, Virginia Tech's Logan Thomas, a 6'6", 250-pound sophomore some NFL draft analysts had already touted as a future number one overall pick. Whitfield structured his week so that Manziel and Thomas would work out separately. Manziel, though, knew of Thomas's rep from having seen the Hokies play Michigan in the Sugar Bowl and convinced Whitfield to let him train side by side with the QB who was a half foot taller. Whitfield compared the dynamic to seeing a Kodiak bear being sized up by a leopard. Whitfield kept harping at Manziel about many of the same things he preached to Cam Newton about working in his cockpit rather than being too quick to rip the cord and escape. Whitfield shortened Manziel's throwing motion, relying on a shorter stride and keeping the ball closer to his ear.

Manziel left California more confident in his passing skills, but that hardly made him the front-runner to emerge as the Aggies' new starter. A July arrest for drunken street fighting and the fake ID he produced, which triggered a shirtless mug shot being tweeted all over the Internet, nearly cost Manziel his career at A&M. Kingsbury found out while lying on a beach in Cabo with a girlfriend, when he noticed a half dozen missed calls from his mercurial young QB. Sumlin lobbied for him with school brass and got him another chance.

Despite Manziel's struggles in the spring, Sumlin and Kingsbury still were convinced he was their best option as they made their debut in the roughest league in college football—the SEC West.

Manziel's father, Paul, told Kingsbury his son would win the Heisman. Kingsbury wanted to roll his eyes. Most parents predicted greatness for their kids, but this sounded different. Cocksure. Like, "No, you don't get *it*." Like when Chief Brody muttered in *Jaws*, "You're gonna need a bigger boat." It was an interesting family, for sure. Paul Manziel was a scratch golfer, had a black belt in martial arts, and sold cars for a living. Johnny's grandfather would later proclaim himself to the *New York Times* the 1983 world champ of cockfighting.

Turns out, Paul Manziel was prescient when it came to his boy's football future. The younger Manziel's daring, gunslinger style evoked memories of his favorite QB, Brett Favre. Manziel's first start put a scare into the number twenty-four Florida Gators. At one point, thanks primarily to Manziel, the Aggies had almost as many first downs (15) as UF had run plays (18). Texas A&M didn't beat the Gators, falling 20–17, but by the end of the day everybody around college football was buzzing about the frenetic QB who had made a dormant, stuffy old program must-see TV. Heck, even Sumlin and Kingsbury's chins were on the floor. After all, in practice, plays get whistled dead when tacklers touch the quarterback. Who knew actually tackling Manziel would be such a headache or what magical things he could do after pirouetting away from some three-hundred-pound monsters?

"This is a different animal," Kingsbury said, referencing Manziel. Kingsbury, a former record-setting quarterback at Texas Tech, played in Mike Leach's "Air Raid" spread system. Like other Leach disciples, Kingsbury used a variation of the Air Raid, but there had never been such a running threat at QB in the scheme. With each week came new wrinkles to A&M's souped-up Air Raid. By the time Manziel played his next SEC game, at the end of September, he threw, for a school record, 453 yards, and ran for 104 yards to break the SEC record for total offense in a 58–10 win over Arkansas. Two months later, Manziel had emerged as a Heisman contender. His team, which hadn't finished in the Top 10 in almost twenty years, went into Tuscaloosa ranked number fifteen to face the top-ranked Alabama Crimson Tide.

Two hours before kickoff, Manziel, who as an A&M freshman (per Sumlin's policy) had been off-limits to the media all season, tweeted to his 25,000 Twitter followers a line from the action movie *300*: "Give to them nothing, but take from them EVERYTHING."

As had been the norm for A&M, Manziel and company jumped on the Tide early. Manziel scooted his way around defenders and zipped passes to give the Aggies the early lead. A&M outgained Alabama, 172 yards to 34 yards in the opening quarter. The Aggies put up 20 points on Coach Nick Saban's D before the opening quarter was over, and Johnny Football wasn't just trending, he was becoming the sports world's hottest new thing. All season no player had a run go for longer than 22 yards against the Tide. Manziel, though, gashed the Tide for runs of 29 and 32 yards. More impressive: Manziel started the game 21 of 22 as a passer.

The play that made all the highlight shows and became the signature Johnny Football moment occurred in the first half, when A&M faced third-and-goal from the Alabama 10-yard line. The Tide collapsed the pocket with a four-man rush. Manziel tried to squeeze through what he thought was a crease in the right side of the line. But Alabama's defensive end shoved Manziel's right tackle, Jake Matthews, back into him. The QB caromed off Matthews, into A&M's right guard, which caused the ball to pop free from Manziel's hands for a heartbeat. Manziel re-gathered the ball while twisting his body back to his right, so he had his back to the other twenty-one players on the field. He hunched down and snagged the ball while wheeling to his left, escaped the scrum, and fired a pass with both shoulders parallel to the goal line to a wide-open Ryan Swope in the back of the end zone.

"You can't teach that, can you?" howled CBS analyst Gary Danielson, a former longtime NFL QB, on the telecast. "And you can't defend that, either."

The play Manziel actually relished the most came later in the game, after Bama battled back, scoring 17 consecutive points to get within a field goal going into the fourth quarter. Manziel had driven the Aggies to the Tide 24-yard line. A&M came out in a five-receiver set with an empty backfield. Alabama put eight defenders up at the line to crowd the Aggies. Manziel glanced left and noticed his inside receiver, Malcome Kennedy, had beaten the Tide's top cover man, Dee Milliner (a guy who later became the ninth pick in the 2013 NFL Draft), off the line by getting the DB to think he was going inside. Even though Milliner and Kennedy seemed to be running in a cluster toward the left corner of the end zone, Manziel lofted a pass that came down just over the receiver's left shoulder. A diving Milliner couldn't reach it with his outstretched arm. Touchdown. Alabama's best DB had tight coverage, and Johnny Manziel still beat him. "Still think I can't throw from the pocket?" Manziel laughed to himself.

"No moment is too big for him," Sumlin said of Manziel after the game. "He gives our players a sense that anything can happen. It's a contagious feeling."

One month later, Manziel would win the Heisman, becoming the first freshman ever to do so; his Twitter followers increased tenfold, and he helped generate a whopping $37 million in exposure for Texas A&M. He set an SEC record with over 5,100 total yards, captivating fans and media—both old media and new media—and also appeared to be the anti–Tim Tebow.

Manziel was completely unfiltered with his after-hours persona, from the shirtless mug shot to the Halloween pictures of him dressed as Scooby-Doo dancing with leggy blondes in lingerie and hanging with LeBron James or rap star Drake to sniping back at trolls on Twitter. His free-flowing artistry resonated with the hip-hop generation, while his Texas Hill Country roots connected with the good ol' boys, giving Manziel a unique platform as an overnight sensation—the rare guy who could present at both the CMA and the BET Awards.

Manziel's off-season, though, would bring new challenges: coping with his escalating rock-star status and trying to hone his pocket-passing skills while not short-circuiting his improvisational wizardry. Kingsbury was gone, too. The young coach's stock had soared so fast, Texas Tech had scooped the thirty-three-year-old up to become its new head coach. Sumlin, knowing Manziel's occasionally obstinate personality, was mindful of bringing in a quarterbacks coach his young star would respect. Sumlin hired twenty-seven-year-old Jake Spavital, a Kingsbury protégé who had coached West Virginia star Geno Smith and Brandon Weeden, a recent first-round QB—although "Johnny Football 2.0" would be a radically different experience for the young coach.

THE NFL WORLD WAS fascinated to see how Manziel would develop. His emergence came at a time when the League had begun to rethink rigid views that had been in place for generations.

"There are gonna be two seminal moments in changing the landscape of every quarterback having to look like Ben Roethlisberger or Troy Aikman," said longtime *Sports Illustrated* pro-football writer Peter King on the eve of the NFL Combine. "One happened in 2006, when New Orleans was recovering from Katrina. The Saints had to get a quarterback, because they didn't have one. [Head coach] Sean Payton and [general manager] Mickey Loomis see that there is only one free-agent quarterback who is even remotely good, and he has a major shoulder issue, and Nick Saban wants him in Miami. It's Drew Brees, but Saban was being a little bit waffle-y on him, because his doctors didn't really like him. Sean Payton does not want a 5′11¾″ quarterback. He wants Peyton Manning or Tom Brady. He wants a big guy, but there were no big guys available. So Sean, who is really a smart guy, said, 'Look, we have to cast our lot with this guy, even though he has this shoulder issue—and we don't know when he'll be ready—because we need somebody.'

"Sean had enough faith in his ability to develop quarterbacks that he said, 'Shit, I'll take a 5′11¾″ quarterback, and I'm gonna make something of him.' Drew Brees works, but until 2012, he's really an anomaly. How many other great quarterbacks at 5′11″ or 6′0″ or barely taller than 6′ had any success?"

The second seminal moment for the League's quarterbacking enlightenment, King said, occurred when the Seattle Seahawks blew out Peyton Manning and the Denver Broncos to win the 2014 Super Bowl. Seattle's budding star was twenty-five-year-old, second-year QB Russell Wilson, a 5′11″, 205-pound, onetime two-star recruit.

"John Schneider had scouted Russell Wilson earlier at Wisconsin, and he'd told [head coach] Pete Carroll after the Big Ten Championship game in Indianapolis, 'I'm telling you, you're gonna love this guy. You gotta believe me. Don't reach a conclusion because he's 5'11" [technically 5'10⅝"].' " Schneider, the boyish-looking Seahawks GM in his early forties, raved to Carroll about Wilson's leadership skills, competitiveness, and ability to extend plays. It also didn't hurt that Wilson put together a sterling 109-to-30 touchdown-to-interception ratio in college. The moment that really won Schneider over occurred on a two-point play late in the game, when Wilson was flushed from the pocket, scrambled left, got to the left hash mark, then wheeled around back to the middle of the field and threw a strike on the move to the Badgers tight end Jake Pedersen in the middle of a pack of Michigan State defenders for the score. Schneider also really loved that Wilson was voted team captain at Wisconsin despite having arrived at UW as a transfer from North Carolina State only a few weeks earlier. That told Schneider a lot, too, even if NFL rationale said not to invest in quarterbacks shorter than 6'0" tall.

"John Schneider is this optimistic, bright, fun, cool guy but also this guy who doesn't give a flying fuck what anybody else thinks about what his decisions are," said King. "Luckily, he didn't have a sedate, traditional NFL head coach who didn't believe in 5'11" quarterbacks." Schneider's mentor from his days in the Green Bay Packers organization was Ron Wolf, another freethinker. It was Wolf who, in his first season, traded a first-round draft pick to Atlanta for Favre, then the Falcons' 248-pound, heavy-drinking, hard-living, third-string QB.

"Ron Wolf could give a shit about what anybody else thought about his decision, and he taught John Schneider, 'Have a conviction, and if anybody disagrees with you, fuck them. You're the one hired to build this team. You build this team.' "

Wilson's size would have been a turnoff to Carroll back in his USC days. The shortest Trojan quarterback Carroll signed was John David Booty at 6'3". However, Carroll, a guy who loves to talk about "doing it better than it's ever been done before," trusted Schneider's instincts, and Seahawks brass exhaled when their third-round pick—

seventy-fifth overall—was up, and Wilson was still available. Most outside of the Seahawks' football complex didn't think too much of the pick. The selection of Wilson, along with the rest of the Seattle draft choices, was ridiculed, being handed C-minuses, D's, and F grades by the major media sites.

"Pete Carroll is proving why he didn't make it in the NFL the first time . . . Seattle selecting Russell Wilson, a QB who doesn't fit their offense at all, was by far the worst move of the draft," wrote a *Bleacher Report* columnist.

Part of the skepticism stemmed from the fact that the Seahawks had just signed free agent Matt Flynn to a $26-million deal with $10 million guaranteed to challenge the 2011 starter Tavaris Jackson. As most expected, Carroll named Flynn the starting quarterback for the first two games of the pre-season—although he still maintained that there was competition for the job.

"I asked him in the pre-season how he thought [Jackson] would react when he's told he's not being named the starter," recalled Yogi Roth, one of Carroll's former assistants at USC and the co-writer of the coach's *Win Forever* book. "Pete goes, 'It'll be hard for him to deal with it.' I said, how will it be for Russell when he's told he's not The Guy right now?' He goes, 'He won't even flinch.' It was 'OK, cool. I'm going to show you.' And he was right, and the rest was history."

Carroll started Wilson in the Seahawks' third pre-season game, and he led the team on scoring drives on the first 6 possessions and wasted little time winning the starter spot. As a rookie, playing in a system run by offensive coordinator Darrell Bevell (Favre's old QB coach at Green Bay under Rossley), Wilson tied an NFL rookie record with 26 touchdown passes and led Seattle to an 11–5 record. In Wilson's first two NFL seasons, he completed 64 percent of his passes and threw 52 touchdowns against only 19 interceptions while rushing for over 1,000 yards and making the Pro Bowl each year. Three days after the 2014 Super Bowl, Wilson tweeted out a picture from the Seahawks' locker room of him and thirteen teammates: "The 2012 @Seahawks draft class. They graded us as an F. Now we are World Champs!"

Carroll said, thanks to Schneider, Wilson's performance "expanded" his thinking, as he suspects it has for many others around the NFL now.

"We just wanted great football players and unique football players, and Russell fit that to a T," he said. "I was excited when John was so fired up about him. This was a chance to see what would happen and realize that the magnitude of this style of play could really be a factor for us, which it turned out to be. As I'm growing and moving forward, I would think more that way, too. I was closed to the idea to some extent. We never had a six-foot QB. I think it's proven to all of us, we gotta be more open-minded and expand our thinking if we want to do great things."

Johnny Manziel was one of many quarterbacks who didn't fit the old prototype, which was now being looked at in a new light.

_ _ _ _ _3.

# THE PAGEANT
# WORLD FOR BOYS

The 1983 NFL Draft is known for producing the greatest crop of quarterbacks in League history. Three of the six first-round QBs—John Elway, Jim Kelly, and Dan Marino—are Pro Football Hall of Famers. In all, there were sixteen quarterbacks taken in the twelve-round draft. But it was a quarterback who got bypassed in that draft and signed on two days later who may have made an even bigger impact on young QBs than any of the NFL stars.

Undrafted free agent Steve Clarkson, a three-year starter and Academic All-American at San José State, lasted one season on the Denver Broncos roster, then two more years in the CFL before he walked away from football.

In college, Clarkson was an unconventional (for his era) dual-threat QB. As a junior, he was a shockingly nimble 6′0″, 254-pounder whom Mike Singletary literally bounced off of when Clarkson led the Spartans to rally from a 15–0 hole to a 30–22 victory over number ten Baylor. Clarkson said he hung out with his Samoan teammates and ate like them, too, but then, at the request of head coach Jack Elway, he shed forty-five pounds before his senior season and sparked State to road wins over Oregon, Oregon State, and Stanford, featuring Elway's son, John. It was the second season in a row Clarkson's team had beaten John Elway's squad.

"If I came along today, I'd definitely be at the top of the charts," Clarkson said. "The things that we held back on are my biggest strengths. I was very fast, but I didn't do a lot of that for fear that they'd make me a wide receiver or a running back. I did everything I could to look like Joe Namath. Wearing his number 12 in high school. Had I come out now, I'd have been in vogue. I wasn't as fast as Michael Vick, but I think I would've been a bigger version of Russell Wilson."

Clarkson's pro career, statistically, consisted of his completing one pass for the CFL's Saskatchewan Roughriders. He was about to head off to training camp for a USFL team in Arizona, when he realized he couldn't take any more rejection. His playing career was over at twenty-four, but it ended up triggering the now-thriving QB tutoring business that helped him generate tens of millions of dollars, as wealthy parents hope some "guru" can turn their kid into a star.

The whole industry actually started with a backflip.

In 1987, Clarkson was divorced with two children and back in his native Los Angeles. His playing career was over at age twenty-four. He was working as a manager for Black Angus Restaurants, when his aunt noticed a newspaper ad seeking a Pop Warner league football coach. She answered the ad, giving a wealthy businessman from Malibu her nephew's number. When the man called, Clarkson told him he had no interest in being a youth football coach.

The businessman, Danny Klein, remembered Clarkson from his days as a star quarterback at Wilson High in LA and told him his own son was a fifteen-year-old aspiring high school QB. Coaching at the high school level sounded better to Clarkson, who offered to watch Klein's son play a flag football game at Westchester High the next day.

The kid, Perry Klein, was really more of a volleyball player at the time. He had a spindly frame and threw the ball OK, but Clarkson wasn't particularly impressed by his potential. Clarkson told the younger Klein to stay in touch, wished him luck, and then headed back to his car. He got to the door, unlocked it, and was about to get in, but then, for some reason, he turned around and glanced back to the field and noticed Klein doing a backflip. Clarkson paused and watched him do another flip, this one with his body twisting in the air, and, once again, the kid perfectly stuck the landing. Clarkson's mind raced. He wandered back over to Klein.

"You mind doing that again?" he asked.

Klein flipped. The gears inside Clarkson's head spun.

"What other kinds of flips can you do?"

Klein, who had grown up in a family of gymnasts and had been doing flips since about the time he got out of diapers, proceeded to go through an array of vaults and corkscrews and cartwheel flips.

"I thought, 'If I can teach this kid to play quarterback, and he does one of these flips after every touchdown, we'll be famous,'" said Clarkson. "That was my logic. I came from a marketing background."

IN THE MID-1980S ANDY Bark, a former San Diego Chargers wide receiver, bought *Cal-Hi Sports* magazine, a glossy publication that maintained the state high school record book for California. One day Bark got a call from Steve Clarkson, whom he knew from their high school days in Los Angeles. Clarkson predicted that his quarterback was going to rewrite the record book. Bark was skeptical. He was plugged into the local high school football scene and had never heard of Perry Klein.

"What makes you so sure?" Bark asked.

"I've changed the offense," Clarkson replied. "It's going to be so wide open. We're throwing it every play."

Clarkson's overhaul of Palisades football had been in the works for months. It had grown from the first time he got Perry Klein out of school at lunchtime and rode with him to the family's home in Malibu. Soon, it felt as if Clarkson and the younger Klein had formed a big brother–little brother relationship, Perry Klein said.

"I think Steve was pretty enamored that we lived on the beach," Klein recalled. "Steve never asked to get paid, but Steve doesn't do anything for free. I think he thought it'd turn into something, but I'm not sure if he knew what. He's a flashy guy. He liked the idea that he could bring girls up to the house."

Klein actually spent a lot more time at Clarkson's place than the twenty-six-year-old did at his. In the spring of Klein's sophomore year, he started bringing his receivers to Clarkson's house in the valley. Klein usually slept on the floor. Clarkson taught Klein how to read defenses and tightened his mechanics. The former standout QB also explained to Klein and his buddies the concepts of a Shotgun-Spread attack that Clarkson had devised as an offshoot of his godfather, Dennis Erickson's, offensive scheme. As payback, the sixteen-year-old washed Clarkson's tricked-out Datsun 280-Z and bought him lunches.

"It was sort of like Mr. Miyagi," Klein said. "And then we'd run this offense that he was installing."

With Clarkson's help working as the high school's new volunteer offensive coordinator, Klein did put up staggering numbers. And, just as Clarkson requested, Klein punctuated every touchdown with a backflip.

"He promoted the showboating," Klein said. "To this day, he's all about flash, and he understands the entertainment value. That's his biggest strength. He understands it's a business, knowing that there's a lot of guys who can throw a football. How do you build a guy's name? That's Steve's genius, too."

In Palisades' first three games, the junior quarterback averaged over 435 yards passing and 4 touchdowns, generating plenty of buzz around Southern California. It also didn't hurt that Klein had quite the hype man in Steve Clarkson:

"If he stays healthy and keeps his head, I think he will develop into the best quarterback in the history of high school football," Clarkson told the *Los Angeles Times*, adding that Klein reminded him a lot of John Elway.

Clarkson transformed previously unknown Perry Klein into one of the hottest quarterback prospects in the country, with big-name schools suddenly in pursuit. Relying heavily on shovel passes and short throws, Klein put up jaw-dropping stat lines. In one game, he smashed the national single-game record for most completions and the state record for most passing yards by going 46 of 49 for 562 yards and 6 touchdowns. Klein went on to set a state record with 3,899 passing yards while leading the Dolphins to the city title game.

The following year, Clarkson—and Klein—switched high schools, going from Palisades, which didn't have many starters returning, to California prep powerhouse Carson, the team that was pre-season ranked number two in the nation by *USA Today*. The longtime coach at Carson had just witnessed his high school team get beaten by a less-talented school with a more advanced passing game. Carson High coach Gene Vollnogle wanted Clarkson to come in and incorporate his offense. Clarkson liked the bigger stage and the better group of receivers and running backs but wanted to bring his QB—Klein—with him to pilot the offense. Klein's father was against the move, but his mom was in favor of it, because she thought it would better him.

The switch caused quite a dustup in the LA sports scene. The longtime Palisades high school coach told the *Times* he felt used. "I would quit coaching before I would ever let a Klein on my field again. They stabbed me in the back twice," Jack Epstein said.

The Kleins navigated the clunky local high school transfer rules by establishing an apartment for Perry to set up residence. The quarterback and his parents lived in a nearby two-bedroom apartment during the week and spent the weekends at their beach house in Malibu. "We came up with a story that it was closer to work for my dad, and that my parents were getting a divorce—even though they weren't," said Klein. "Turns out, we didn't even need to have the story."

At Carson, the QB and his private coach won over their new teammates as Klein amassed more eye-popping stats, leading the Colts to a city championship and the state title. Then, after football season, Klein transferred in the winter to Santa Monica High, where he played on the volleyball team. "It was made out to be such a big deal," Danny Klein recalled. "It was, like, here is this rich father who would do anything to make his kid a better quarterback. But it was a good experience for Perry, and now they're all doing it, transferring to different high schools because they think it will make them better.

"If he was a violinist and wanted to go to a special high school to get better at violin, would anybody be upset? No one would care. It really upset me. One day my wife was in the Malibu market, and some lady who had a son who knew of Perry came up to her. She started chastising my wife for taking him away from Palisades High School."

As keen as Clarkson's marketing sense was, it took some advice from Klein's father, a self-made man who never went to college and had made a fortune in the scrap-metal business, to open the former quarterback's eyes to something bigger.

"We were talking, and he pulls down his bifocals to the tip of his nose and goes, 'By the way, you're missing a great opportunity here.'" Clarkson thought the elder Klein was talking about some potential real estate boom, since they'd spoken about that before.

"'Look,' Klein continued, 'there are [private] tennis coaches and golf coaches and pitching coaches. You could be the first quarterback coach.'"

Given all the potential Danny Kleins out there—the rich dads of Southern California—Clarkson's mind kicked into high gear. He took a leave of absence from Black Angus, because he knew he was on to something bigger in the football world. Clarkson didn't need to put any ads in the newspaper or spring for a TV commercial. The visibility of Perry Klein in high school worked better than any advertisement Clarkson could've had. Klein accepted a scholarship to Cal, while word of the coach's impact on his protégé had other parents scrambling for Steve Clarkson's number.

"The college coaches helped me the most," said Clarkson. "They'd run into a high school kid at their camp, and they'd recommend me."

In 1994, Klein, who also transferred in college (to Division II C.W. Post) was the third quarterback selected in the NFL Draft, behind Heath Shuler and Trent Dilfer. By then, Clarkson's QB business, the Air 7 quarterback academy, was booming. Eager parents saw Steve Clarkson as their sons' ticket to stardom, and Clarkson saw many of them as his ticket to a lavish lifestyle. Several of his pupils had dads worth eight and nine figures. Clarkson was raking in $700 an hour and had some parents paying him $10,000 a month for private lessons for their sons. Many of those kids he trained did blossom into college quarterbacks. Later, one of his clients, Kevin Feterik's dad, not only funded hundreds of hours of tutoring but was also the subject of rampant speculation that he bought a CFL team, the Calgary Stampeders, so his son could play quarterback in the pros.

The zest to cultivate a budding NFL quarterback taps into the vanity of many, especially the type A big-business leader conditioned for success. For some dads, syncing up with the top quarterback guru for the teenage QB—or preteen QB—is akin to a business student's getting accepted to Wharton or a journalism student going to Medill. Only there is no accreditation for this education. Instead, they have to sort through hype, hope, and hearsay.

"The QB dads are like nomads in the desert," said Rick Neuheisel, the former head coach at UCLA, Washington, and Colorado, who started out his coaching career at UCLA in the late '80s and early '90s. "If you tell 'em there's water, they're gonna drink it. They want their sons so badly to have the instruction, so if you have any sales ability at all, you can make them believe they have to know what you know.

"All you have to do is tell 'em, 'Hey, he's got *It*.' And they'll keep spending. And spending. And spending. That's all it takes."

Greg Biggins, a former personal trainer based in Southern California who spent more than a dozen years handling playing personnel for the Nike Football Training Camps and also was on the Elite 11 selection committee for thirteen years, says the Little League father is tame compared to the quarterback dad. Biggins says he's been offered $5,000 by some fathers just to rate their kids higher. (Biggins didn't take the money, he said.)

"The nuttiest species on the planet is the dad of a quarterback," said Biggins. "He is the most myopic. They have such blinders on toward their son. If the kid's 5'10", it doesn't matter, because, well, Drew Brees is 5'10". But these guys are paying an expert to 'like' their kid, so that gives them even more reinforcement."

Many parents, eyeing Division I dreams for their sons—and their families—schlep their boys to one college summer camp after another, sometimes hitting six campuses in seven days. In some cases, the dads seem to want it a lot more than the kid does. The dads hope their kid will pick up a few key tips from famous college coaches and get noticed in these mini auditions in hopes of landing a big-time scholarship or at least generate some recruiting buzz, but they usually just end up with a half dozen T-shirts. Steve Clarkson, though, had history on his side . . . at least enough history to make things very tempting for a lot of dads.

ANDY BARK'S BUSINESS, WHICH became Student Sports, Inc., spread into sports camps. After the 1990 high school season, Bob Johnson, a veteran Orange County, California, high school coach and onetime Fresno State quarterback, told Bark he was retiring so he could watch his sons, both QBs, play college football. The older, Bret, had been a starter at UCLA before transferring to Michigan State, while Rob was set to play football at USC.

When Johnson asked Bark if he had any work he could give him, Bark offered him a part-time gig as the lead instructor at the weekend camps he had scheduled throughout the football off-season. He also gave the salty coach some advice: "You had [Stanford quarterback Steve] Stenstrom and your sons; you ought to coach QBs, because this Clarkson guy is killing it."

Johnson had amassed a lot of clout among college coaches for building a powerhouse in Orange County at El Toro High. He was up front about planning on going back to coaching in a few years, but he wasn't sure if it would be back at the high school level or in college.

"We were a really small, lean option—we couldn't pay Bob very much," said Bark. "Two things naturally came to my mind: Steve Clarkson. Kids need it [coaching]. My deal was, when they're eighteen and off to college, it's too late."

By the early '90s, Bark had emerged as perhaps the most influential person in the Southern California youth sports scene, both through his publications and the camps, combines, and 7-on-7 tournaments he was running. Back in the '70s, when he served as ball boy for the USC football team, Bark first noticed the advantage a budding quarterback could gain from growing up around high-level coaching.

He saw it firsthand with Trojan QB Pat Haden, who was best friends with J. K. McKay, his go-to receiver who happened to be the son of USC head coach John McKay. During Haden's senior year of high school at Bishop Amat, he even lived with the McKays. "I saw [that the] coach's kids had a huge advantage," Bark said. "My dad was a surfer. I'm not complaining. But I realized, the earlier you're exposed to it, the quicker you make decisions, and the more reps you get, your feet are better. Your release is better."

That message was reinforced for Bark when then-University of Miami offensive coordinator Gary Stevens in the late '80s told him that the way the college game was structured, with the NCAA limiting coaches to only twenty hours of practice a week, it was too much of a time crunch to develop a quarterback. "Unless you've got Bernie Kosar, who is basically smarter than the coaches, you can't make up for your lack of fundamentals," Stevens said.

"He told me, 'You gotta get your drops early. You really can't get 'em up to speed in twenty hours,' " Bark recalled. " 'You need to come in as an eighteen-year-old ready to learn your plays and be a dude in the locker room.' We'd write about it, but I'd keep thinking, 'Where do I go to get this coaching? My high school coach is still running the Veer.' "

Bark also researched that more than 40 percent of NFL quarterbacks were the sons of either former quarterbacks or coaches, a number that was staggeringly high to the former college receiver. But the more Bark examined it, the more it made sense—and the more it bothered him.

"You shouldn't have to be a coach's son or a player's son to be a quarterback," he said.

Bark recruited Johnson to handle the fundamental work at his roving camps. He also provided Johnson with the player who would eventually become his most successful protégé—a tall fourteen-year-old named Carson Palmer. At the time, the big seventh-grader's dad, Bill Palmer, a successful Orange County financial planner, called Bark, asking for advice on developing his son, who he thought had a good arm and lots of potential. Bark mentioned a couple of viable options: Steve Clarkson, but that would probably mean a ninety-minute drive each way; and Bob Johnson, who four years later helped turn Carson Palmer into one of the country's biggest recruits in 1997 and a future Heisman Trophy winner for USC. By 1999, when Bark created the Elite 11, a week-long quarterback "campetition," Johnson was installed as the head instructor, which over time certainly elevated his "guru" status as Clarkson's brand was flowering in the grassroots football world.

"Steve always tried to figure out a way to scale himself," said Bark. "Bob didn't care about scaling his stuff at all. He charged $20 for a couple of hours. He liked being in the limelight as the Quarterback Guru."

The competition among Clarkson and Johnson and their protégés created an awkward dynamic with some residual effects. A few Clarkson protégés supposedly steered clear of the Elite 11 because they didn't want to be coached by Johnson for a week—out of loyalty to their coach. Another Clarkson QB approached one of the Elite 11 coaches, Yogi Roth, and asked whether changing his personal QB coach would "help me with the Elite 11, since I know you guys don't really like him." (Roth, a former USC assistant, told him no and not to worry about it but was stunned a kid would be so direct about the tension.)

Clarkson also had a pipeline into arguably the most fertile QB factory in the country, Mater Dei High School in Santa Ana, located right in Johnson's backyard in Orange County. Clarkson began working with Matt Leinart when he was a fourteen-year-old freshman after the Monarchs coaches connected the two. Clarkson also groomed future Mater Dei stars Colt Brennan, a Heisman Trophy finalist at the University of Hawaii, and Matt Barkley before he went off to be the four-year starter at USC.

"Steve's whole deal is, he made average guys good, and good guys very good," said Bark. "And he generated hype and sizzle. [Mater Dei head coach] Bruce Rollinson doesn't let anyone touch his athletes except Steve Clarkson."

In Northern California, another onetime college QB, Roger Theder, also got involved in the private quarterback coaching game.

Theder was older than Clarkson and Johnson and had a richer coaching pedigree. As an assistant at Stanford, he had coached Jim Plunkett to consecutive Rose Bowls and a Heisman Trophy; at Cal, he had developed Steve Bartkowski into the NFL's first overall pick in the 1975 draft, and later he helped make unheralded Jeff Garcia from San José State into a future NFL star.

"I drive a Honda Prelude station wagon, the same car that I drove for some twenty years," said Theder, when asked if he thought his approach to the business was similar to Clarkson's. "I don't think we're opposite. My goals are different. My goal is just to make the kid a better quarterback. I think he [Clarkson] wants to make a lot of money."

By all accounts, including his own, Clarkson had.

Google Steve Clarkson's name and you'll find a litany of jaw-dropping monetary amounts parents have paid him at different times over the past two decades, depending on the frequency and time he's invested with a kid. A 2004 *New York Times* story said that tutoring for a year at Clarkson's camps cost up to $60,000. In a 2008 *Men's Journal* story on Clarkson, which detailed how he trained, among others, the sons of Will Smith, Wayne Gretzky, and Snoop Dogg, Clarkson got $700 an hour for private sessions, with a minimum commitment of a year. (Clarkson pointed out to me that he's also coached the sons of FedEx founder Fred Smith and talk-show legend Larry King . . . yes, that Larry King. Both men have sons named Cannon.) In a 2009 *Philadelphia Daily News* story, Clarkson's "cheapest" deal was $625 a month, which included forty-eight sessions a year but no actual one-on-one instruction. Clarkson told me his best bargain deal was now actually $650 a month, which included thirty-six sessions a year, not forty-eight.

That deal was separate from what Clarkson made on the private-instruction side, where he had about two dozen quarterbacks, he said, adding that he had clients nationwide and in Germany, England, and Japan. According to the 2009 *Philadelphia Daily News* story, the starting price for his private instruction was $8,000 a month. And that didn't include the two-day evaluation that each young QB must pass, which costs an additional $3,000 plus traveling expenses. Clarkson steered clear of getting into too many specifics about his rates.

A friend of Clarkson told a story about how the private QB coach spent much of his fall of 2005. Clarkson would get on a plane on Friday (usually from Los Angeles) and fly to Philadelphia, where he coached a ten-year-old quarterback. He'd call plays in the kid's game Saturday morning and then fly to Boston later in the day to review film and work with Harvard QB Richie Irvin, the son of a Southern California attorney. Then on Sunday morning, he'd board the first flight up to San Francisco so he could go over the high school film of a Bay area quarterback, Nate Montana, the son of NFL legend Joe Montana. Clarkson's friend said the coach was making around $75,000 a week for the road swing.

Clarkson chuckled when asked if the $75,000-a-week price tag was accurate. "That would make it legendary," he said. "It wasn't nearly that much—but I was paid very well."

Steve Clarkson's marketing savvy resonated with eager parents *and* with media hungry for hyperbole and the next big thing, and it made him a go-to guy. In truth, he wasn't just marketing his protégés but himself as a brand, too. He credits reading the 2001 Bernard Goldberg book *Bias* for opening his eyes to handling the media. "I don't read many books, but it's one of the greatest books ever written," he said. "It talks about how media basically runs the world. I truly use it as a practice. You can almost anticipate how emotions will turn before it actually happens.

"There is a story line and a script that you have to create, because there's too many kids out there. How do you say this kid is better than that kid? I mean, who the hell knows? You don't really know till they get up there [to college] and play, and then you have to hope they get to a program where their coach believes that this kid's talent is gonna help get them their contract extension or their next big job. And if they don't have that, they're just another guy."

Clarkson's Sistine Chapel was quarterback Jimmy Clausen, the youngest of Jim Clausen's three boys. Before owning an insurance business, Jimmy's dad was an assistant coach at Cal-State Northridge. Jimmy's oldest brother, Casey, and middle brother, Rick, were quarterbacks at Tennessee, and both were longtime Clarkson projects. Casey was a four-year starter for the Vols, but he had underwhelming physical tools. Scouts saw him as an immobile pocket passer lacking arm strength, which was backed up by Casey's going undrafted.

Clarkson loved to tell the story for reporters about how he noticed young Jimmy's prodigious arm in the distance while sitting with Jim Sr. at one of the Clausens' high school games after the kid supposedly took an errant pass and fired it back—on a rope, 55 yards across the field, according to *ESPN The Magazine*. "Who the hell is that?" Clarkson asked.

"That's my other son," said Jim, referring to his fifth-grader. "He wants to be a linebacker."

"He's a better quarterback than both your other boys right now," Clarkson replied. Once Jimmy got into the seventh grade, he, too, started training with Clarkson. It's worth noting that Jimmy, like Jim Clausen's other sons, was considerably older than the other students in his grade. Jim Clausen started Jimmy in kindergarten late, at age six, the same age his other children had been. He also held Jimmy back in the sixth grade, again to allow his son to mature more, just the way he did with Casey and Ricky. It was as if Clausen Sr. was redshirting his kids in grade school. Twice.

By Jimmy Clausen's sophomore year of high school in 2004, Steve Clarkson was practically writing the headlines for journalists. "If there were a LeBron James for football, it would be Jimmy Clausen," Clarkson told the *New York Times*. "He's truly a freak. It's ridiculous."

Cynics snickered at the quote, especially the part where Clarkson used the word "ridiculous" in comparing Clausen and a basketball prodigy who'd already earned Rookie of the Year honors and become the youngest NBA player to ever score forty points in a game. A year later, Clarkson evoked the names of other iconic athletes to describe his latest high school QB project.

"Jimmy has the leadership of Casey, the intangibles of Rick, and the skills of Dan Marino," Clarkson told *Sports Illustrated* in 2005 for a story titled "The Kid with the Golden Arm."

The elder Clausen wasn't shy about giving Clarkson credit for making his sons into college quarterbacks and conceded to the *New York Times* that all three of his sons were actually average athletes. "Steve Clarkson is a dream maker," Jim Clausen said, using a term he also used about Clarkson in *Los Angeles Magazine*'s 100 Most Influential People issue. [Clarkson liked the description so much, he changed the name of his company from Air 7 to Dreammaker.] "There's no way that any of my three sons ever get an opportunity to do the things they've done and have the experiences they've had if it isn't for someone like Steve Clarkson."

In 2006, when Jimmy Clausen announced that he would be attending Notre Dame, he did so at a news conference at the College Football Hall of Fame in South Bend after arriving in a stretch Hummer limousine with a sixteen-person entourage. There was a press release touting the news event. Clausen waved around three bulky high school championship rings. "In terms of entrances, Jimmy Clausen outdid Don King, Don Corleone, and Don Quixote combined," wrote CBSSports.com's Dennis Dodd.

Clausen never did get any championship rings at Notre Dame. The best he could do was lead the Fighting Irish to a Sheraton Hawaii Bowl victory, and his team went 16–21 in his three seasons in South Bend. He had a good career but hardly a great one, throwing 60 touchdowns against 27 interceptions. His team was just 1–6 against ranked opponents. After the 2009 season, he entered the NFL Draft and was taken in the second round. The NFL career of the QB once compared to LeBron James amounted to 3 touchdown passes, 9 interceptions, and 9 fumbles for a Carolina Panthers team that went 2–14. Two seasons later, Clausen was cut.

Jim Clausen may have paid Steve Clarkson a small fortune for a decade-plus of private QB lessons, but he probably made that money back in unspent college tuition, thanks to all three of his sons getting scholarships. After Jimmy Clausen signed with Notre Dame, Charlie Weis even recommended Clarkson to Fighting Irish legend Joe Montana, who was looking for someone else to train his own sons. The Montanas flew Clarkson out to their place in Calistoga Ranch, watched him work with their eldest boy, Nate, and after ten minutes were sold and told him he had the job. Nate Montana transferred to longtime Bay Area powerhouse De La Salle but couldn't win the starting job. He attempted just 19 passes as a backup for his senior season and was completely off the recruiting radar. Well, almost completely.

"When I moved back to California as the new head coach of UCLA, Steve Clarkson calls me," Rick Neuheisel recalled. "He wants to make deals. If I take Montana's kid, he'll make sure that we get the next great one he's got to come to UCLA. I said, 'I can't really do that, Steve.'"

Nate Montana ultimately decided to be a walk-on at his dad's alma mater but then transferred to Mount San Antonio Junior College in California, then to Pasadena City College, before re-enrolling at Notre Dame. He lasted there one season before ending up at West Virginia Wesleyan, a Division II school. (Montana also had a short stint at the University of Montana, too.) His younger brother, Nick, also became a Clarkson disciple and even transferred down to Southern California in high school to play at Oaks Christian, Jimmy Clausen's alma mater.

Asked to size up the ability of the younger Montana for an ESPN.com story about the famous sons on the Oaks football team in 2009—Joe Montana's son, Wayne Gretzky's son, and actor Will Smith's son—Clarkson replied, "How good is he? He's Joe. He's Joe with a stronger arm." Nick Montana also ended up bouncing around in college, beginning his career at Washington before he, too, transferred to Mount San Antonio Junior College and then resurfaced at Tulane.

The run of Jimmy Clausen stories in the media also caught the eye of a wealthy commercial developer and contractor in Delaware, who kept calling to ask Clarkson to train his nine-year-old son, David Sills V. Clarkson says he was initially reluctant, because he'd never worked with anyone quite that young, but he eventually relented, because the "experiment" of seeing how much the kid could retain intrigued him.

Even though Clarkson and his new protégé lived three thousand miles apart, they met regularly, usually for one weekend a month, weekly in football season. The coach often was flown back east, but sometimes the Sillses trekked to California to visit Clarkson. Other times, they connected at various places in between, depending on wherever Clarkson was conducting a clinic. By the time Sills V was an eighth-grader, his dad estimated he'd already spent around $100,000 on Clarkson.

Soon, Clarkson was gushing about his "Next Big Deal." One of the people who listened was then-USC head coach Lane Kiffin. Clarkson and Kiffin were chatting over the phone about recruiting, and the "dream maker" told the Trojan coach that he had a thirteen-year-old kid who was going to be better than Jimmy Clausen and Matt Barkley, USC's starter at the time. Before saying good-bye, Clarkson directed Kiffin to a YouTube video.

Curious, Kiffin called Clarkson back after watching the clip to find out more about Sills. Clarkson explained that the boy had been training with him for three and a half years. A few hours later, Kiffin was on the phone with the kid and his parents, offering a scholarship that wouldn't become a reality for another five years. None of these scholarship commitments are binding until the player puts his signature on a National Letter of Intent on Signing Day, which comes on the first Wednesday in February of his senior year of high school. Regardless of all that, the story of Kiffin offering a scholarship to a thirteen-year-old seventh-grader became national news, and Steve Clarkson and his Dreammaker brand swelled even bigger.

_ _   _ _ _4.

# DQ

**Trent Dilfer cringed as he** started to discuss the five-star quarter-back he'd let his staff talk him into inviting to the 2012 Elite 11 in his second season running the event. Dilfer lamented that he wasn't at the Elite 11 regional where the QB had worked out. Instead, he was attending one of his daughter's volleyball matches.

"The kid was the recruiting guys' guy," Dilfer said, referencing a prospect who gets so hyped by the online recruiting analysts so early that the kid practically gets anointed, which often skews his self-worth and breeds a sense of entitlement. This dynamic had only become thornier as the social-media world had grown. Five years ago, thousands of fans weren't flocking to some seventeen-year-old's Twitter feed, fawning and telling him how much their school needed him. It was bad enough that high schoolers had become mindful of their status being measured in recruiting stars; now they could quantify it in a different metric: followers.

Dilfer said he would never pick the kid—or allow him to get invited again.

"Joey told me, 'Trent, you're really gonna struggle with this kid,'" Dilfer said. "Joey" was Joey Roberts, Dilfer's twenty-six-year-old assistant. The onetime Elite 11 ball-boy-turned-undersized-wideout for Bob Johnson's powerhouse Mission Viejo high school program makes a point of taking a three-mile walk with his old coach near his parents' place just to talk high school football every time he returns home to California. Roberts's title with the Elite 11 was general manager. He was also a right-hand man for Dilfer and ESPN's NFL reporters Chris Mortensen and Adam Schefter. Roberts evaluated QB tape, just as the Elite 11 coaches did, and also had a keen sense of the personalities of the quarterbacks.

Roberts was right. The kid arrived at the week-long Elite 11 event in Southern California and recoiled at the competition. At one point, the QB even retreated to a bench along the sidelines and just sat there observing while the other blue-chippers kept playing.

Asked if the young quarterback was reachable, Dilfer leaned back in his chair. "No," he said. "Maybe he might be three years from now, but he wasn't at the time."

Dilfer said the problem went deeper than a lack of maturity.

"I think that's 'nature' at home, like the environment you grow up in," he said. "There are some of these kids who have, like, 25,000 Twitter followers. So 25,000 people are telling them how great they are. Even if 10,000 were haters and 15,000 were admirers, they['d still] grow up with this weird perspective or paradigm that 'I'm better than everybody.'"

Dilfer was done inviting kids like that. In his first season with the Elite 11 in 2011, the staff had already invited the QBs. They had selected another five-star "recruiting guys' guy." In the presence of the other touted quarterbacks and coaches, that kid wilted, too. "He turtled," said another Elite 11 staffer, invoking a now-often used MMA term for when guys just tuck their heads to avoid battling and wait for someone else to end things mercifully.

It used to be that the highest-ranked high school QBs in the star system were pretty much guaranteed invites to the Elite 11. The staff felt that they essentially had to have the high-profile kids there for political reasons or to quell outrage from fans questioning the authenticity of the camp if some five-star guy was neglected. Those days were over, Dilfer said, adding that event founder Andy Bark loved the fact that "we don't *have* to invite anybody."

Perhaps more than anything else, Dilfer wanted quarterbacks with "DQ," as he's termed it, as part of his ever-expanding QB glossary.

Dude Qualities.

Those other two five-star quarterbacks who made it through the old Elite 11 screening process weren't *Dudes*. They were just *guys*.

*Guys* don't lead. They don't inspire. They don't draw people to them. In coach-speak, there's a term for average players—JAGs. As in "Just a Guy." Guys don't have presence. A Dude does.

DQ is a handy Dilferism that old football personnel folks might have classified under the scouting umbrella of "intangibles." There is no position in sports more dependent on the intangibles than quarterback. Competitiveness. Toughness. Leadership. Resilience. Moxie. Grit. There are all sorts of buzzwords coaches use when it comes to sizing up the man they'd feel most confident flipping the keys of their livelihood to. Of course, none of those traits can be measured with any stopwatch or tape measure, which is a big reason the draft, much like the college recruiting process, is such a crapshoot, especially when it comes to quarterbacks.

Dilfer spoke a lot about quarterbacks either being "thermometer" leaders or "thermostat" leaders. If you're a "thermometer," you react to the climate of the room. If you're a "thermostat," you *set* the climate. Different coaches have different gauges for this quality. Broadway Joe (Namath), Joe Cool (Montana), and Tom Brady all had *It*. Little Russell Wilson has *It*, too.

Great coaches could bring the Dude out of some quarterbacks, Dilfer believed. He felt he was proof of that. Dilfer played high school ball about a decade before the star system was in place, but if it had been, he wouldn't have been even close to a five-star prospect. He was a big athletic quarterback who played in a Wing-T offense, meaning he threw the ball about ten times a game. He didn't even make all-league his senior year. The first-team all-league QB ended up as a punter at San José State. Dilfer landed at Fresno State after one of the assistants saw something in him. In 1992, in his first full season as a starter, the Bulldogs were preparing for their next opponent, Louisiana Tech, when FSU offensive coordinator Jeff Tedford summoned Dilfer into his office the Tuesday before the game. Tedford was watching film of Tech's D, which had just held Alabama, the defending national champs, to its worst offensive game of the season. The Tide managed just 167 yards of offense and 0 offensive touchdowns in a 13–0 Bama win.

"We were ranked near number one in the country in offense at the time, and he goes, 'I'm gonna be honest with you. I trust you, but I don't know if we can get a first down on 'em,' " Dilfer recalled. His heart sank. His own coach didn't even think he had a shot?

Three days later, Tedford called Dilfer to his office again. Dilfer, a self-admitted "knucklehead" in those days, figured he had gotten into some sort of trouble. Jeff Tedford said it wasn't anything like that.

"I want you to know something," Tedford said. "I never should've said that to you Tuesday, because what I didn't remember about this game is that we have you. We have the best player in college football, and that's you. And we're gonna go beat these guys because of you."

Dilfer went out and threw 5 touchdown passes against Louisiana Tech the next day, including a 57-yard touchdown pass less than one minute into the game. Fresno State won, 48–14. "I played perfect football," said Dilfer, who called that week a signature moment in his life. "And was I the best? I wasn't even close to the best player in college football. But I was the best player that night."

Fresno State went on to lead the nation in scoring that year. FSU began the next season ranked in the Top 25. The opener was at Baylor. The Bulldogs took a 20–0 lead as Dilfer was on his way to a 31-of-38 performance with a career-best 483 passing yards. "The [fans in the] stands were chanting 'Dildo, Dildo . . . ,' and that's a rough crowd for a Christian school," Dilfer said. "We lose the game on a reverse pass where I fumble and I separate my throwing shoulder. I'm crying like a baby up in the rehab room, because it was bad, and it was the first time I had really gotten it bad. Everybody's panicked. I'm a Heisman Trophy candidate, and the coaches are all throwing things. Jeff [Tedford] comes in and looks at me. 'You need to stop crying,' he said. I was, like, 'It hurts so bad, and I love the team, and I'm not gonna be able to play.' "

Tedford asked Dilfer if he wanted to play the next week against

Oregon State. Dilfer, who couldn't even lift his hand off his hip, nodded that he did.

"OK, now stop crying, because you're probably going to really be crying in the next few days as we try to get this shoulder right," Tedford told him. "You gotta trust me."

Tedford had Dilfer do a grueling set of arm raises with weights while the QB's whole body was shaking. "I'm tearing up, I'm in so much pain," Dilfer said. "He kept saying, 'Trust me.' That Thursday, I threw. Friday, I was cleared, and Saturday, I played against Oregon State."

Dilfer threw 4 interceptions and only 1 touchdown pass, but the Bulldogs were so fired up, they hammered the Beavers, 48–30.

"I'll never forget his teaching after that game," Dilfer recalled. "'Nobody knows what you did to play in this game, and we would never have won without you.' I didn't play good. But his point was that you're awesome because of what you did leading up to it, not in the game. Of course, I remember the next Monday and him just ripping me for the four interceptions, but I also remembered what he'd just said after that game, and that was genius. I listened."

Dilfer only tossed one more INT over the next ten games, while throwing 25 touchdown passes to lead the nation in passing efficiency. After the season, he opted to skip his senior season to enter the NFL Draft and was selected by the Tampa Bay Buccaneers with the sixth overall pick in the first round.

During Dilfer's time at Fresno State, Tedford refined his mechanics, tightening up his motion—and his mind-set in the pocket—coaxing the big QB to use his legs to buy time, opting to try to find the twenty-yard pass play rather than the six-yard scramble. Dilfer called Jeff Tedford the best coach he ever had in his football career.

"He simply turned the light on," Dilfer said. "He enlightened me that consistency comes with doing the little things, mechanics, discipline; all that will allow your athleticism to come out. You can't just run around and be an athlete, be tough, have crappy mechanics, be inconsistent."

Years later Dilfer's family repaid Jeff Tedford. Dilfer's stepdad, an old football coach, had a former player whose son was pretty good. That kid, Garrett Cross, played tight end at Butte College. Dilfer's stepdad told Tedford, then the head coach at Cal, he should check out Cross—at a junior college in Northern California—to recruit the tight end. Tedford liked Cross but loved the quarterback. Aaron Rodgers was 5'2" when he began high school and didn't sprout to be 6' until his senior year, and by then it was too late for him to get on college football recruiting's radar. Locally, no one doubted his arm—he was clocked at 91 miles per hour on a radar gun—and he had a 3.9 GPA. Regardless, Rodgers didn't receive a single scholarship offer coming out of Pleasant Valley High School in Chico, California.

At Butte, Rodgers threw 28 touchdowns and just 4 interceptions in his freshman season. Tedford offered him a scholarship as soon as he had a chance to visit him. To say that Rodgers emerged from the recruiting process with a chip on his shoulder would be an understatement.

"A huge chip," said Dilfer.

Dilfer himself lost the edge he'd had at Fresno State once he made it to the NFL. "The biggest mistake was feeling like I'd gotten there," Dilfer said, "like it was about the culmination of the hard work instead of the beginning of the hard work.

"I had the worst three years any quarterback's ever had in his first three years [in the NFL], and then I was humiliated, and from humiliation comes humility, and then I worked really hard, got back to who I was." He earned a trip to the Pro Bowl in his fourth season, becoming the only Tampa Bay QB in franchise history to get selected, and led the Bucs to their first trip to the playoffs in fifteen years, but two seasons later he was benched for journeyman Eric Zeier by Coach Tony Dungy.

The knock on Dilfer in Tampa, according to a *St. Petersburg Times* columnist in 2001 was: "The greater the pressure grew, the tighter he seemed to play. It is generally acknowledged that Dilfer is sometimes too smart for his own good. He overanalyzes his life. He thinks, when he should react."

Dilfer said he'd agree with the criticism after the first sentence. "I actually played pretty well in big moments if you look at my career," he said in regard to a column written days before he became a Super Bowl–winning quarterback for the Baltimore Ravens. "But I do think I overanalyzed. I out-thought the room. Very true. I did tighten up, but I still won games. If I could go back and change anything, I'd try to be more reactive, more instinctive. Less analytical. Looser in big moments. My tightness wasn't pressure. It was more people-pleasing. I tried to do it the right way instead of doing it the way that works."

Dilfer had signed as a free agent with the Ravens in 2000 as a backup to Tony Banks before taking over the starting job at mid-season. Despite the championship season, Baltimore still opted to sign free agent QB Elvis Grbac to a $30-million deal. Dilfer signed with the Seattle Seahawks, where Matt Hasselbeck was the expected starter. Dilfer won the starting job, but a knee injury and then a ruptured Achilles tendon derailed him again. He bounced from Seattle to Cleveland to San Francisco, starting twenty-nine games before retiring and joining ESPN as a commentator in 2008. His biggest contributions to some of his NFL teams came in locker-room pep talks, such as the one he delivered before Super Bowl XXXV.

"I was always scanning the room, monitoring," Dilfer said. "I've always had that awareness [of], 'OK, what needs to be said? What is everybody waiting to hear? What do people need to have?' I love self-help books and love reading great speeches and quotes. Those things resonate with me. I think they resonate with most people, just not all the time, right? So I'm always looking to give you the one thing that resonates in the now for you."

Dilfer was a natural on TV for some of the same reasons folks reasoned he struggled in his NFL playing career. He was analytical and thought before he reacted. He wanted to talk about the smarter stuff in the game of football but present it in a way that someone who didn't play could grasp what he meant.

"I think a lot of people make the mistake [of] trying to show how smart they are," Dilfer said. "That's not the goal. I don't care how smart they think I am. I want you to love football more than you already do. Because I love it. I love the purity of it. I want you to love it as much as I do."

He referenced again the 2001 *St. Petersburg Times* column observing that he was sometimes too smart for his own good and over-analyzed his life: "A lot of my core values come from that, and I've been very transparent. I teach 95 percent from my failures, not my successes.

"I can handle all the criticism as a coach and as an analyst, but I hate it when I get criticized in a way of, 'Oh, he thinks he was better than [the player he was discussing], so that's why he said that.' I never come from that [place]."

Dilfer was complimentary about all the former-QBs-turned-analysts, from Troy Aikman to Phil Simms to Ron Jaworski, and he also said he was grateful to studio hosts Rich Eisen, Chris Berman, and Trey Wingo, but the guy he said he learned the most from about TV was Mike Holmgren—his old coach in Seattle—a guy who had never done TV.

"Mike Holmgren is the most gifted person I've ever been around at taking the super-complex and making it digestible," Dilfer said, adding that the two of them would laugh all the time, because he often did the opposite. "I could overcomplicate anything—still can to this day, if I want to.

"I can sit and talk to the Malcolm Gladwells of the world, or the professors, and talk these highly theoretical, complex, multilayered things, and I love it. It's stimulating to me. Nobody else gets it; you're living in a little bubble in these conversations, right? Mike could take a Fire Zone Blitz and the genesis of it from [longtime Pittsburgh Steelers defensive coordinator] Dick LeBeau and make it sound simple. And here I'd be, where I would give you the whole history of it, the different shades they used and disguises and why, and he's just, like, 'At the end of the day, this is what they're doing.' "

Mike Holmgren, like most of those close to Dilfer during his playing career, figured he'd go into coaching. Jeff Tedford tried to hire him for his coaching staff at Cal. Other NFL friends offered him coaching jobs, too, but Dilfer declined all of them. He told Tedford it was a job he was not ready for. Dilfer recognized that he didn't have the ideal temperament for coaching at that level.

"All these great head coaches, they're so patient," he said. "Holmgren is so patient with dipshits."

In the first two years after his football career ended, Dilfer spent much of his time—when he wasn't on TV or on the golf course—taking inventory of his life. His office inside his Saratoga, California, home was littered with yellow notebooks filled with Dilfer's random thoughts probing the issue of "What am I supposed to be doing?"

Steve Stenstrom, the former NFL quarterback who took over as the president of Pro Athletes Outreach (PAO), a Christian program for athletes and coaches, became a mentor for Dilfer. Stenstrom also lived in Northern California and had kids around the same ages as Dilfer's. They'd go out to eat and discuss what would be the best direction for Dilfer's energy and spirit. The more they spoke, the more Dilfer came back to coaching, because, as much as he relished being as connected to football as he was while doing TV, there was still a void for him. That was right about the time ESPN asked Dilfer if he'd like to be involved with their program Elite 11, which the company had bought from Andy Bark. Bark had studied Dilfer's work on TV. He was blown away by Dilfer's knowledge of quarterbacking and his ability to communicate it.

"I think he knows the position better than anyone I've ever been around," said Bark, who had been around a long list of coaching innovators over the past three decades.

Dilfer was fascinated by the opportunity. He'd always believed he could be a good coach but that he could be an even better mentor. The Elite 11 setting afforded him a chance to do that, but if he was going to get involved, he wanted to flip the model on its head.


TO DO THIS THING right, to make the Elite 11 even more substantial in its space, Dilfer said, he had to incorporate some "soul-building stuff" into the process. "That was, without a doubt, the number one thing I wanted to address," he said. "I wouldn't be part of a 'camp,' because camps are lame. Camps determine whether you're good at camping or whether you're good at drills. There are very few transferable traits that come from traditional camps. You learn how to thrive in controlled environments without random elements being thrown at you. I said, if I was gonna do this, I wanted to discover the soul of the player as much as the talent. I wanted to create environments where you'd see them fail. That way I could find out about them.

"The only kids we've missed on since I've taken this over are the ones who had faked the Dude Qualities, that when they were really put into the tough situations, they were broken emotionally and mentally. They just didn't have it in them, yet."

Dilfer was still trying to determine what his best barometers and revealers for DQ were in the regional Elite 11 workout settings. Those events tended to feel like cattle calls. He credited Joey Roberts, his protégé from TV, for being a good resource. "He played a big part in getting a behind-the-scenes look at who a kid was, because people still didn't know who Joey was," Dilfer said. "They'd just think he was a friendly face walking around writing down notes. Joey became a lot of the reconnaissance on the kids. We were doing a lot of the drills I guarantee a lot of them hadn't done, because I know I didn't do them until late in my NFL career. We watched how they interacted with their competitors, how they interacted with their parents, with their coaches."

The Elite 11 finals afforded Dilfer more control and a clearer window to see Dude Qualities. In his first year running the Elite 11 finals, he made the QBs pull an all-nighter. The quarterbacks were summoned to the hotel lobby just before midnight and told they were responsible for knowing the rest of their playbooks, which meant they had to cram on three times the information they were supposed to have gotten down by that point. The next year, Dilfer called in the Navy SEALs for a surprise 4:45 a.m. workout that involved three-hundred-pound logs, chilly ocean water, hundreds of push-ups, bear crawls through the sand, and a bunch of determination. He wanted to see them tapping into their personal reservoir, he said. Better still, Dilfer wanted to observe how they responded in the practice sessions right after they were the most physically and emotionally drained.

"We're looking for guys who have 'figure-it-outness,'" he said. "Go figure it out. Now I'll guide, and we as coaches need to help, but if we create robots, those guys are gonna fail. They have to be empowered to figure it out. We can give them some of the answers but not all the answers. They have to discover those answers."

The more Dilfer delved into the quarterback culture, researching the great ones—and not great ones—from the past three decades, the more he'd become convinced that it was much more "nurture" than "nature" that produced top QBs.

"I'm 100 percent sold on nurture, 'cause the streets are littered with talented kids, and the Pro Football Hall of Fame is littered with guys who aren't that talented. They have great 'figure-it-outness.' They make great decisions. They develop."

Dilfer learned a lesson from his early work as an NFL analyst that he factored into how he structured the Elite 11 and his perspective on evaluating and developing quarterbacks. He admitted that he'd been fooled as an NFL analyst by how some quarterbacks came across in their interviews. Dilfer cited a guy in his first few years as a TV commentator he had pegged as a first-pick-of-the-draft talent, a guy he thought had "serious Dude Qualities."

"My biggest whiff," Dilfer said. "I got sold. I had really never been around him. I took other people's word for it. I said, 'I think he's the best quarterback in the draft,' and I based my evaluation on hearsay, not personal experience. Now I don't do that. That's one of the reasons we bring the counselors to the Elite 11. They don't know that. You're an idiot if you don't come be a counselor for me at Elite 11. It's just that simple. You have a chance to show me who you are for four days in a great environment. It's priceless for my evaluation. Johnny Manziel proved so much to me with what he did the three days I was with him. I don't think he's the most talented. I don't think his size is ideal. I don't think a lot of things about Johnny are ideal. But Johnny has the Dude Qualities for when the moment's big, when the pressure is on; when the shit hits the fan, it brings out the best in him. It brings out the worst in others, but it brings out the best in Johnny Manziel. And Johnny will be successful, because the shit hits the fan every day in the NFL.

"You have to see them in adverse situations. You have to see them struggle. I think Dude Qualities come out best when you see them fail, so from an Elite 11 perspective, that's why we create environments where they will fail. All these other camps put them in these other drills that they've done a thousand times. You don't find out if the kid is a good quarterback. You find out if the kid is good at drills. We've created graduate-level drills, where they will fail. They're designed for these kids to fail, so that we can get a gauge on how they're going to respond to coaching while they're failing, on how much can they adapt, how pliable are they. Do the Dude Qualities show up when they're irritable or only when they've just dropped a dime?"

He also figured out that, upon exiting the NFL, he didn't even know what he didn't know when it came to evaluating quarterbacks. "No way I would've been able to see this in 2011, let alone 2008," Dilfer said. "I had no wisdom in this space while I was in the League. This is why, when some 'Coach A' says something, I say, 'Wait a second. Why is he the expert on this? Coach A is wrapped up in being Coach A in his little space that he's focused on. There is no thirty-thousand-foot perspective.' It wasn't until after that I got out and embraced my role as analyst and global thinker in this space that I realized I had a lot of work to do.

"I'll spend twelve hours a day watching college quarterbacks. You have to do the work from a global level, not just a micro level. It was a process of learning how to look at this position differently and taking the best from Mike Holmgren, the best from Mike McCoy, the best from Norv Turner and spending time with all the quarterbacks. What are the commonalties, and what are the biggest things that cause guys to miss? Just wrestling with all this stuff. This has been an evolution. Hopefully, I'll do a lot better in 2014 than I did 2013, which is better than I did in 2012."

THE EVALUATION GAME, PARTICULARLY when it comes to things such as draft analysis or even recruiting ratings, often gets clouded with snap judgments.

"Can't play."

"Coach killer."

"He was a two-play guy," as in, "I watched him for two plays and saw all I needed to see."

Perhaps it's human nature to rush to judgment. Perhaps it's about egos striving to be authoritative voices. Definitive talk does sound best in the media marketplace. Gray areas are seen as wishy-washy analysis. They don't drive headlines or attract eyeballs. The same can hold true in war-room settings, where assistants are looking to impress their boss—same with Dilfer's Elite 11 staff. Dilfer was self-aware enough to know it was a temptation he'd have to battle, especially since in his day job as an NFL analyst for ESPN, he was studying grown men who had been playing the position for decades. That was the world he'd lived in as a player for almost twenty years before immersing himself back into high school football.

In the online recruiting rankings, where a level of groupthink seemed to fester, since most of the evaluators had only worked outside the college coaching system they covered, the evaluators often leaned on which schools were showing which kids interest. The evaluation process was even sketchier, since it related to teenage football players still maturing into their bodies and playing in a wide variety of systems and against levels of competition that were all over the map. In the face of all that, attitudes and egos got shaped about who was a "five-star" and who wasn't.

Former USC assistant coach and self-described "AdventurePreneur" Yogi Roth was often the most reasoned voice in the Elite 11 war room. The thirty-two-year-old former Pitt wideout, who also works as an analyst for the Pac-12 Network, was best friends in college with Panthers tight end Brennan Carroll, Pete Carroll's son. Roth co-authored the Super Bowl–winning coach's *New York Times* best-selling biography/motivational book *Win Forever* and had become an ambassador for Carroll's message, which can best be summed up as relentlessly upbeat. Roth tried to never lose sight of the fact that these kids were just sixteen or seventeen years old, he said. Roth's style was formed from his first day on the practice field as a Trojan coach: "My first practice, I was running around like a maniac. Pete said, 'Why were you doing that yesterday?' I said because I saw that's what [fellow Trojan staffers] Kenny [Norton] and Brennan were doing.' He goes, 'How about you run around with a purpose today? Better yet, how about you don't run around at all? Instead, how about you watch and observe a couple of days, and observe why guys do what they do? Let's develop a way for you, because it really matters. Do everything with a sense of purpose.' That sounds really easy, but it blew my mind, especially when it came to coaching. It was always, 'Go! Go! Go!' But go where? Instead, it should be, 'Go here. Step this way.' No kid is trying to throw three picks in 7-on-7 on the Nike campus on ESPNU. So why are you gonna get on his case? He already feels bad enough about it. Let's coach him up. Let's talk to him about it. Let's give him some real truths."

The dynamic with recruits had become more complicated with the ever-escalating visibility of recruiting and with kids getting offered so much earlier than just two or three years ago.

"We're gonna blame a high school kid for getting loved up because he's committed to a major university that has an insane fan following?" said Roth. "We're gonna potentially discredit a kid because everybody loves him up every day? I think we have to A) guard against that and B) be aware of it. That does not mean we need to break him down to build him back up again. This is not old-school coaching. This means, how do we communicate with him? What type of learner is he? Is he auditory? Is he visual? What is the best way? Is it calling him out in front of a group? Probably not. Is it pulling him to the side and seeing how [his] life is? We have to find that out.

"We always say, we think we're the new generation for the next generation of athlete, because the athlete has changed. We have to be aware of it. They've had more hype. They have more self-confidence. They're part of a millennial generation. They have the world at their fingertips instantly. We have to be aware of how that affects their emotions. We have to be aware of how emotional some of these kids are and how they mask those emotions, because they're supposed to be a guy with Dude Qualities, because Trent Dilfer in a tweet said, 'This weekend I'm looking for guys with DQ! Own the environment!' None of those kids have a clue what DQ is or what it means to own the environment. They've been doing it, but once they start to try too hard is usually when the majority of them fail."

Roth said for many of these hyped high school quarterbacks, they just want to land the golden ticket to the Elite 11 so they can exhale and think, " 'Whew! Glad I proved everybody right.' And it's our job in Coaching 301, 401—graduate-level coaching—to make sure that we communicate really cleanly with these guys in this developmental aspect of their lives, because this is probably one of the first times they're going to hit some adversity, since they're [now] around other alpha males, but we need to remember that it's really not the kid's fault if he doesn't know how to deal with not being The Guy.

"If I had to define quarterbacks, they're like models. They're very fragile. A model on the runway, when [she's] walkin', nobody can touch her. But the models I've known or dated are very self-conscious, and 90 percent of quarterbacks are the same way. It's the Oedipus complex. They all want to prove that they're The Guy and want someone to tell them that they're good. I can't think of one quarterback who isn't self-conscious, because they have such high expectations and high standards. [Speaking] as a coach, the little nuggets—'Nice job,' 'Good throw,' 'Way to be accurate'—do build your confidence, because when a coach isn't saying them, you're wondering. And if you're saying the opposite, it's even worse. The power of your language is massive. You have to elevate them. That's your job. You gotta coach them hard, but be aware."

Just in the first three years running the Elite 11, Trent Dilfer had learned to become more patient with the young quarterbacks, he said.

"Oh, God, yeah," Dilfer said, "but I came into this thing late, and I had a lot of cleaning up [to do] my first year. That first year [2011], there was a lot of damage control. It just wasn't what it intended to be. I had to change the culture and make sure it would align with my core values. I was very harsh. I only got to choose about five of the kids the first year. I was very impatient, to a fault, but I think some of that was necessary in order to prove a point to everybody involved that this was going to be very different.

"One of the biggest things was eliminating the stars from the rankings and the offers from the evaluation process. It's hard to say I know more than Scout[.com], Rivals[.com], 247[Sports], ESPN's *Recruiting Nation*, but I said, 'We're gonna do it better. We have to stick to our guns, even if it's about some kid who has five stars.' All the things I showed to our staff about how you evaluate a quarterback, I said, 'They [the online recruiting analysts] don't do this, so we are right. We are more comprehensive in what we are looking at because of our experience, because of our process. So, we are willing to say that just because a kid has a bunch of stars by his name, that doesn't mean he's good.'"

NEAL BURCHAM, A SHAGGY-HAIRED kid from Arkansas, arrived at the 2011 Elite 11 finals unknown to even the national recruiting reporters. Burcham had just one scholarship offer—from FCS-level Central Arkansas. He was, literally, a no-star recruit. The 6'2", 175-pounder got assigned to room with Jameis Winston, the strongest personality among the twenty-four QBs invited, and Burcham never seemed awed by anything. Not Dilfer's late-night cram session. Not the more-hyped, higher-profile quarterbacks with their supposed rocket arms. Not being surrounded by elite wideouts and defensive backs everywhere he looked.

The more perfect passes the kid threw, the more he picked apart 7-on-7 defenses, the more he rose to jump at any challenge, the more annoyed Dilfer got, knowing that Burcham had been so overlooked in the recruiting process.

"That shows how stupid some of these people are in college football," Dilfer told reporters at the finals. "If you're in that region, and you haven't offered this kid, you're stupid."

Burcham left the West Coast sharing MVP honors with Jameis Winston and Tanner Mangum. The most-hyped quarterback prospect invited to the camp, five-star QB Gunner Kiel, struggled in Dilfer's setup and wasn't even selected as part of the top eleven—news that left many recruiting analysts bewildered.

A few days after Burcham returned home, he received his first FBS scholarship offer, from Arkansas State. The bigger college programs, though, either already had settled on their quarterbacks or weren't believers in Burcham, which didn't sit well with Dilfer.

"Neal Burcham is QB w/no major offers. Shows the absolute

dysfunction in NCAA recruiting. Coaches need to work harder and study QB pos more," he tweeted on the eve of the 2011 college football season.

June Jones became a believer in Burcham a couple of months after Trent Dilfer did. The SMU head coach, a former NFL quarterback, has his own measure for DQ. Only his letters of preference for his QBs are "ESTP" from the Myers-Briggs Type Indicator, the psychological prism based on the theories of psychiatrist Carl Jung. The sixty-one-year-old Jones first became intrigued by Myers-Briggs in the spring of 1998, in the midst of football's biggest QB debate. Jones was in his first season as the San Diego Chargers quarterbacks coach and had spent months with his colleagues trying to sort out the dilemma facing them about which QB the organization wanted: Peyton Manning, the cerebral son of football great Archie Manning; or Ryan Leaf, the rocket-armed country kid from Montana who had just led Washington State to the Rose Bowl. Jones took a break from draft prep one night and turned on *20/20*, the ABC newsmagazine show. It was featuring a man claiming to be an expert on brain-typing. The man, Jonathan Niednagel, is a lay scientist whose academic credentials are rooted in finance, not science or psychology. In the *20/20* episode, Niednagel was asked to size up Manning versus Leaf. He said one of the two guys has *"It."* One doesn't.

"Which one?" Niednagel was asked before saying, "I can't tell you. I'm being paid by an NFL team."

The next day, Jones walked into the office of his boss, Bobby Beathard, the Chargers' GM. San Diego had the second pick of the draft. Beathard admitted it was the Chargers who were paying Niednagel. "He says Peyton Manning has *It*. Ryan doesn't," Beathard told Jones. Manning was ESTP. Leaf was ESTJ.

"I said, 'Are we going to take Ryan Leaf, even though we know he's not one of *those* guys?'" Jones recalled. "He said, 'Well . . .' and then he hemmed and hawed and said something about how the owner made the call." The Colts shrewdly drafted Manning first. The Chargers, against Niednagel's suggestion, drafted Leaf, who wasted little time alienating his teammates. Leaf opened the season throwing just 1 touchdown pass and turned the ball over 15 times. Head coach

Kevin Gilbride was fired after six games. Jones became the interim head coach. A few days after taking over the Chargers, Jones met Niednagel.

"He scared the piss out of me the first time I ever talked to him," Jones recalled. "We talked for two and a half hours. He said, 'Let me tell you four things about yourself,' and they were things that nobody else would know. He said, 'When you don't prepare, you're at your best.' I'd just become head coach of the Chargers. Tony Gwynn and Ted Williams are there. I prepared for it and wrote a speech, put it in an envelope, and I get called up and realize I'd put the wrong deal in there. I gave the greatest speech I'd ever given in my life. Standing ovation. Two days later, he tells me that."

Jones's team, the Chargers, had just signed Leaf to a four-year, $31.25-million deal, including a guaranteed $11.25-million signing bonus, the most ever paid to an NFL rookie. Jones won his first game over a hapless 1–5 Philadelphia Eagles team, 13–10, thanks to Natrone Means's 112 rushing yards. San Diego won in spite of Leaf's only completing 9 passes but for the first time not committing a turnover.

"Ryan Leaf can't play, and I know it," said Jones. "Knowing he can't do it, you call a different game."

The next week against Seattle, Leaf had what would prove to be the best game he would ever have in the NFL, going 25 of 52 for 281 yards. "We have our final drive first-and-goal from the 3, down 27–20," Jones said. "We have time for four plays. He misses every pass. I shouldn't have thrown it, but we were struggling running the ball."

A week later, at Kansas City, on the opening drive, Jones predicted to his team that they'd spring a receiver wide open on a deep route. Too bad Leaf overshot the guy by five steps. "The whole sideline's crushed. I said, 'Ryan, I don't think I'm going to be here at the end of the year. I'm going to play this [backup Craig] Whelihan guy. You just take your licks and get ready for the next year.'"

Jones was correct. He was canned after the season, and Leaf went down as one of the biggest busts in NFL history. Jones left the NFL and has since become one of the most successful coaches in the college game. In his first season at Hawaii, he sparked the biggest improvement in NCAA football history. He led the Rainbows to a

23–4 record in his last two seasons at Hawaii before accepting the SMU head coaching job. In Dallas, he took over a team that went 1–11 in his debut season and the following year went 8–5, making a bowl for the first time in twenty-five years since before the Mustangs got slammed by the NCAA's Death Penalty. Jones also had become one of Niednagel's staunchest supporters, along with Danny Ainge, the president of the Boston Celtics, who said, "You can take Red Auerbach, Jerry West, Phil Jackson—I'd take Jon Niednagel."

Jones had Niednagel "brain-type" his players at Hawaii and at SMU for more than a decade. Jones always had a list of seven or eight players for Niednagel to evaluate when the coach brought him out to his practices. The players were usually good athletes who should have won starting positions but hadn't because they didn't respond well, Jones said. Niednagel then gave him direction on what positional moves should be made to better fit each player to his more "natural" position.

"It's fascinating stuff," Jones said. "I had some guys playing positions who I thought should be better than they were. He talked with them and then told me, 'OK, this guy [Reagan Maui'a] needs to be a running back,' and I had him playing defensive line. He was a 380-pound backup nose guard. I went to him. He had one year of eligibility left. I said, 'You're gonna have to trust me on this. If you lose a hundred pounds, I'll get you into the NFL as a running back.'

"[Maui'a] looked at me like I was crazy. But he lost a hundred pounds. I put him at running back, and he got drafted in the sixth round, and he's still playing in the NFL. And he'd never played running back in his life.

"He's been 100 percent right on every kid we've talked to him about."

Niednagel said he could talk to a person and gauge how his mind was wired by his voice inflection and diction as well as by eyeballing his facial features.

"Their eyes are more hawkish or more narrow, which is a telling factor," his son, Jeremy Niednagel, said of ESTPs. "Even their hair, their gait—whether they go up on their toes when they walk—are indicators."

Niednagel, who worked out of a tiny south-central Missouri town (population: 453), met with much skepticism from the science community, who took issue with the fact that he had no advanced scientific degree. Instead, he had a BS in finance from Long Beach State and had previously worked as a commodities trader. But he was quick to point out that he'd had almost forty years of research. He maintained that 60 percent of athletic ability came from personality type, and the other 40 percent stemmed from external factors, including how they were coached. He first started noticing the variances in motor skills when he coached his kids' Little League soccer and baseball teams. Soon, he was testing out his theories.

"I'd draft certain kids even though they'd never played before," he said. "I'd talk to the kid. I knew that, by halfway through the season, just by my coaching him, he'd be better than a kid who'd looked ten times better in the workout." Niednagel, then living in Southern California, had so much success as a Little League coach, there were stories about him in the *Los Angeles Times*. Word spread about Niednagel to pro sports teams always desperate for an edge.

Niednagel loved his connection to the sports world. Even though the Celtics paid him a reported salary in the six figures, Jones had never actually paid him for his guidance.

"I just fly him over," Jones said. "Jon sensed that I got it, and he wanted to help, and that I was more open than any coach he'd ever talked to." Jones, in his second season at SMU—after he'd led the Mustangs to their best season in twenty-five years—tried to get Niednagel hired as a professor in the Sports Management department.

"If he was a professor, I could run the recruits by him, but they wouldn't let me do it," Jones said. "[Niednagel] wanted to do the science to give validity to what he was doing, and being a professor at the university would do that for him. [SMU athletics director] Steve Orsini approved it, but we didn't have the money in the department to do it."

Jones had become well-versed in the sixteen personality types from Myers-Briggs, which were at the root of Niednagel's work. The letters are based on the pairings of psychological attributes:

*E-extraverted versus I-introverted.*
*F-feeling versus T-thinking.*
*J-judging versus P-perceiving.*
*N-iNtuitive versus S-sensing.*

Niednagel tweaked the older verbiage and came up with his own terminology, which he officially went with in 2011 when he published a book about parenting. Extraverted (E) became Front (F); Introverted (I) became Back (B); Sensing (S) became Empirical (E); iNtuitive (N) became Conceptual (C); Feeling (F) became Animate (A); Thinking (T) became Inanimate (I); Perceiving (P) became Right (R); Judging (J) became Left (L). Niednagel also reduced the profiles even further with numbers, as if the players were dishes off a fast-food menu, along with one buzzword. "ESTP," the type Peyton Manning is, became "FEIR"—Front Empirical Inanimate Right—or a #5, the "Opportunist." The full definition: "smooth operator," deal-maker, tactical, enterprising, adaptable, persuasive, energetic, seeks fun and excitement, athletic, enjoys the moment, realistic, good-natured, self-focused, body- and clothes-conscious, entrepreneur, negotiator, promoter, fine motor skilled.

"I took it out of that bogus Myers-Briggs world and tried to take it into the brain and what it's really representing," Niednagel said. "More than anything now, I just use numbers, 1–16. They all have a logical sequence in terms of the mind and the motor skills. And it's more memorable. I'm finding that dumbing down as much as I can helps them to learn it and retain it better."

Jones could rattle off the names of all the great quarterbacks who were ESTPs (FEIRs): Joe Montana, John Elway, Johnny Unitas, Joe Namath, Jim Kelly, Troy Aikman, Terry Bradshaw, Fran Tarkenton, and Brett Favre. An eye-catching majority of the Hall of Fame quarterbacks who played in the past thirty years are this one personality type. So were other Super Bowl–winning quarterbacks Ken Stabler, Phil Simms, Joe Theismann, and Trent Dilfer. Jones used the famous NFL Films anecdote of Joe Montana, the moment before beginning a last-minute, game-winning, touchdown drive in the Super Bowl, walking into the huddle and matter-of-factly pointing out John Candy in the crowd to one of his linemen as an example of a guy wired to thrive under pressure.

"ESTPs, under pressure, play their best," said Jones. "Whether it's a two-minute drill or we have to win the game on this drive, they play their best. Manziel—I would guess that he's ESTP. When the game is under pressure, he makes a lot of plays. I watched him in the Alabama game, and he made big play after big play. I'm pretty sure he is.

"I had this conversation with [former Denver Broncos head coach] Dan Reeves. He wanted to get rid of John Elway. He said Elway couldn't learn the playbook. But guess who was so great in the two-minute drill? John Elway. Guess who was calling all the plays then? John Elway.

"Can another guy who doesn't have the same brain type perform at a very successful level? Yes, he can, but you have to know that he's not one of those guys, and you have to be able to manage the game so that you don't put him into situations to lose the game, and you take some of the weight off him in pressure situations."

The latter is a key point that both Jones and Niednagel stressed. As much as it was ideal to find an ESTP quarterback, it was vital to ID what kind of personality type your QB had, so you could alter accordingly how you coached the guy.

Peyton Manning had the "best QB package of all time, thanks to his smarts, tactical spatial logic, peripheral and stereoscopic vision, body balance, and fine motor fluidity and prowess and decision making, etc.," Niednagel wrote on his blog on braintyping.com. "These DNA attributes also radically separate him from baby brother, #2 BT Eli, who we predicted from his NFL start would never consistently play to the excellence of prodigy Peyton."

Jones was stunned when he learned that Tom Brady wasn't ESTP (a #5) but rather an ENFP (a #9). ENFPs typically are too smart and empathetic to thrive as quarterbacks, because they have so much exuberance and passion. They, too, like ESTPs, are right-brain dominant, meaning perceiving and not judging. Translation: He was less likely to dwell on things and freeze at crunch time. The left brain has a more methodical bent, Niednagel said. "It is self-critical, and when it makes a mistake, it dwells on it." Drew Brees also is an ENFP.

"Brady and Brees are very atypical for their wiring," Niednagel said. "Most #9s end up as major busts. Brady was as good as anybody Belichick could ever coach as a #9. He's a team guy who wants to please, whereas Peyton [Manning], because of the way he's been raised, wants to please, too, but his inborn nature is more tough-minded in the moment, and he wouldn't be as apt to not toe the line [the way] Favre was. That's why when [then-Packers Coach Mike] Holmgren said in Super Bowl XXXI, 'Don't you dare mess with the plays,' and then on the second play, Favre audibled, and they scored a touchdown. That's just the nature of #5s. It's how they function in the moment. They have incredible vision. They don't script anything. They just can improvise. That's why Peyton Manning is so superior at the line of scrimmage. Peyton Manning just has that tactical mindset that is off the charts. #5s are not super-cerebral typically. Peyton is regarded as that, but of course he was taught by his dad, an NFL player who is a #13."

Niednagel's example of Favre's Super Bowl audible proved to be one of the biggest moments in a Hall of Fame career. Favre, then twenty-seven, uncorked a 54-yard touchdown pass on the game's second offensive play to torch Bill Parcells's New England Patriots defense in what would become a 35–21 Packer win.

The play was supposed to be 322 "Y" Stick, a pass designed to go to tight end Mark Chmura on a short, sideline pattern, but instead Favre opted for "74 Razor," which enabled him to connect with receiver Andre Rison on a deep post pattern.

"As I came to the line, I saw the safeties cheating up, and the linebacker over [Chmura] looked like he was coming," Favre told *Sports Illustrated*. "I figured they had seven guys rushing me. Incredible. We had never seen this from the Patriots on film, and if I couldn't get out of the play, we'd be in trouble. I checked to see that we had enough time on the clock to audible—you need at least seven seconds to change a play and get everybody to hear you—and we did. I knew I had to check to something with great protection and something that attacked the area the safeties were leaving open.

"It's not like I have a Rolodex in my head and just flip through plays till I get to one I like. After you've been in a system for a while—boom—the right play just comes to you. And 74 Razor just came. [Chmura] and both backs stayed in [to block]. And the second I took the snap, both of the safeties charged to cover a back and [Chmura]. The linebackers came. They had seven guys rushing and only two corners covering deep. That second, I thought to myself, 'Yeah! Just what I expected!' "

Even more curious about Favre's audible was, according to Packers assistant coach Gil Haskell, the team hadn't even practiced 74 Razor one time all season.

Jones actually was the Falcons' offensive coordinator when the team drafted Favre in the second round in 1991, years before he'd ever heard of Jonathan Niednagel. Favre lasted one season in Atlanta before he was traded to Green Bay for a first-round pick. He attempted four passes, had two of them intercepted, and the other two went incomplete.

"I thought Favre was inaccurate and drunk for eighteen straight months. [Atlanta starting QB] Chris Miller was in the Pro Bowl, and we needed help on defense," recalled Jones, who wasn't surprised to learn that Favre was wired to thrive under pressure. "If you go back in college, he won so many games on the last drive. In two years, I think he had thirteen wins, like, ten of them came on the last drive."

Jones said if he knew then what he knows now, the Falcons never would have traded Favre to Green Bay. "I[t] would've been different if I knew and I knew how to coach him," he said. "In two-minute situations, let him call his own plays. In those heated situations, Kelly went no-huddle; Favre, Elway, Marino—they all called their own plays. Let them lead."

Jones has never had an ESTP in college. He admitted he tried to type guys all the time, especially quarterbacks, and he always ended up wrong. "They all end up my brain type, ENTPs. I've looked for 'em. I tried to find 'em, but I haven't had one, but what Jon [Niednagel] does, which is really important for coaches, is he can tell you how to say things to a particular brain type that will be received better, and they will respond better. Basically he teaches you how to coach them better. He'll tell you, 'For him to play at the highest level under pressure, this is what you need to say and how you need to say it as a coach. Don't tell him what to do. Ask him what he thinks, even if you don't want to do that; then you trigger it this way to get him to see it in a timely fashion.' I did that with [NCAA career passing leader] Timmy Chang, and it really changed him."

"Type #13s are typically the ace on baseball pitching staffs, but their wiring isn't optimum for quarterbacks," Niednagel said. Still, it seemed that as the NFL was becoming more open to mobile QBs, more and more #13s were thriving. Aaron Rodgers was a #13, and so were Andrew Luck, Russell Wilson, Colin Kaepernick, and Robert Griffin III.

"Most of those #13s have squirrelly mechanics, because they don't have dominant motor skills," Niednagel said. "They're so loosey-goosey. They can get a whip [motion]. They have the biggest serves in tennis, the longest drives in golf. When they learn, with a lot of practice, how to use their whole bodies, they can get a whip in terms of club-head speed or arm speed—that's why they can get their fastballs to move a lot."

According to Niednagel, Johnny Manziel—despite Jones's suspicions—was a #13, too. So was touted UCF quarterback Blake Bortles.

Niednagel said he wasn't surprised that Tim Tebow struggled in his NFL career: "He's a #1, which is what a lot of great running backs are. Walter Payton and Emmitt Smith are #1s. Randall Cunningham and Donovan McNabb are #1s, too, but most #1s are busts, because they don't think the game real well. That type needs to be really relaxed to loosen up the big muscles. They need to be in the flow. Quarterback is not the consummate spot for Tebow, because he won't see the game the way the Mannings and Favres and Marinos do. When [#1s] get nervous and uptight, the feelings take over, and they can go haywire. With Tebow being left-handed—when you use the left side of the body, the right hemisphere is triggering so much of that; it's one thing to be a right-handed #1, but it's another thing to be a left-handed #1—it made him much more cumbersome in his delivery."

Jones was perplexed that he couldn't find ESTP quarterbacks

anymore. He asked Niednagel, who offered up a theory. "He said, 'June, if you and I went to the juvenile-detention home, 50 to 60 percent of the kids are ESTP.'" Jones at first thought Niednagel was joking but found out he wasn't. Niednagel explained that ESTPs often hate school and recoil at structure. Jones thought back to many of the great quarterbacks he knew and was convinced.

"Even look at Joe Montana's career at Notre Dame with [head coach] Dan Devine," said Jones. "That's why he didn't play for a while there."

Even if, as Niednagel said, ESTPs do recoil at structure, many of them have proven to be some of the world's greatest leaders. Winston Churchill, Teddy Roosevelt, FDR, George S. Patton, Douglas MacArthur—all were ESTPs. So were Malcolm X, Dale Carnegie, L. Ron Hubbard, and Ernest Hemingway. Studies estimate that somewhere between 4 and 10 percent of the population are ESTPs.

Jones thought Neal Burcham was an ESTP, "because every time I put him in a live setting, he completes every ball," Jones said a few months before the QB's freshman season. "I'm very anxious to see him play." Turns out, the young quarterback was actually ENTP, another right-brain dominant profile and the most common of all the personality types. Burcham ended up starting the Mustangs' final two games of the 2013 season, both losses, throwing 1 touchdown pass and 3 interceptions.

"I made a mistake in how I handled him," Jones said. "I should've slowed the game and talked to him between plays and nurtured him. I didn't do that, and he failed miserably. Against UCF, I told [SMU QB coach] Dan [Morrison], I'll go back to what I know works. He completed over 70 percent of his passes. I'm convinced if he didn't have a concussion with eight minutes to go, we['d have] beat[en] UCF, and we'd be talking about him a lot more. I know he would've made a couple of plays for us."

But Jones has another quarterback on his roster, who he now thinks is an ESTP, a freshman named Kolney Cassel.

"He reminds me, with how he acts in the huddle, of Jim Kelly [whom Jones coached with the USFL's Houston Gamblers]. Jim was

[an] ESTP," Jones said. He said by the fourth day of training camp in 2013, he turned to his QB coach, and both of them started believing Cassel might be an ESTP. "He didn't have any idea of what we were doing but still completed all the balls when we ran no-huddle. Even though I'm frustrated that he's not picking it up as fast, and he's not where he should be, he has something about him. He doesn't care. He thinks he's the best. Same thing Jim Kelly had."

Jones said if he finds out that Cassel's an ESTP, he'll let the kid call his own plays.

Usually by this stage, Jones (who has since resigned from the SMU job) would already know a player's type, but for the past three years Niednagel has been unavailable, battling Stage IV melanoma. The cancer started out on his arm, then jumped to his back, and then to his chest. He's had to battle two bouts of pneumonia and arsenic poisoning that he got, he said, from eating so much wild rice.

"I'd seen top experts in the field but ended up creating my own protocols," Niednagel said. "I was two weeks from death, but I've come back a long way."

His recovery comes at a time when he believed he, along with some help from a company in Orange County, was on the brink of a scientific breakthrough, that through DNA analysis he had four of the sixteen personality types defined. "The neat thing is, we're bringing out the science now in a way that is irrefutable," he said. "But, hey, anything that has been noteworthy over the ages has been scoffed at. I'm looking at this as a way to change mankind, not change NFL teams. It's far bigger."


ESTP OR ENTP, TRENT Dilfer was rooting for Neal Burcham. If the kid blossomed into a college star and made it to the NFL, it would help validate his model and his evaluation savvy. But his connection to the young quarterback ran deeper than that, just as it did with all the quarterbacks he had bonded with, whether they made it to the Elite 11 finals or not. He's told the kids who don't get selected that nothing would make him happier than "if you prove me wrong," and it doesn't seem like mere coach-speak when you see how choked up or moved to tears he sometimes gets around the high school quarterbacks.

"I'm always aware that some kids are gonna leave very disappointed. I don't want them to be crushed. I want them to be motivated," he said, adding that he often ends up texting back and forth with some of these kids more than with the ones he does invite to the finals. Walk into the office at his home, and you begin to understand why. The room is jammed with books, trophies, game balls, photos, and hard drives. There is also one of those giant cardboard checks, the kind contest-winners get. Dilfer's was a $25,000-prize check for winning the 2001 Stan Humphries Celebrity Golf Classic. Dilfer shot a course-record 62 to beat former Major League pitcher Rick Rhoden, the guy who was dominating the celebrity-golf circuit, who shot 67 the final day. On the wall facing Dilfer's chair is an antique dresser with a marble top covered with a half dozen trophies, including a two-foot replica of the Super Bowl trophy next to a game ball commemorating the Baltimore Ravens' Super Bowl XXXV win over the New York Giants. Above the dresser is a large flat-screen TV mounted to a built-in wall unit, and above that are three more game balls. The ball in the middle, directly above the Super Bowl trophy, commemorates the Ravens' 24–23 road win over the Titans in Week Eleven from mid-November 2000, which handed Tennessee its first loss in the thirteen-game history of Adelphia Coliseum.

The game was tied at 17 late in the fourth quarter. The Ravens just got a turnover and had the ball deep in the Titans' territory. In good position for the go-ahead field goal on a third-and-7 from the Tennessee 19-yard-line, Dilfer tried to force a slant intended for Patrick Johnson, but Titans defensive back Perry Phenix stepped in front and returned it 87 yards for a touchdown. Dilfer gathered himself on the sideline, said a prayer, and returned to the field to start a game-winning drive from his own 30 with 2:19 remaining after Tennessee's kicker missed the point after. Faced with another third down, Dilfer relied on some of his old athleticism after being flushed out of the pocket to his right, and he found Shannon Sharpe along the sideline for a 36-yard gain. On the ninth play of the drive—with 25 seconds left—Dilfer looked to Johnson again. This time, he connected on a 2-yard touchdown pass for the win.

"What I've learned from playing this game is that you never let circumstances around you affect what you do," Dilfer told reporters after the game. "You have to keep fighting. I'm from the old school. You play as hard as you can until you die out there. You leave everything on the field. I can't believe something this good happened to me. It's been such a long time."

The Ravens won the next nine games in a row to win the Super Bowl. That game proved to his new teammates in Baltimore that the guy who was run out of Tampa Bay could win big games and that he could shine in the spotlight after being slammed with adversity.

"I threw the worst pick of my life," he said, staring at the game ball. "Came right back and made a big play to Shannon Sharpe on third and long and then threw the game-winning touchdown pass in the two-minute drive. *That's* my career. Some good and some epic failure."

That game was more significant than even the Super Bowl win, which is why Dilfer aligned the game ball above the replica Lombardi Trophy. But there is something even more meaningful than that Ravens–Titans game ball. Above it is a framed picture of a smiling little boy, Dilfer's only son, Trevin. In 2003, the five-year-old boy began to feel sick on the second day of a family vacation to Disneyland. At first, doctors thought it might be asthma or bronchitis. Then other doctors thought the boy might have hepatitis, so they sent him to a children's hospital, but en route Trevin's heart failed in the ambulance. Doctors revived him. They stabilized Trevin and put him on a heart-lung bypass machine. They needed to transport him to the hospital at Stanford University. He required a heart transplant, but they couldn't put him on a waiting list until they could prove he still had brain activity. One day, Trent put his finger in little Trevin's hand and started talking to him. A tear rolled down the boy's face, and he squeezed his daddy's finger, which gave doctors enough proof to put Trevin on the list. That led to twenty-five more nerve-wracking days of hoping, but before the family could get more good news, they were told that Trevin appeared to have a systemic infection. On April 27, 2003, after a six-week battle, Trevin Dilfer passed away.

Over two thousand people, including dozens of NFL coaches and players, came out for a "Celebration of Trevin's Life" at People's Church in Fresno three days later.

That picture of Trevin perched near the top of the wall means everything to Trent Dilfer. Trevin would now be almost the same age as many of the high school quarterbacks Dilfer was grooming.

"I get to have a second chance," he said. "I get to pour out everything I have into young men's lives. I now have a bunch of sons. I get to do what I would've done with Trevin. I wouldn't have been the overbearing dad, but I betcha I woulda been close. I mean, good thing my daughters are strong."

Dilfer also had become a big brother and father figure to some of his Elite 11/TDFB staffers as they set out on their own coaching careers. "I think I like the coaching more, but I'm better at the mentoring," he said.

"He is [as] emotionally connected to these kids as anyone I've ever been around," said Yogi Roth, who has a Master's degree in communications management and who, before going into coaching, worked in the Pittsburgh mayor's and state representative's offices. "That's a combination of 1) the loss of his son, 2) his unapologetic, pure love of the game of football, and 3) for his desire to prove that he's the best in the world at understanding the quarterback position.

"I've watched him truly grow. He has gone through the process of self-discovery of how he coaches, how he speaks. His awareness of how he challenged the [players]. The greatest thing he brought to the Elite 11 is, he raised the standard. They [think they] can't handle more than twenty-five plays. What do we have? Eighty-three? Eighty-seven? Their minds can expand. He's raised the stakes. I watched him grow so much as a head coach. When Jameis [Winston] stood up [at the 2011 Elite 11 Finals] and said, 'Hey, we know you lost your son, but you've got twenty-five sons in here'—I still get a chill thinking about that right now. I think that's when he realized not only the power he has in shaping young men but also in shaping young men who then have the opportunity to shape lots more people. These are the crème de la crème, right? These are the CEOs. The BMOCs. They're the Dudes. They are going to take some element of what they learn from Trent and carry it on in life. And it's the same with his coaches, who not only look up to him as a player who won a Super Bowl, but also for where he goes philosophically. The thing is, he doesn't miss what he gets back from this, either. Other coaches I've been around—they don't take a moment to recognize that, because they don't have the time. This is one of those jobs where it's not thankless. It's thankful. I think that's why he really loves it."

# 5.

# THE QB WHISPERER FROM DIME CITY

JUNE 5, 2013.

Twelve year-old Chase Griffin was up before 5:00 a.m., dressed in his workout gear, waiting for his dad to make the two-hour drive from Austin to Bryan, Texas, on a steamy Wednesday. The Griffins were headed to see young Chase's private quarterback coach, George Whitfield, the guy who in what seemed like just a fortnight had replaced Steve Clarkson as top guru in the private-QB-coaching world. In truth, young Chase was giddy because he was also going to see Johnny Manziel, the reason Whitfield had come from San Diego to Allen Academy, a tiny Christian school that played six-man football a ten-minute drive from Texas A&M. Whitfield was set to train Manziel, Griffin, and three other college QBs, including the starters at Syracuse and Memphis, in Dallas, but the Heisman Trophy winner said he needed to stay local for his workouts with his Aggie teammates, so Whitfield audibled—and the other college QBs scrambled to relocate three hours south on a day's notice.

Manziel's separate one-on-one with the thirty-five-year-old Whitfield was scheduled for 8:00 a.m., but the Aggies star was twenty minutes late. He arrived in a dark SUV, flanked by two of his buddies. Whitfield was already annoyed with the star for being tardy.

Watching Manziel's pals each stroll up and snag a bottle of water from an ice chest set out for the half dozen high schoolers who had shown up to play receiver for the day only irked the coach even more.

"What's up, playa?" Manziel said as he spotted little Chase, whom he had met two months earlier at the Dallas Elite 11 regional when he spoke to the high school QBs.

Whitfield handed Manziel two Chinese Baoding balls to maneuver through his hands before they trotted onto the field. They were the same kind of therapy balls Whitfield recalled from his childhood that his dad used. His old man said they helped regulate blood flow and that great Chinese warriors used them before they went into battle. Whitfield bought a set (price: $80) for all his QBs. In fact, he had bought so many online from a certain company that its owner called him to ask if Whitfield was re-selling them on his own. Whitfield explained that he was a coach who gave them to his athletes, and he asked who normally bought them. He was told that musicians and surgeons used them to help develop dexterity, which got Whitfield thinking about how most athletes grab and clutch things with their mitts but seldom hone skills with their fingers to have a more acute touch. He bought so many more sets since then that the guy gave him a deal for nearly half the price he had been paying.

As Manziel sleepwalked through Whitfield's drills, one of the QB's buddies, a twenty-year-old whom the A&M star called "Turtle"— just like the name of the pal-turned-gopher in the HBO comedy-drama *Entourage*—tried to explain the player's mind-set.

"It's his instinct to *not* listen to anyone trying to tell him what to do," said Turtle a.k.a. Nathan Fitch, an old high school classmate who had just dropped out of A&M to manage Manziel's life.

If anyone had Manziel's trust, it seemed to be Whitfield. The son of two high school teachers in Ohio, Whitfield was the king of accessible metaphors; for example, he might coax a quarterback to use more of his body and less of his arm in his delivery by telling him, "The body pays the tab. The arm pays the tip. If the arm takes the whole bill, the arm can bankrupt you. The body can't bankrupt you."

If a quarterback was doing a drill and got too far up on his toes, Whitfield might tell him, "We don't want you to go Michael Jackson here." To remind a quarterback to keep good posture, it was about "keeping your suit and tie on." When he prodded Michigan State quarterback Connor Cook to pull his lead elbow (left arm) through in his throwing motion, Whitfield crouched behind the Spartan standout and told him, "Just imagine there's a midget talking shit right here. You don't want to decapitate him. You just wanna make him spit his gum out."

One drill Whitfield created to fine-tune Manziel's instincts or, more specifically, to retrain them, he called the Jedi. In order to get Manziel to work lower in his base, a tendency the A&M star worked against as his adrenaline revved, Whitfield said he wanted to "rob" the quarterback of his sense of vision by putting a blindfold over his eyes, so his instincts would kick in. His analogy was to the way someone wakes up in the middle of the night in a dark room and tries to, cautiously, be more anchored as they feel their way to the bathroom. "It put him in more of a controlled, predator position," Whitfield said. In the Jedi, Whitfield lined up two receivers, one off to the QB's left, the other to his right, and pointed for one of them to clap, triggering Manziel to plant his feet and get set to fire. Whitfield actually didn't intend for Manziel to try to throw the ball. "I didn't want him to throw, because I didn't want the ball to dictate 'success.'" Manziel couldn't help himself, though. He connected on 26 of 28 throws while blindfolded.

While Whitfield was best known as Manziel's Svengali, the former small-college quarterback trained QBs on six of the top eight teams in 2013's pre-season Top 25. This dynamic can make a lot of college coaches uncomfortable, knowing that an outside guy—a celeb coach—is tinkering with their school's most important player. One college coach admitted he's uneasy with the relationship and is skeptical of Whitfield's creative teaching methods but is afraid to say no.

"The one thing I told [my quarterback] I never wanna hear is, 'But George says . . .' And the good part is, they believe they're getting better, and added confidence is always a good thing."

Regardless, that college coach said he cringed when he saw Manziel on ESPN's NFL Draft coverage in 2013, a few months after winning the Heisman. Manziel was asked on the set if he thought he might leave college (two years early) to go to the NFL, and he responded by saying, "Coach Whitfield will know when the time is right for me."

"Coach Whitfield?!? What about his coaches at A&M?" the college coach groused.

GEORGE WHITFIELD JR. GREW up in a football family with a defensive pedigree. His father, George Sr., was a linebacker at Wichita State before a successful run as a high school coach in Kansas and Ohio. His uncle, David Whitfield, played defensive end for Woody Hayes's 1968 national championship team at Ohio State and was a captain on the Buckeyes' 1969 squad. George Jr. was born in Wichita but raised in the football-obsessed town of Massillon, Ohio. Massillon loves to brag that it's the place where all newborn boys are given a little orange football. The old rust-belt town (population: 32,000) fills its high school stadium, which seats 20,000, to root on the most storied high school program in the nation, the Massillon Tigers. The younger Whitfield's first job was in football. He was in second grade; he served as the Tigers' water boy. He was the eighth Whitfield to play football for Massillon but the first who wanted to play offense. The previous seven all were team captains and played on state championship teams. His dad, once the linebacker coach of future football great Chris Spielman, figured little George would grow up and become a linebacker, too, but his son would tell anyone who'd listen that he was a quarterback. The younger Whitfield imagined when he played with his buddies in the backyard that he was John Elway or Major Harris or former Notre Dame star Tony Rice.

His father, sensing how determined his son was, drove George four hours to Fremont, Ohio, three times a week the summer before his senior year of high school, just so he could learn the nuances of the position from Tom Kiser, a keen football mind who also worked as an engineer.

Whitfield went on to star as quarterback for the Tigers and

to spark Massillon to four fourth-quarter comebacks. He made honorable-mention all-state. Whitfield was offered scholarships by Iowa State and Indiana and several MAC schools and the Air Force Academy, he said. But every offer was to come to college and play defensive back. Whitfield didn't want to hear that. His heart was set on remaining a quarterback. He signed with Youngstown State to play for Jim Tressel, then the coach at YSU. Whitfield redshirted his freshman season and then starred in the Penguins' spring game, which gave him hope he might win the starting job. Tressel, though, had other ideas.

One day Tressel waved Whitfield into a staff meeting in a conference room.

"How many guys at this table would love to have George in their position room playing for them?" Tressel asked his assistants. The linebackers coach, defensive backs coach, and receivers coach immediately raised their hands. In fact, as Whitfield looked around the table, he noticed that every coach except for the offensive and defensive line coaches raised their hands. Whitfield reached down and playfully pulled up Tressel's hand, too. Tressel doubled as Youngstown's quarterbacks coach.

"Your vote's bigger than theirs," Whitfield said, smiling at Tressel before ducking out of the room.

Tressel later told Whitfield that he couldn't give the keys of his offense to a nineteen-year-old.

Whitfield thought about transferring to Ohio State as a walk-on but instead opted for Division II Tiffin University, in large part because he would be down the street from Kiser, so he could continue working with him. "He taught me that results aren't always the reality of what happened after he deconstructed it," says Whitfield, who went on to become the school's all-time leading passer.

After graduation, Whitfield figured that college coaching should be his next stop. He landed an entry-level job on Kirk Ferentz's staff as a weight-room graduate assistant at the University of Iowa. However, after one season, the pull of being a quarterback was too strong. Whitfield worked managing a bar in Iowa while driving all over the country to open tryouts at various levels of football. In 2004, he was one of 250 aspiring players who drove to Pittsburgh to try out for the Arena Football League's Chicago Rush. Head coach Mike Hohensee kept only two players from the tryout. Whitfield was one of them.

"I remember specifically saying at the end of the camp, 'Unfortunately, I'm only gonna keep two of you guys.' George said to me, 'Coach, when you said that, I was wondering who the other guy was.' That's how confident the kid was," recalled Hohensee, who said that Whitfield had a good arm but probably relied too much on his arm strength at the time at the expense of his touch, which was more of a premium in the Indoor Football League for some of the "specialty" throws.

"He needed to learn the game," the coach said. "That was his first experience with [arena football], so I recommended he play at one of the lower levels. He was a student of the game with a great attitude. He took coaching well, and he applied it quickly. He just didn't have the experience. I remember, I made a couple of calls for him."

Whitfield moved on to the Louisville Fire, where he threw a couple of TD passes in an exhibition game, but that was as close as he ever got to playing in a regular-season game.

Asked why his playing career never really took off as a quarterback past the Arena Leagues, Whitfield said that, as ironic as it might sound now, he never had the 30,000-foot view as a quarterback. He was a strong-armed, 220-pound guy with 4.5-speed, but he'd never been exposed to anything like the Elite 11. He'd only participated in a few local camps.

Law school started to sound good to him. Whitfield, who had relocated to San Diego, began studying for the LSATs. To help pay his bills, he applied for a marketing job with a local company, when he was presented with a different opportunity: The family that owned the business Whitfield contacted, the Green Flash Brewing Company, knew he played football and asked if he'd be willing to train their son. The dad had become the coach of a Pop Warner football team. His son was a fourth-grader and his team's new quarterback. His mom told Whitfield they'd pay him $40 a session.

"It was about a forty-five-minute drive to get there, so I probably spent half the money on gas," Whitfield said. The workouts took place on a Little League baseball field.

Whitfield's efforts with the kid proved to be a hit. By the end of Mikey Hinkley's Pop Warner season, Whitfield was coaching more than a dozen other kids. "I realized how cool it was whenever there was an 'Aha!' moment, when a little kid gets it," said Whitfield.

Whitfield essentially stumbled into a profession he hadn't even realized existed. He also had no clue that he had landed in perhaps the perfect spot to do it—in a QB haven with wealthy families and year-round sun that happened to be outside the driving distance of Steve Clarkson and Bob Johnson in the LA area. "I didn't know who Steve Clarkson or Bob Johnson were," Whitfield said.

He pulled the plug on his struggling playing career and on law school. His outgoing nature and gregarious personality also helped him get an internship with the San Diego Chargers in 2006, where he assisted offensive coordinator Cam Cameron, who also happened to be the son of a former Massillon football coach. Whitfield had actually first met him back when Cameron was Michigan's quarterback coach and he was a thirteen-year-old QB who had talked his dad into letting him attend the Wolverines' summer football camp. In San Diego, Whitfield cut film, charted practice, and got to observe how Cameron and the staff studied minute details that the former Arena QB had been oblivious to.

"It was like being a junior high science teacher sitting in at NASA, working with government scientists," Whitfield said.

Details Whitfield had taken for granted as a player, he was forced to reconsider. These became his 'Aha!' moments. "A snap is a snap," he said. "I just thought guys put their hands under however they're most comfortable. But they [the Chargers] had a systematic reason for doing it a certain way."

The Chargers would have one cameraman lying on his belly filming up next to the center, and a second cameraman, also on the ground, four feet behind, filming up through Philip Rivers's legs to see exactly how the quarterback clasped the ball when he received it. The team would spend forty-five minutes twice a week filming these

exchanges during their OTAs, Whitfield said. Cameron became consumed by details dating back to his Michigan days in the mid-'80s, he
told Whitfield, after learning how then-Wolverine baseball phenom
Jim Abbott, despite being born without a right hand, excelled as a
high school quarterback and never fumbled a snap.

Another example of the level of attention to detail: All his life
Whitfield had been coached to drive off his back foot in his delivery.
With Cameron and San Diego QB coach John Ramsdell, it was "drive
off the *inside arch* of your back foot."

Whitfield began to grasp the mechanics of things he had never
contemplated when he was in the middle of doing them as a QB.
For instance, how a quarterback's whole body needed to be engaged,
starting from the inside of his right shoe (if he is a right-handed quarterback), and then the hip goes through. Then the core goes through
as he rides that energy, and then his arm rolls into it.

"They were splitting hairs, splitting atoms—everything," Whitfield said. "There was a science to it, because if you're not specific,
something can mean different things to different people."

THE FIRST TIME WHITFIELD flashed onto the national radar as a private QB coach was in 2009, at the Nike high school football training
camp being held on the USC campus in Los Angeles.

Whitfield, then thirty-one, was part of a caravan of four car-
loads of QB hopefuls who made the two-hour drive up from San
Diego. Among the quarterbacks Whitfield brought was the guy many
of the recruiting analysts expected to be the top quarterback at USC
that day, a chiseled 6'5", 220-pounder from San Diego with J. Crew
looks who reminded scouts of a young Brady Quinn. Pete Thomas
reportedly had scholarship offers from Maryland, Arizona State, and
Northwestern, among others.

Whitfield explained to one of the two camera crews working on
a pilot that would eventually become ESPN's *Elite 11* TV show that
he had been training Thomas since the kid was in the eighth grade.
Whitfield also gushed about another QB he'd brought, a spindly 6'6"
quarterback with zero offers. But the kid was about to break out,

"like a submarine ready to rise," Whitfield said. Penn State coaches were coming in the next week to check him out.

Whitfield was engaging, a natural on camera. He certainly appeared a lot more relaxed than his protégés were that afternoon: Thomas struggled with his accuracy. The other quarterback, the sleeper Whitfield was touting, was overwhelmed by the scene. At one point during the day the kid wandered into the group of top QBs the camp's coaches had put together after about an hour of observation. The main coach overseeing the drills noticed the taller kid trying to blend in before getting his turn to throw. He called the kid out and told him to point out who had sent him over. The kid pointed in the general direction of about twenty people, but when the coach demanded who, specifically, the kid dropped his head and slunk away to a group of younger kids. It was a heartbreaking scene to watch a kid get crushed like that.

Whitfield, at the very least, seemed like a heck of a salesman, but was that all he was? Just another fast-talking character in the growing fringe surrounding the college football world?


IN 2010, A FIFTEEN-MINUTE video Whitfield posted online got some traction with the national media fixated on Florida star Tim Tebow's transition to the NFL.

"My name is George Whitfield, and I'm a quarterback builder," he said as it began.

Whitfield broke down Tebow's mechanics, as well as drills that he explained would shorten the Florida star's elongated throwing motion via some before-and-after clips of adjustments he'd made with former Louisville QB Hunter Cantwell and other former college QBs.

Tebow's camp never contacted Whitfield, but later that year, after Ben Roethlisberger was suspended for the first four games of the 2010 season and was prohibited from working with the Steelers coaches, he hired Whitfield to keep his skills sharp. Roethlisberger's agent became sold on the coach after seeing his work with Cantwell, one of his other clients.

Whitfield learned plenty from the Pittsburgh Steelers star, too.

He studied with Roethlisberger and realized how much the QB did "off-script"—in situations where plays broke down because there was so much conflict in the pocket, Whitfield said.

Roethlisberger was just improvising and solving problems on his own. Whitfield realized how all those conventional, regimented drills that QB coaches had been doing for years often ran counter to the reality of the game. They just weren't applicable. Whitfield started scripting situations that were the *un*scripted scenarios of actual football. Whitfield showed Roethlisberger a bunch of new drills, one in which Whitfield simulated oncoming rushers swarming the big QB by swatting at him with a garden rake that he'd bought at a local hardware store. (Whitfield covered the talons in some pipe foam to avoid the risk of gouging the Steelers star.) The drill—"Chaos," as Whitfield titled it—was something he'd picked up from watching former Nebraska assistant Shawn Watson at a camp years earlier. Watson had swept a broom along the grass to get his quarterbacks to move their feet. Whitfield had seen other coaches chuck volleyballs at their QBs. Whitfield combined the two concepts. It was a way to influence a quarterback without being up on him, simulating evading pressure with his feet or with his upper body while he kept both hands gripping the ball up at his chest with his eyes focused downfield.

Roethlisberger loved the drill. He went on to lead the Steelers to the Super Bowl, and Whitfield finally had a big-game client on his résumé; but more than that, the 6′5″, 250-pounder was a big, playmaking quarterback. Whitfield was able to sell his handling of "Big Ben" to football's latest phenomenon at the time, Cam Newton. Days after Newton finished leading Auburn to the national title, he and his father, Cecil, tabbed Whitfield to orchestrate the Heisman Trophy winner's pre-draft training.

With Newton heading to be the first pick in the NFL Draft, the spotlight on Whitfield grew, and his unconventional training methods became a curiosity inside the growing industry. His training regimen targeted a quarterback's base and stressed footwork. Whitfield was creative in his ways to develop those elements. One day he brought Thomas and another high school protégé out to train on North Pacific Beach. What better place to work on their drops than in the soft, thick sand, Whitfield figured. Once there, Whitfield noticed how the surfers struggled in the water, walking with their boards, and got another idea. Why not have his QBs practice their drops in the ocean, where the waves would surge in and rush them at mid-thigh?

"You can't take any step for granted in there," Whitfield said. "With the ocean, there are gonna be times where the waves come in on you in mid-drop, and are you strong enough to continue dropping [back] against the weight of that water? If your steps aren't true, you're gonna fall in."

Whitfield's training philosophy was emboldened after he watched *Moneyball*. "That movie was such an eye-opener," Whitfield says. "I loved how *Moneyball* let what happened on the field set the course."

The movie, based on Michael Lewis's *New York Times* best seller about how Billy Beane transformed the hapless Oakland A's franchise by relying on new-age analytics, dovetailed with something Whitfield had picked up that winter from an AFC scout at the NFL Combine in Indianapolis. The veteran NFL personnel man told Whitfield that his team had done a study and found that only 48 percent of the time had his team's quarterback taken his prescribed drop from center and run the pass play as drawn up. More times than not, the QB had to adjust—or escape pressure and then try to unload the ball.

"And that guy was with a team that had a good offensive line, so I'm thinking, in college, the percent where the QB has to improvise and scramble out of trouble is probably even higher," Whitfield said. "I was thinking about that scene in *Moneyball*, where Brad Pitt [playing Beane] and Jonah Hill are at the backstop, and he goes, 'So, do you believe in it or not?'

"It was alarming to me. So we tried to build in a protocol. We had to teach them the proper response and throw all these variables at them—slide, move, dodge, retreat, now hop over something. We talk about matador escapability. You gotta be just like that matador, so when the bull gets about a foot away, you make one subtle, decisive move, and that bull rumbles past, and you're still right there. You gotta get as close as you can in what you practice to it seeming as real as possible."

To remedy that, Whitfield came up with drills he called "Havoc," "Chaos," and "Surge" and used brooms, tennis rackets, rakes, and bean bags to enhance them.

At Andrew Luck's Pro Day in 2012, televised from Stanford live on ESPN, Whitfield made his national TV debut. To most sports reporters he was simply "the Broom Guy," the dude built like a linebacker chasing—and flailing at—the expected number one overall pick of the 2012 NFL Draft.

"[Andrew] Luck being pressured by a guy with a broom while he throws. Really. Hilarity ensues among press corps," tweeted one NFL writer.

"Unexpected development: Man w/ broom is charging Luck as he throws, simulating pressure of a very skinny NFL defensive end," wrote another NFL reporter.

But by the end of the day, Whitfield had some ninety messages from college coaches and quarterbacks asking if he'd have time to train them, too.

"The data is real," Whitfield said, "and I quit worrying about people calling these drills 'hokey.' "


DEALING WITH CELEBRITY CAN be a tricky thing, especially when a person becomes a big deal quite suddenly. It's not just a risky proposition for twenty-year-old quarterbacks but also for a thirty-something private QB coach, too. As Trent Dilfer said, his buddy George Whitfield was "a rock star in the QB space." Being in the quarterback-builder business often means getting deeply invested in each player you coach. Whitfield wasn't shy about defending Newton or Luck whenever someone doubted their abilities, and he tweaked some of Newton's old skeptics after the Carolina Panther won NFL Offensive Rookie of the Year honors in 2011.

After former NFL QB Phil Simms remarked how he just didn't see "big-time NFL throws" from Luck, Whitfield invited the CBS announcer to Stanford for Pro Day. Days later, Whitfield made more headlines when he was asked by an *Indianapolis Star* writer about the possibility of the Colts not using the first pick on Luck, as it appeared that Robert Griffin III's draft stock was soaring, possibly at the Stanford star's expense.

"If they overthink this, they're going to make a mistake they'll regret for years," Whitfield was quoted as saying. When *USA Today* picked up the story, it ran with the headline: *Luck's coach: "If Colts pick Griffin, 'They'll regret it for years.'"*

Whitfield said it bothered him how Robert Griffin III or his family might take that. "I wouldn't take a single quote back, but the headlines made it sound like I was taking a swing at him, and I wasn't. I was just saying that Andrew Luck is a special player. That he is going to continue to get better. I never meant to say anything [bad] about Griffin.

"And it was the same with Cam. I couldn't help it. I wanted to stay on the sidelines, but you read things, and [you] see [that] people said things like, 'Cam's lazy.' It did get personal. Cam's there, and you've seen him put in long days, but then you hear these guys go on TV and say, 'I just think he's a self-serving guy.' And before you know it, you're off the sidelines."

The more high-profile Whitfield got, the more careful he realized he needed to be. Powerful people in the football world knew who he was and that he was a mentor and confidant to many top young football prospects. In many cases, Whitfield also acted as a media liaison for those college players, in a way that their often buttoned-up schools did not.

In addition, Whitfield became a target for some of his competitors, especially those who'd made it further in their playing careers. Former NFL backup Sean Salisbury used his @SeanUnfiltered Twitter account to take a not-so-veiled shot at Whitfield in the spring of 2013:

"Just saw Johnny Football on ESPN being QB trained. Someone tell Manziel that a NEXT level QB trainer awaits his call #dontsettle."

Jeff Garcia, another former NFL quarterback who had jumped into the QB coaching business, echoed a similar tone on Twitter:

"Why would U go to a QB coach who's never played at the highest of levels, who's never exceeded expectations, who's never been a true leader?"

Whitfield just shrugged when others took shots at him. His buddy, Trent Dilfer, got asked a lot by some of his old NFL buddies why he works with "the Broom Guy."

"This guy I was golfing with was very cynical about, 'Why do you have this guy as one of your coaches?'" Dilfer said. "I said, 'That's a great question. Let me give you my three-year history with George Whitfield,' and over a round of golf I explained what I've seen and what is important to me. 'Here's what I've seen this guy do with young people and with people in the NFL,' and by the end of my explanation, the guy said, 'OK, I'm in.'

"I think people see George as self-promoting. I emphasize with my staff, if you're good, you don't have to do the self-promoting. I understand the social networking part of it, where you gotta do Twitter. But to me, George Whitfield might be the most gifted communicator I've ever been around as a coach. He can, on the fly, metaphorically, in a way, get the kid to understand the why [of something]. He changes his metaphors all the time. I once asked him, 'Where do you come up with these things?' He said, 'Honestly, I go to bed thinking about them.' He'll watch the Discovery Channel, or he'll watch a boxing match or watch a sitcom. His mind will get stimulated by something culturally relevant, and then he spends tireless hours thinking of ways he can apply that in a quarterback-building sense. I just think that's brilliant. He's brilliant. Some stuff, I've seen him inadvertently convey the wrong information, but he'll communicate it in such a way that the kid gets that he has to change something, and so the kid naturally changes it, because the message was so crystal clear. It's not the application that changed the kid; it was the communication that allowed the kid to change."

MOST OF WHITFIELD'S DISCIPLES came to him in San Diego, the laid-back Southern California metropolis he's dubbed "Dime City." Whitfield came up with the nickname because he wanted his home turf to be known for quarterbacks who throw perfect passes—"dimes." Dime City also meshed with Whitfield's view that great quarterbacks have a superhero quality to them. Superheroes are born out of adversity, Whitfield said, noting that Aaron Rodgers had no scholarship offers out of high school and was once sent a letter by a Big Ten coach telling him that he wasn't D1 material; Tom Brady was the skinny 199th pick of the NFL Draft, and undersized Drew Brees grew up down the street in Austin from Texas and was passed over by the local Longhorns. Dime City sounded like a place where superhero-QBs trained. Whitfield's visiting protégés also noted the double en-tendre of "Dime City." "Dime" also referred to the stunning women (perfect "10s") who seemed to be everywhere in San Diego.

Whitfield's June road trip to Bryan, Texas, had been in the works for months. Johnny Manziel's late arrival to the session already had Whitfield on edge. After all, these June workouts were supposed to take place at SMU, before Manziel had Whitfield, Chase Griffin, his dad, and the other three college QBs reroute three hours south. Manziel only got his coach more frustrated as Whitfield sensed that his star pupil was just going through the motions. Was Manziel dis-tracted by having two of his buddies there? Was he hungover from the night before? Was he sick? Whatever the reason, Whitfield cut the session off after forty-five lackluster minutes, telling Manziel to get his head right for their afternoon session scheduled for 5:00 p.m. Whitfield's next group was three lower-profile QBs: two transfers, Jacob Karam at Memphis by way of Texas Tech, and Drew Allen at Syracuse by way of Oklahoma, along with Montana State freshman Dakota Prukop.

Manziel and his two buddies headed to a golf course a mile down the road, bringing young Chase with them to get brunch. They were the only diners in the posh country club, in a scene that felt as if it was right out of *Entourage*. The group hung on every breath and move Manziel made. He was in a prickly mood but loosened up a little listening to the precocious twelve-year-old Griffin tell the story of how his father grew up in a single-parent home and made it to Har-vard Law.

Whitfield seemed more annoyed still after Manziel left the high school field to get lunch after the morning sessions. Driving around College Station, Whitfield ended up at a Texas A&M bookstore. He walked in to see that seemingly half the store was hawking Johnny

Football gear—hats, jerseys, T-shirts, all with Manziel's number, 2, or with the Heisman outline.

"The strongest man-love there is is to wear someone else's jersey," Whitfield said, marveling at the collection of colors and styles of Aggie #2 jerseys. "It is admiration more than just respect."

Whitfield had been around star QBs before, but he had never seen anything quite like this or seen it happen so fast. Less than a year ago at that point, almost nobody in the store would've known who Johnny Manziel was if he walked in. Now he was the biggest celeb in their world. Whitfield likened the evolving situation to the movie *Rocky III*, where Rocky Balboa was no longer the gritty underdog out to prove people wrong. Now the hero was surrounded by excess and enablers, and his vision was clouded. His hunger had been satisfied.

"It's like, Rocky's not going as hard, because there's a circus around him," Whitfield said. "Now there's a piano right by the ring. [Rocky's brother-in-law] Paulie's selling commemorative pens. Meanwhile, Clubber Lang's training in someplace with exposed pipes, trying to catch him."

Whitfield's world, too, had changed. In the car leaving the bookstore, he took a call from an unrecognized number. It was the head coach of an FBS program asking if Whitfield had some time to work with his new quarterback. Whitfield tried to say politely that he didn't. Five minutes later, he got a call from the uncle of Brandon Harris, asking if he had time to train the talented Louisiana high school quarterback. Whitfield said if Harris was up for making the five-hour drive over, he'd work him in the next day.

Whitfield still had two workout sessions set for later in the afternoon. The first session went well. Allen and Karam were both in second-chance mode, having transferred to smaller football programs, hoping for strong senior seasons to catch NFL scouts' eyes, while Prukop was just hoping to keep up with the FBS guys. They were riveted to every move Whitfield made. That workout concluded with no sign of Manziel, who was scheduled for the second session.

A half hour later, Whitfield got the Aggies star on the phone. They bickered over what time the workout was slated for. Whitfield was hearing a mix of excuses, apathy, and angst. This was a different side of Manziel than Whitfield had ever dealt with. It was a side he'd only heard about.

"My head's just not into it today," Manziel told Whitfield. "I don't know what it is."

Whitfield was more frustrated than angry. The only reason he'd come to South Texas in the hundred-degree heat was for Manziel. He could've spent more time back in Ohio with his family.

"I'll come back," Manziel told him.

"Nah, I'm not gonna guilt you about it," Whitfield replied.

Twenty minutes later, Manziel arrived in an SUV with Turtle and another buddy. The Heisman Trophy winner was flustered. Whitfield didn't have much to say to his protégé. He looked disappointed. It was hard to tell if Manziel was upset at Whitfield or himself. However, after the QB took his own iPhone and fired it into the ground, it became apparent that Manziel was more annoyed at himself, Whitfield later said.

The sound of the smartphone shattering on the concrete startled an elderly couple walking laps around the school parking lot.

"I had to take inventory," Whitfield said later. "I never knew any of that type of stuff [what Manziel felt he had to juggle]. His family is in College Station. All his friends are in College Station. College Station is his running path. All of a sudden, I'm in *his* town. I'm in his world. Every time he'd come into San Diego, he'd get better. He didn't golf there. There was no leisure. He was there to work."

After Manziel's spectacular first season, Whitfield wanted him to stay in college for more than two seasons playing in the SEC, but after this trip, he started to rethink that. "Staying meant [he'd have to] stay in [College Station] and swim through all that stuff. Everybody had a stake on his time down there. He was a pleaser, and, for the most part, he'd been great at compartmentalizing, but down there it was all colliding together."

Manziel didn't offer any explanation for his outburst or for his lax behavior. He only told Whitfield he'd be ready to go in the morning, before he and his friends drove off again.

Asked if he ever thought that that day might've been his last with Manziel, Whitfield said no. "I'm invested. He was clearly overloaded.

Instead of barking at him and lighting him up, I had to remember that he was only nineteen. His brain must have hurt from how fast he was growing. Of all the people in his world, I know that I'm going to have to have some range and flexibility and some rigidness. So you treat him [the way you would] your kid brother. That's our relationship.

"I think he was trying to let me know how frustrated he was with himself when he smashed his phone. He's carrying all this [emotional] stuff from his girl, his next girl, his buddies, his coaches, and then I'm down there, and I can't be all fired up, too."

The next morning Whitfield's other group of college QBs was up first. Two local high school football coaches had driven over to observe the training and learn from Whitfield. One got to play broom man for the Havoc drill.

At 10:07, a truck pulled up, and Manziel got out, barefoot. He was wearing a Dallas Cowboys shirt and some basketball shorts that hung down below his knees. He wandered over to the far end zone of the field, where Whitfield was working with Allen, Karam, and Prukop. He slapped hands with the other quarterbacks and made small talk with Allen and Karam. Manziel's mom, Michelle, drove up, as did a longtime family friend who brought his nine-year-old son, whom Whitfield was also helping to train. Manziel was in an upbeat mood. Problem was, his buddies had his cleats in their truck, and they were no longer around.

"Where are they?" Manziel asked Whitfield.

"Huh? They're not my crew," Whitfield replied.

A few minutes passed as Whitfield joked with the other QBs.

"How long does it take to get Taco Cabana?" Manziel muttered to himself.

Whitfield ignored Manziel until he put on his shoes.

Of the eight training sessions Whitfield had scripted for the trip, he later said, Manziel really only got one in. However, Whitfield added, "We got a nice understanding of who 'we' are. I think I would've pretty much lost him if I let him set the training or if I was just more of a fan. I didn't want that. I came down for the progress. I told him, 'You and I can hang out any old time.' I think he was wandering all over the road, and you gotta be a guardrail at some point."

# 6

# THE MAD SCIENTIST

**Ground zero in the quarterback** coaching world was a dark weight room set underneath the left-field bleachers of Dedeaux Field, the USC baseball stadium. Here, a sixty-six-year-old man in a hooded sweatshirt gave lectures while seated on a large lime green exercise ball. On a particularly crisp Thursday morning in early December, the audience was a dozen pitchers, three New York Yankees' front-office executives, a javelin thrower, a junior college quarterback, and one female golfer.

The man in the sweatshirt in front of the group had salt-and-pepper hair, a bristly mustache, and a wry grin. Tom House looked a lot like the brainier of the Smothers brothers. In the 1970s, House pitched in the Major Leagues for almost a decade with the Atlanta Braves, Boston Red Sox, and Seattle Mariners. He finished his career with a 29–23 record and a solid 3.79 ERA, although he was best known in his baseball career for something that happened off the mound. In 1974, as a twenty-seven-year-old relief pitcher with the Braves, House was standing in the Atlanta bullpen when teammate Hank Aaron whacked his record-breaking 715th home run over the outfield wall. House barely had to move to catch it. If he didn't reach up, the ball would've clunked him right in the forehead.

House began his lecture by asking each of the pitchers in the room what was the hardest they'd ever thrown a baseball. They went around the room, touting numbers that would make baseball scouts' hearts race: 98 miles per hour, 98, 97, 95, 92, 97, 98.

Even seated on a group of weight benches in a loose semicircle around the former Major Leaguer, it was obvious the pitchers dwarfed the 5'9" House. He nodded to the Yankees front-office guy sitting with two colleagues, asking, "You're having your big meeting tomorrow. What're the three things you look for?"

There was a five-second pause.

"I'll help you out with the first one," House said. "Pitchability."

"Yeah, right," the Yankees personnel guy replied. "Stuff. We're always looking for command, control. Deception. I'd guess athleticism. Being able to repeat it."

House: "And then velocity, right?"

"Oh, yeah, velocity is last."

"Here's something that I know pisses you off, Tommy," House said in the direction of a lanky 6'5" career minor league pitcher in his late twenties who was moonlighting as a substitute teacher. "My best was 82 [mph]. I got nine years in the big leagues. I signed before they had [radar/speed] guns, or I would've never signed. What are the three kinds of velocity? Do you have any idea? If not, that's OK. That's why we're here."

The minor leaguer House was speaking to answered, "Perceived?"

HOUSE: That's not my first one. It is one. But the first one is real—what the gun says. Unfortunately, to play college baseball, you gotta throw 90, unless you're left-handed. But tell me about perceived velocity.

"How it looks to the hitter?" said another pitcher.

HOUSE: Close.

He called on another guy, who proceeded to guess.

HOUSE: OK. What is one foot of distance to the hitter? Three miles an hour? It's how close you get. So, what is *effective* velocity?

"It's how [the hitter's] brain interprets the speed of the pitch based on his experience with the previous pitch?" ventured another pitcher.

"An 88-mile-per-hour fastball up and in is actually 92 to the hitter's eye. Down the middle of the plate is actually 88. Down all the way is . . ."

"Real close," House said. "That's a B-plus. It's 6 (miles per hour), not 3, not 4. Basically an 86-mile-per-hour fastball down the middle is 92 up and in and 80 down and away. Guys like me have to pitch backwards. What does pitching backwards mean?"

One of the Yankees personnel people who should have been well-versed in the answer offered up with a hint of hesitation in his voice, "Starting soft? In hitter's counts, throwing soft, and in advantage counts, throwing hard. If I was behind in the count, I'd throw a changeup."

House responded by asking, "What's a lockout pitch?" House was big on answering questions with more questions and also liked responding to answers with more questions even before letting people know if their answer was right or even on the right track. His ability to survive in the majors by keeping people off balance had not diminished with age.

"The only reason I pitched in the big leagues is because I was left-handed and could throw a curveball," House told me a few minutes before starting his lecture. "If I was right-handed, I wouldn't have pitched past high school. There's a level of talent that has to be there, but with that talent, the ceiling is pretty high."

House became a Major League pitching coach after his playing career ended when he was released at the age of thirty-one. In the past three decades, he had shepherded the pitching careers of everyone from Nolan Ryan to Randy Johnson and is the co-founder of the National Pitching Association. House, who wore glasses while on the mound in his big league career, had earned a PhD in performance psychology, a Master's degree in marketing, an MBA, written almost two dozen books, and was now known to many in the sports world as "The Professor." "Sports are games of failure, coached by negative people in a misinformation environment," he told me. "These guys are surviving in spite of themselves."

Baseball is the biggest game of failure out there, followed by hockey, in House's view. "You can make a million dollars in a month as a hitter and fail seven out of ten times. Pitchers fail half the time.

In all sports, there's a lot of good intentions but not a whole lot of science-based information. We call it, 'Fail Fast Forward.' The guys who get ahead are the ones who aren't afraid to fail, but they don't fail the same way too often. The fear of failure—especially with smart, middle-class, white kids—is usually what holds them back, because they are so afraid to screw up.

"I was blessed because I was right in the crease between what they called the Old School and what is now the New School. Yogi Berra said it best when he said '50 percent of baseball is 90 percent mental.' I saw guys with great tools who never made it because of what was going on between the ears. I went ahead and got my PhD in science because too many guys were failing with mental, emotional issues, and I had no clue what to do. I figured if I could bring in some academic help, maybe that'd give me some direction on what to do with my practical experience."

WHETHER SOMEONE IN HIS weight room had provided a correct answer or not, House kept volleying questions at the group.

"Anyone know who Warren Spahn was?"

Silence.

"Big old bowlegged guy with a dip in his mouth," House said. "Smelled like a goat, couldn't trap a pig in a ditch, winningest left-hand pitcher in baseball."

"*House, get over here!*" House said, his voice deepening as he imitated Spahn, right down to pretending he was spitting out a mouthful of tobacco juice. "Don't throw a short-armed man in. Or a long-armed man away. You gotta be before the bat. Or after the bat. You just can't be during the bat."

"I thought, what the fuck is this guy talking about? I didn't have hard [a good fastball]. I had to make my fastball look better. So when you say you throw 98? Awesome, but it's not 98. Anybody remember the Julio Franco story?"

No one in the weight room knew the Julio Franco story. And it was probably better that way for House—and for everyone else in attendance. Franco, a three-time All-Star and former American League batting champ from the Dominican Republic, reportedly used to take batting practice with a weighted donut still on the bat while in the cage. In baseball circles, there was something of a mythology rooted in Franco's, um, machismo. Franco played for the Texas Rangers from 1989 to '93, at the same time House was the team's pitching coach.

"So we're at old Arlington Stadium. Good old days. It's a rainout. Everyone's talking. And Julio likes to talk. *'Da' big boy,'*" House said with a Latino accent as he took his palm and started pounding his chest. "*'He could hit hundred thuuuur-tee mi' per hour fass-bo.'*

"So the other guys are, like, 'No chance. No way.' Everyone started throwing money onto the table. Pretty soon there's four grand. We go down to the cages and put the JUGS [pitching machine] up to 130.

"*Whhhooosssssh!* It's bouncing off the back wall like I've never seen. And Julio swung that forty-ounce monster bat. He fouls the first one off and then fouls the second one off. Then he starts making contact and starts ripping it. Then," House continued, his eyebrows arching in astonishment, "he starts moving closer to the machine. And before you know it, he's hitting 130-mph fastballs from ten feet in front of home plate.

"How?

"Timing," House said, answering another of his own questions. "Sequencing and mechanical efficiency," he added before breaking back into the Franco-Latino accent, "If I know a fastball's coming, I can hit a *boo-lettt*."

TOM HOUSE WAS IN his mid-fifties before his coaching career found a new industry. Or, more specifically, the new industry found him. Whitfield's old mentor in San Diego, Cam Cameron, then the offensive coordinator for the Chargers, was at a local basketball camp with his three sons (ages eight, six, and four), where House's name kept coming up. That got Cameron—himself once a multisport athlete in college at Indiana University as a quarterback for Lee Corso's football team and as a guard on Bob Knight's basketball team—curious.

"Tom's remarkable," Cameron said. "I'd heard about his baseball work, so I went on the Internet to learn more about him. Then I read his books."

Cameron showed up with his kids to watch House conduct one of his workouts in the San Diego area. Cameron was amazed as he watched House coaching Major League pitchers, guys rehabbing, high schoolers, and even Little Leaguers.

"He was everything I'd read and heard about, so I mentioned him to Brian Schottenheimer, our quarterback coach, and said, 'Why don't we introduce [Chargers starting QB] Drew [Brees] to Tom and see if they hit it off.'

"Eventually, we just said, 'Hey, Drew, we're not suggesting Tom. Just meet him. You might be interested.' And those two formed a bond that's been tremendous."

House asked Brees what he thought he needed, strength-wise, to be a great quarterback.

"I guess I need a strong arm and strong legs for power," Brees replied. House said from looking at Brees, he could tell the Chargers quarterback lacked some back-side shoulder strength.

"You're very front-loaded," House explained. "You have more muscle in the front of your shoulder than in the back, which has created an imbalance." House added that if the front of Brees's shoulder was strong enough to throw a ball 100 miles per hour, but the back could only muster 80, he was only going to throw 80, since you're only as strong as your weakest link. Brees was amazed that House could ID all that just from observing his posture.

House also examined Brees's diet. The former Purdue star thought he ate well, since he rarely touched fast food, but House had him take a food-allergy test. He had Brees and his wife fly up to Portland to see a specialist. The test revealed that Brees was, in fact, allergic to nuts, dairy, wheat, and eggs—many of the things he was eating, which caused him to often feel fatigued and have problems sleeping. House overhauled Brees's diet as well as his musculature and, in the process, his throwing mechanics.

House has an acronym for his process: "STATT"—Screen Test Access and Then Training.

"First, we got him healthy," House said. "We were far [enough] along with baseball to know you can only accelerate what you can decelerate. We had a mechanical model that was balance and posture and weight shift, opposite and equal. These things that were translating. Football and pitching are pretty similar, only a little bit different timing. We just took the pitching model and overlaid it on quarterbacking. Did a lot of mirror work, got him on the computer, and we did everything we do with pitchers. Problem identification is half the solution.

"Football players are more dynamic, but the same rules apply. Instead of it being a six-foot stride, they have a two-foot stride, so their timing and the foot strike has to be about one-third, but after the front foot hits—whether somebody's chasing them or not—it takes .25 to .35 [seconds] to get the football out of your hand, and you have to do it with balance and posture. All the same things apply. So with pitching, it's a very stable environment; with rubber and mound, it's a very unstable environment, but all the same rules apply with dynamic movement as they do with static movement."

Brees's transformation was startling. In his 2010 book titled *Coming Back Stronger*, Brees detailed how he'd once lacked confidence and was afraid of making mistakes. He went from throwing 11 touchdowns and 15 interceptions with a 58 percent completion rate in 2003 to a 27 TD-7 INT year with a 66 percent completion rate that earned him a Pro Bowl invite in 2004. He went on to make seven Pro Bowl appearances in the next nine seasons, even overcoming major shoulder surgery.

"It was easy," House said. "I'd like to say we helped him a lot, but percentage points is what we did with him.

"That was two years, and then he got hurt during his free-agent year, and then we really got serious. Dr. [James] Andrews did the surgery and the rehab, and he wasn't sure how he'd throw again. So we pulled out all the stops. And that was the beginning of Functional Fitness for Quarterbacks, just like we did for baseball. And then from there, Drew has success, he mentions my name here and there, and that leads to Tom Brady and Matt Cassel and Joe Flacco. We don't market. It's just word of mouth."

House would like to say he had the foresight to know that this other avenue—training elite quarterbacks—was out there, but he said he didn't. "A blind squirrel can find an acorn," he said. And, as a life-long baseball guy, he isn't too proud to note the differences he found after working with both pitchers and QBs.

"Quarterbacks are way smarter," he said. "Those elite guys are so friggin' smart. You [only] have to tell them once. Pitchers you have to tell fifteen, twenty times.

"Until quarterbacks started coming by here, I had no clue who they were. And they're all pretty good at what they do. They knew what to do, but not many knew why [certain] things were happening. We're kind of the 'Why' guys. I'm not a quarterback coach. We're what we call movement specialists or performance analysts. We complement, very much, what [Steve] Clarkson is doing and what Trent [Dilfer] is doing and what these quarterback coaches are doing. One of the guys who works with me, Adam Dedeaux, can tell you about footwork and route trees and stuff like that. I can't. I just look at the body when it's throwing and what it needs to be good at throwing a football.

"The reason why we're at where we're at is because we knew nothing about quarterbacking, but we knew a lot about throwing. There are rules you have to follow, but everybody looks different following those rules. Everybody."

According to House, one of the big mistakes quarterback coaches make is getting too caught up in trying to make all their QBs throw exactly the same way. Bodies are different. Physiognomy. Conditioning-wise. "They're wired differently. What you need to do is identify the critical variables. And do you have a fix for the variables that aren't efficient? Then, if they're efficient and effective and they're repeatable, they play. And we do as well with quarterbacks who are just trying to get better to go to college as we do with Drew Brees and Tom Brady, who just want to get 1 or 2 percent better."

The commonality among all top quarterbacks, he's found, actually happens at their release point. "That's when all the good ones look the same," House says. "Eyes level. Release point is eight to twelve inches out in front of the front foot. Non-throwing hand is somewhere in front of the face. They all look the same, but how they get there is a little different. Brady has closer to a 'classic' delivery, whereas Drew Brees is a tiptoe guy, a short-armer who throws off his toes."

Trent Dilfer calls Tom House sports' greatest biomechanics guy to ever walk the Earth. His impact on what Dilfer taught and looked for in quarterbacks was significant. When Dilfer ramped up to try to become a presence in the quarterback coaching world, he first spent a couple of days observing House in Los Angeles.

"Even House told me, 'Man, by accident you kinda understand the biomechanics of this,' " Dilfer said. "I'd never studied biomechanics. I don't have a degree in anything. I've asked a lot of questions. Before I went to Tom the first time, I think I probably understood intuitively 70 percent of the biomechanics. I think Tom has filled in the other 30 percent. And it's a very important 30 percent, because if you get 30 percent wrong, it's gonna mess up the 70 percent.

"I think we both have very similar passions behind us."

House said he is a big fan of the work Dilfer does with quarterbacks, too, especially since their perspectives are so different. "I think we're going to work together one of these days," House said. "I hope we do.

"Trent is really good, but he is guessing at stuff based on looking at video. When you look at video, don't your eyes lie to you?" House asked, alluding to the fact that the speed of the video is inhibiting and, therefore, misleading. "I've been where he is, where he's really good at what he does, but he's not defendable. He can put it out there, and his instruction capabilities are off the charts. He can really teach it, but his information is based on his experience. But it's not science coming from his side. We have science."

House credited Greg Rose, from the Titleist Performance Institute, for opening his eyes. "He's more responsible for me getting out of the box and changing my paradigm than anybody I've ever been around." About fifteen years ago Rose called House out.

"I thought I was a science-based coach. He said, 'Tom, you're a great coach, but you've got a little bit too much BS in your system. You have no science.' So Trent is where I was. He's doing all his empirical research with his eyes and with current technology in high-speed video. Science is basically hypotheses that you test with an IRB—an institutional review board—looking over your shoulder, so you're defendable with a peer group. That's the thing that separates us. We are science-based with our conditioning, with our nutrition, with our mental and emotional and our biomechanical stuff. I think we offer the only independent coaching in the world. Now there's medical research and academic research, but I think we're the only real coaches to do research and actually come up with hypotheses and protocols and defend them and do a number of studies and reviews. Not many coaches write books or get published. We do."

HOUSE'S OFFICE AT USC was two cubicles above the third-base bleachers. The back cube looked as if someone was ready to move out. The desk was bare save for two radar guns aimed at each other. A half football that is a staple of House's training regimen sat on a shelf. (The ball, which is pointed on one side and flat at its widest end, is ideal for throwing into a trampoline, since it'll bounce right back to the thrower.) On the floor in one of the corners were two large black cases the size of dorm-room refrigerators. Inside was $220,000 worth of technology that processes House's data-capturing and motion analysis. Next to that were five hard drives. "That's thirty years of shit right there," House said sheepishly. "The cool thing is, people can argue with me, but they can't out-research me."

The front cube had a coffee table, and its walls were covered with poster-sized action shots of past pitching clients, including Nolan Ryan and Randy Johnson. On the wall closest to the door was a smaller framed photo of Brees. The building used to be the Trojans' old snack shack, which led House to joke that he had come full circle. His mom used to work the snack stand when he was growing up in California. House's father was a civil engineer. They taught him, "Don't ever be embarrassed to ask why," House said, "and ever since I was a little kid, we asked, 'Why? Why are we doing this?' What do I need to do to get an A?' I think 'Why?' kinda shortens your trials."

That sense of wondering—and asking why—explains how a lot of athletes end up as coaches, House said.

"Superstars don't have to be that way, you know?" he said. "Most of the elite athletes are *unconsciously* competent. And they're really, really good. If you're *not* an elite athlete but you're trying to be, you have to know why things work or why they don't work. I think people like me, who struggle every day to survive—they have to know why."

House was always looking for any edge to elevate what he believed was his below-average arm. He was a self-described "pitch-backwards" guy. He relied on his off-speed stuff and then would finish with a fastball. "None of my pitches were any good, but in combination I was OK," House said. "Sinking fastball, curveball, screwball . . ."

He also got a little creative, and that included taking performance-enhancing drugs.

"We tried everything," he said. "Our basic tenet was, 'You don't get beat, you get out-milligrammed.' If someone was beating you, you found out what they were taking, and you took more of it. That was the '60s and the '70s. It didn't work for me. I got bigger, but I didn't throw any harder. I was off PEDs before it became the thing to do. I took Dianabol, which was primitive, but it was what weight trainers were doing. We didn't know."

House tried PEDs for two and a half years, he said. He bulked up from 180 pounds to 220.

"It didn't help my fastball. I've had seven knee surgeries. I had too much weight for my structure." But that doesn't mean he's against the PEDs in baseball under different circumstances. "In retrospect, I would level the playing field and say, take whatever you want to take under a doctor's care," House said. "Telling them not to take them— well, there is that risk-reward: If they have a good year, they get a $100 million contract, and then you fine them $2 million."

After he got released by the Seattle Mariners in March 1979, House tried working in the "real world." He sold signage on buildings and made between $300,000 and $400,000 in six months, he said, but when an old baseball friend, Bob Cluck, offered him a job as a minor league pitching coach in the Houston Astros organization,

House jumped at it. For the next eighteen seasons, House worked as a pitching coach for the Astros, San Diego Padres, Texas Rangers, and the Chiba Lotte Marines of the Japanese league. He also coached in Latin America. In 1984, the year before he was hired by the Rangers, House got a call from a buddy named Coop DeRenne, a third-generation professional baseball player and also an academic.

"There's this new thing called motion analysis," DeRenne told House about the system Kodak had developed.

They both thought the concept was really cool. "Three dimensions, a thousand frames a second," House recalled. "Your eyes lie to you. We only see thirty-two frames a second. When you look at TV or standard video, you only see thirty-two frames a second. Now we know all the critical parts for a rotational athlete in the throw or swing or kick; it takes places at about .250 of a second to about a .700 of a second. We're coaching on what we think we see, but we're really not looking at it.

"The Kodak system was great, but it wasn't user-friendly. Six months later, we ran into a guy named Gideon Ariel at Coto De Caza [California] with [Hall of Fame tennis coach] Vic Braden. We looked at his system, and it was actually user-friendly. So we got a system. We mortgaged houses. Borrowed money. Whatever. And we started capturing data. Had no clue what we were doing. I probably had two years of data before I started to realize, 'OK, there are some common denominators here.' But just because you have motion analysis doesn't mean you can do anything with it. The next step in our progression was coming up with the instruction."

House's penchant for always asking why didn't just lead him into areas beyond the expanding technology. He once wrote a six-hundred-page doctoral thesis on the "Terminal Adolescence Syndrome" of professional athletes, which was something he had observed from his six seasons riding buses in the minor leagues to his near decade as being, in his own words, a "marginal-to-horseshit" major league relief pitcher. The root of his findings were how, in the world of big-time athletes living lives of privilege and entitlement, a staggering percentage were unequipped to cope with life as ex-athletes, when real losses take place. The impact of a life born essentially out of being "rewarded for what they are and criticized for who they are" rendered most players "dysfunctional heroes." House said that all professional athletes have OCD (obsessive-compulsive disorder)—since they essentially have to. If they didn't, they would not have gotten as far as they did, but the "checkpoints in pro sports" are not what they are in the real world, since those are merely a function of what happens on the field. Then again, to most pro athletes, House noted, that *is* their real world, especially since such adolescent behavior is the norm inside the locker-room culture. House also cited divorce rates that were below the national average during the players' career, when they seemingly were awash in temptation, yet in their post-playing career soared beyond the norm. In 1989, House had a version of his thesis published, titled, *The Jock's Itch: The Fast-Track Private World of the Professional Ballplayer.*

The book was about five hundred pages shorter than what House had submitted for his thesis. "There was a lot more to that book than they printed, because they [Contemporary Books] didn't want another *Ball Four*, with all the sexual stuff, the drug stuff, the alcohol stuff, though I wasn't naming names."

House's own marriage also became a casualty of his baseball life. His first marriage had lasted twenty-two years. "She wanted a real life as the kids were getting older," said House, who has since remarried. His life, though, even in his mid-sixties, is still centered around sports—and the question why.

"This is my vocation, avocation, and passion," he said. House stopped short of saying that his circumstances as a marginal pro athlete and the time he came along were part of some grand plan to make him a pioneer in the field of athlete development. "I wish I could say there was some master plan, but I think I just stumbled into it. Right place, right time. I know I've been an avid learner, and I'm always searching for a way to get better."

The biggest misconception about House as a coach is that he's just a biomechanical expert. Actually, even referring to House as a "coach" feels like a misnomer. He rolled his eyes at the "guru" label, although of late that has become a handy way for media folks to

ID a guy who seems about as far removed as possible from having a whistle around his neck. He'll tell you he's "a rotational-athlete evaluator," but that also seems too limited, even though he's quick to point out that the title opened his shingle up to baseball players, football players, golfers, tennis players, and so many others, since all rotational athletes have similar timing and kinematic sequencing—hips, shoulders, arms, and implement. But, as Drew Brees learned, there are many other components to House's program.

"Mechanics are the easiest things to teach," House said. "Conditioning? Well, it takes no talent to get in shape. Nutrition is the toughest sell, because these kids can eat cotton balls, and they'll survive. When it comes to the mental/emotional [development], unless you tell stories and recruit the audience, they'll gloss over on that. I went ahead and got my PhD in [Sports Psychology] because too many guys were failing with mental, emotional issues, and I had no clue what to do. I figured if I could bring in some academic help, maybe that'd give me some direction on what to do with my practical experience."

House, though, is skeptical of many of the sports psychologists who have flooded the marketplace in recent years: "A lot of them are useless. They talk about visualization without explaining what it does. Seeing versus feeling."

House said he could transform an average high school kid into a college quarterback.

"And there's research behind this, too. It's called Windows of Trainability," he said. "If your base [of knowledge] is broad enough, you can teach anything. You heard about the two Indian kids, right? That was us here. They'd never thrown a baseball in their lives. and then six months later, they signed pro baseball contracts."

House's "two Indian kids"—Rinku Singh and Dinesh Patel—were the first athletes from India to sign a professional baseball contract. They were the products of a reality show, *The Million Dollar Arm*, the brainchild of J. B. Bernstein, a sports agent from LA.

Bernstein figured that in a country with more than a billion people, there had to be some baseball talent. The two nineteen-year-olds were picked from a group of more than 37,000 who tried to throw a baseball in all sorts of curious ways. Singh and Patel, both former javelin throwers, each clocked faster than 85 mph on the radar gun to earn a ticket to Southern California, where they'd end up being trained by House for six months. Five years later, Singh was still with the Pirates organization, and Disney made a movie called *Million Dollar Arm* starring Jon Hamm as Bernstein and Bill Paxton playing House.

Asked if, knowing what he knows now, he could have turned himself from an average high school quarterback into an NFL quarterback, House said no chance.

"I didn't have the physical tools. I didn't have the arm speed. I might've been able to throw [the ball] accurately, but I couldn't throw it far enough. An 82-mile-per-hour fastball doesn't translate into a 75-yard pass. Foot speed, arm speed, being able to jump—those genetic things—I could refine it and make it very efficient, but my top end would be on the low end of what was acceptable."

HOUSE WAS SURROUNDED BY believers. The fifty-something-year-old guy who stood behind him jotting down key points on a sandwich board while House gave his morning lecture was really in the import/export business. He'd been helping House out for three years. He got into it after he brought his son, who had become a pitcher at USC, to him. House's "football guy" was twenty-seven-year-old Adam Dedeaux, whose grandfather was legendary USC baseball coach Rod Dedeaux, the man the stadium was named for. The elder Dedeaux won eleven national titles before passing away in 2006, when his grandson, Adam, was a left-handed freshman relief pitcher for the Trojans. The younger Dedeaux was a product of Orange County's storied football-powerhouse program Mater Dei High, the high school that produced Heisman Trophy–winning QBs Matt Leinart and John Huarte. Dedeaux had been a quarterback until Jason Forcier, one of a trio of brothers from San Diego whose family had spent thousands of dollars on private quarterback training, transferred in, prompting Adam's move to tight end. Dedeaux majored in policy planning and development at USC, figuring he'd go into real estate if a career in sports didn't work out. In essence, he's gotten a graduate degree in coaching from being at House's side for the past five years.

"Going to school would certainly be beneficial, but I'm essentially learning everything I could possibly want from him," said Dedeaux.

House was at his best when his students had just enough knowledge to be informed on a topic but not spot-on. That created the epiphanies, when 300-level students became 500-level students, exploring the nuances, much more than the basics of top athletes.

HOUSE: What's the most important pitch in baseball?

"Strike one," replied one of the minor league pitchers. Sounded like a good answer.

HOUSE: Wrong. The next pitch. The *best* pitch in baseball is strike one. What's the most important count?

"1–1," the Yankees exec in the wraparound shades answered. "You either go way ahead or way behind."

The guy was correct. But . . . House was quick to quantify what way ahead or way behind actually meant.

"A .250 hitter becomes a .300 hitter if you throw a ball," House said. "If you throw a strike, he becomes a .200 hitter."

House's questions came rapid-fire, sandwiched in a mix of science, psychology, and personal anecdotes. "What are the four outcomes based on process? Do you have any idea?" he asked, looking around the weight room. "In a game of failure coached by negative people in a misinformation environment, you have to create your own confidence. What's the difference between being confident and cocky?"

Silence.

"If you take care of process, results are going to happen," House said. Results, yes. Good results, not necessarily.

House's breakdown of process:

*If you have a bad process and end up with a bad outcome, well, you deserve it.*

*If you have a bad process and end up with a good outcome,
you're lucky. Ever been around a player who says, 'I'd rather be
lucky than good?' Run from 'em.
If you have a good process and end up with a bad outcome,
you're unlucky.
If you have a good process and end up with a good outcome—"*

House doesn't finish the sentence. Instead, he downshifts. "How do you succeed in baseball?"

"Fail one time less than your competition," said the minor leaguer/substitute teacher.

HOUSE: Say it again.

"Fail one time less than your competition."

"Let's go broader," House said. "Can anybody tell me the difference between stress and anxiety?"

"One's panicking, and—" answered one of the pitchers.

HOUSE: Stress is a ten-pound load for a five-pound box. Anxiety is hormonal. Stress is physical. Anxiety is adrenaline and all that good stuff. You want to be a little anxious. It's the feeling you miss the most. When you're walking between those lines, and you're going EREREAAAA! That doesn't happen in the real world. Choking is thinking too much, and panicking is not thinking enough. If you think you can or you think you cannot, you're right.

How many thoughts do you have a second? Forty. Your subconscious processes eleven million a second. What's gonna win, your thinking or your feeling?

I did better up than I did down. You have to know yourself. Is it OK to be afraid? Yes.

That led into the "Thinking Triangle"—the person you are, the person you want to be, and the person people see.

"Why did coaches leave me alone?" House asked.

"Because you threw strikes?" one of the younger pitchers responded.

HOUSE: Because they didn't give a shit. I was the tenth or eleventh guy.

"The thing that screws all you guys up is, you care too much about what other people think. You care more about results than process. How much time do you care about the last pitch? Thirty seconds? We call that 'anchor.' And then you're not ready for the most important pitch of your life. The only pitch that matters is the next pitch.

"One of the best things about Nolan Ryan is, right after his seventh no-hitter, he went to the ice and the bucket and started preparing for the next one. He told the media, 'I'll talk about it, but this game is over.' Brees had one of the worst games of his career Monday night in Seattle. We're texting back and forth. Their plane had a mechanical failure. They were sitting on the tarmac at 7:00 a.m. He wasn't sitting on the loss. He knew, 'We have a short week.' He was already looking at game film of Carolina."

[Brees led the Saints to a 31–13 win over Carolina in the game by completing 30 of 42 passes for 313 yards and 4 touchdowns.]

"Why is Drew Brees so good? His process. He manages the process. It didn't happen last year. He threw back-to-back pick-sixes last year. He'd never done that before. He called me and said, 'This is driving me nuts. I can't figure out what I did wrong.'

"I said, 'Believe. Close your eyes. What's the difference between visualizing and seeing? Try this, and look at the pick-six, and turn it into a touchdown. Ninety trillion cells aren't anchoring on a pick-six. We just reprogrammed a touchdown.'

"It's the 'Optimism Bias.' You can't change reality, but you can change your perception of reality. The people who can take reality and put a positive spin on it—and that's called 'Learned Optimism'—they're the guys who survive in baseball if all things are equal. You're your own island. Not every coach has your best interest at heart. Remember Occam's Razor: the simplest solution. Don't overthink it. The best players don't always win. The best prepared players always win."

Near the end of House's lecture, he asked for everyone in the room to say one thing they'd learned from the session. He later said he learns from the kids more than they learn from him. "Why do I ask questions? Sender-receiver feedback. You can learn from people who aren't even quite right."

Just as House's students got off their weight benches to begin their workouts, his most famous protégé entered the weight room wearing a Jockey T-shirt. A muscular 6'3", 230-pound Tim Tebow stood out from all the tall, lanky pitchers with their faces barely visible under their ski hats and ball caps pulled down to the bridges of their noses. Tebow arrived beaming. He literally couldn't seem to stop smiling. House was busy chatting with a thirty-one-year-old pitcher from Australia and didn't notice that Tebow was in the building until he heard the laughter.

Tebow broke out his Tom House impression for the import/export guy. It was equal parts House and the old Dana Carvey *SNL* spoof of John McLaughlin.

"Tim, what is a hot girl?" Tebow asked himself. "Well, Tom, it's any girl who is at least an eight—"

"WRONG! It's a . . ."

House laughed for a few seconds. Then shook his head, saying, "The fact that he's making fun of me means I'm getting through to him.

"OK, Tim, what do you want to do today?"

TEBOW: Get better.

HOUSE: How are you going to get better?

TEBOW: By working on the process. Harder.

That was exactly the kind of answer House wanted. He smiled as he exited the weight room while Tebow began to stretch.

BY EARLY DECEMBER, AS NFL teams geared up for the playoffs, Tim Tebow had been in LA training with House for three straight months, going at least four times a week. The former first-round draft pick showed up right after he got released by the Patriots. Prior to his stint with New England, Tebow had spent one season with the Jets before they released him.

"I will remain in relentless pursuit of continuing my lifelong dream of being an NFL quarterback," Tebow wrote on Twitter.

The merits of Tebow as an NFL quarterback became the most polarizing topic the league had had in years. In college at Florida, Tebow was a hero to many. He helped spark the Gators to two national titles. In 2007, he won the Heisman. His style was that of a throwback. A bruising runner, Tebow was the Gators' power back, bulling his way for yards in an offense that often operated like the old Single Wing with a few modern-day wrinkles tacked on.

Tebow's throwing mechanics, with his elongated motion, left many football men shaking their heads, but he still put up gaudy numbers, leaving college as the SEC's all-time leader in passing efficiency, and he was second on the NCAA's all-time list. Tebow also was the SEC's career leader in completion percentage and touchdown-to-interception ratio. NFL analyst Jon Gruden, a former Super Bowl–winning coach, told the *Orlando Sentinel* that Tebow could "revolutionize the game." Another Super Bowl–winning coach-turned-TV-analyst, Tony Dungy, said he would use a Top 10 pick to select Tebow, even though he "doesn't have the classic throwing motion" and "doesn't have the accuracy."

Others were more skeptical. Jimmy Johnson told Sporting News Radio, "I don't think Tebow can play in a pro style of offense—not quarterback," adding that he viewed the former Florida star as more of a candidate to play H-back. The anonymous quotes from NFL personnel men were even less flattering toward Tebow, whose well-publicized religious views only made him that much more of a hot-button debate subject. For many, Tebow resonated because of his clean-cut image and because he was devout. He spoke about his faith in public settings, visited prisons, and even referenced Bible verses in the eye black he wore on his face during college games. He was a bona fide phenomenon, but that came with an undertow. Many recoiled at Tebow—or at least the idea of Tebow—as if he was some over-saturated pop-music act. He was like a one-man version of Duke basketball or Notre Dame football.

Despite all the speculation that Tebow didn't have the skill set to be an NFL quarterback, the Denver Broncos traded up to select him with the 25th pick of the draft. He started three games as a rookie in 2010. Tebow began the 2011 season as the Broncos' backup QB, but after a 1–4 start, Kyle Orton was benched at halftime, with Denver trailing the Chargers by 16 points. Tebow rallied the Broncos, but they ended up losing 29–24. Tebow, though, emerged as Denver's new starter, and the struggling team started winning. With Tebow starting, the Broncos won seven of their next eight games, even though his passing skills were, at best, shaky. Denver even made the playoffs and won its wild-card game over Pittsburgh after Tebow connected with Demaryius Thomas on an 80-yard touchdown pass in overtime. The next week, Denver was blown out by New England, 45–10. Tebow finished the season with the lowest passing completion rate (46.5 percent) in the NFL. Two months later, he was traded to the Jets for a couple of middle-round draft picks but was cut after one season, being used primarily as a special teamer.

Right around the time word started to spread that Tebow had been cut by the Patriots, House got a call from Tom Brady: "I think Tim is gonna call you, because he feels like you might be the last option he has." Two days later, Tebow showed up at USC ready to work. Tebow had actually worked with House for a week in 2012 right before he went to the Jets.

"We actually had him throwing correctly, but he didn't have enough reps, and he went right back to the old neuro-pathway programming as soon as the intensity hit," said House. "He was worse when he showed up this time around than before he went to the Jets. He was all over the place."

House was just one of many private quarterback coaches who had a crack at "fixing" Tim Tebow. Coming out of Florida, Tebow worked with college QB coach Noel Mazzone (who was the offensive coordinator at Arizona State at the time) and his son, Taylor. In 2013, he spent a few weeks training in Bradenton, Florida, at the IMG Football Academy with former Florida State Heisman Trophy winner Chris Weinke, who tweaked how Tebow's feet were aligned when he began his motion. There was also a stint with David Morris, Eli Manning's backup at Ole Miss, who has a quarterback-training business based in Mobile, Alabama. Then, before Tebow went to camp with the Jets, he trained with Steve Clarkson, who said he solved Tebow's slow, "looping" throwing motion by changing his footwork and incorporating some Tai Chi into the workouts. A few weeks later, more Tebow coaches spoke out about their tweaks with the former first-rounder. Dennis Gile, a protégé of Trent Dilfer, and Mike Giavondo told reporters they'd worked with Tebow for three months in Arizona, while Clarkson actually only came down for one day and went to the media claiming credit.

"We are getting tired of Clarkson taking credit for guys, going on radio stations," Gile told the website SB Nation. "I don't want to get in a war with him. We put in a lot of time and effort for nothing to really help this guy. [Tebow] became a good friend of ours, and he is a good guy."

NFL teams probably didn't doubt whether he was a good guy. A good quarterback was a different story. Worse still, he was a quarterback who came with a legion of media in tow. That had become Tebow's baggage. And that made him not worth all the drama.

"Everybody's afraid of Tim," House said. "There's too much stuff that comes with Tim. When he showed up here, he was 10,000 reps behind any other NFL quarterback. He'd never been given a tool kit on how to fix [his mechanics]. With good intentions, he wasn't getting any help. Everybody pulls for him, but good intentions with bad information is just as bad as no information at all."

For the first month of training sessions, Tebow asked House not to allow people into the stadium, because the former college star didn't want anyone to know he was there. House didn't bother to look at Tebow's old film.

"I don't look at bad film," he said. "We work with what our statistical model has validated, and then we work from there. It's what we're supposed to be dealing with right now. We know for a fact that he had premature rotation issues on the front side, and his back foot came off the ground too soon, but that shows up when he's throwing. You don't have to look at it on film."

House also examined Tebow's diet and determined that the QB

was taking in too much protein and didn't have enough balance. House wanted to make his body more "quarterback specific, so he doesn't look so much like a linebacker anymore."

For his entire life, Tebow's will had been seen as his greatest attribute. It was celebrated in many features written about him. In truth, House believed, it also had been a detriment.

"He probably has been in muscle failure most of his adult life," House said. "We talked about prepare, compete, and repair. You're more efficient when your body repairs before you start asking things of it." It took a good six weeks before Tebow's body got acclimated. They eventually gave him Wednesdays off to recover.

House picked up on what a "pleaser" Tebow was. House and Dedeaux would tease Tebow sometimes; they'd whisper gibberish to each other out of the quarterback's earshot.

"Hey, what are you guys saying?" Tebow would ask. House and Dedeaux would laugh.

"Feedback is huge for him," House said. "But he doesn't like bullshit."

House dismissed a lot of reasons why people said Tebow struggled, from being too stiff in his neck and shoulders to a penchant for over-striding. "There is no such thing as over-striding, but there is something about not having the right timing in the foot stride," he said. "Guys like Brady and Carson Palmer have much bigger strides than Tebow, but they had better timing with those strides. When we start teaching, we look at timing first, then kinematic sequencing, and then the mechanics of the throw. So if you're not timed right, no matter how good you are with the mechanics, it's gonna look weird. It's called the step-wise regression analysis.

"All of the stuff that they'd criticized him about—there was actually no basis for them to criticize him. The only thing that held true was that he was not accurate. He knew that. [Bill] Parcells knew it. Everybody knew that."

TEBOW WAS THE FIRST high-profile product of House's new 3DQB business, which launched in the summer of 2013 to help leverage the momentum the former Major Leaguer had in the QB-development world. House admitted he didn't know much about the quarterback-coaching space as a business, but Adam Dedeaux did.

"I'm not much of a marketer," House said. "He is. He's helped me in how to market and how to relate to this current generation of athletes.

"There are some really good quarterbacks coaches out there, like the Whitfields, but nobody teaches the throwers, the rotational athletes, like we do."

House was mentoring Dedeaux just as the kid's grandfather once mentored him when he was a USC pitcher back in the '60s. One of House's mantras—Fail Fast Forward—about athletes not being afraid to fail, was something he'd learned from the legendary Trojan coach. In addition to the work they were doing on the USC campus, 3DQB also was branching out into the youth-camp model, which former NFL quarterback John Beck, the other member of the business, was shepherding. They had already done camps in Boston and Utah, and had another one lined up in Arizona in the spring.

"John's helping build a camp model for us, so we can reach more kids, because there's only so many hours in the day," said Dedeaux.

House wanted to throttle down his pace by the time he was seventy and have Dedeaux become the face of 3DQB, he said. That way, he could do more research; House had noticed that things had only gotten more hectic for him in the past year than ever before.

He was at USC every day during the week and then traveled to give similar lectures on weekends. "I just did a golf thing at Ojai Country Club for twenty-five seniors like myself," he said. House mostly stayed in a condo across the street from the Staples Center at L.A. LIVE, a ten-minute drive from USC. He had gotten a nice home on the beach down in Del Mar but lamented that he only got to live in it about two or three days a month.

"I'm surprised how quickly it's grown," House said of his business. "I was happy with three or four guys, and now we have fifteen to twenty. It's cool, because we don't advertise. It's all word of mouth. We've only been pushing [the quarterback business] hard for about a year. I was dabbling in it for fourteen to fifteen years, but it's become a real business with Adam and John.

"Our biggest wish is to be too busy, and our biggest nightmare is to be too busy to deliver a product. I think we're on overload right now. Adam wants size. We're not gonna be a babysitting group, though. I'm not gonna do large numbers. But the most important [thing] to me is that when someone leaves here, they're better."


THE "FIXING" OF TIM Tebow, the quarterback, would take some three months. House's diagnosis of why Tebow was inaccurate all came back to timing issues with his body. Once they could get his body in sync, the mechanics were actually pretty easy to fix, the former Major League pitcher said. "He still does what he's always done with his throwing arm. We just fixed the front side and gave him a better posture to do it and made him time it better." Beyond that, House said Tebow learned why he would misfire whenever he did, which "The Professor" said was vital for anyone to be at their best.

"We allowed him to understand why the ball goes right or left, why the ball goes high or low and how to spin the ball and how to physically prepare from feet to fingertips and to take it out and make the dynamic movement work for you and not against you. Does the term 'muscle-head' make sense? He muscled everything. He can muscle it when he needs it, but now he's got kinematic sequencing. He's muscled down for efficiency."

Another underlying problem that tied into Tebow's issues in the NFL that House IDed: the former All-American quarterback had no confidence in his throwing ability.

"He didn't think he could make that throw, so he went to what he was confident in, and that was his legs."

Dedeaux added that Tebow was particularly flummoxed by timing routes: "If he's supposed to hit a corner, and he thinks, 'Well, maybe I can hit or maybe not, or I can just roll out and let everything become chaotic, and then I'll find somebody.' That's where he found his strength to be."

"He's gone from chaos to total repeatability," House proudly interjected. "If I had never seen him throw before, and then I watched him throw on Tuesday in the Coliseum, I'd say he was right up there with the guys we work with. Is he quite at the level of Drew Brees, Brady? No, but it's pretty frickin' good. He can make all the throws now.

"It's a numbers game. You saw Malcolm Gladwell's book that it takes ten thousand hours for mastery? He's getting close.

"You can be the tough guy here," House said, turning to Dedeaux. "How much better is his accuracy than when he first showed up?"

DEDEAUX: It's a lot better. He knows how to throw now. If he was play-ing a game of catch, and he was 65 percent, the deviations have gotten much smaller.

HOUSE: The problem with identification is half the solution. When he misses high, he knows why. When he misses right or left, he knows why. Without stepping on anybody's toes, I think quarterbacks get less help than pitchers. I don't think they get much help at all. They either perform, or they don't. And if they're not performing, next!"

When told that they were not the first people to work with Tim Tebow and pronounce the big QB "fixed," Dedeaux nodded. "That's why I'm a little bit more conservative."

HOUSE: I'm not. I'm not. We know for a fact that if you block-train X amount of reps, and you random-train X amount of reps, and if you put those two together with skill training, and you can get predict-able consistency out of the skill training, he's fixed. He's fixed! Because he already has the 'It' stuff. His asshole's not gonna slam shut when he goes between the lines.

"What we don't wanna do is send him off, telling everybody he's fixed, and have him poop the bed. But he's not gonna poop the bed. He knows why he's screwing up, and he can tell you why. I think he's ready to go play right now. If we could get him into a system he's comfortable with, he could go play now."

DEDEAUX: He will definitely be better. Right off the bat, what's his biggest flaw? Completion percentage. As we got to know him, we saw that he looked deep and then would check down. Maybe he saw those checkdowns but just wasn't confident enough to make those throws. He just wasn't, so he wouldn't make them. He'd roll out or run.

HOUSE: Why's he more confident now? Because he knows what, why, and how. The best players in the world aren't always really the best players. If you've done your homework, and you've done everything you can possibly do, then you're confident that your process gives you a better chance to succeed—so all those pieces are [now] fitting for him.

DEDEAUX: The only thing we haven't been able to simulate is a defense with rushers, which is a big piece. And that is my only worry: when he's thrown into the fire, does it hold up?

That, of course, *was* a big piece. The knock from NFL coaches and personnel people on Tebow, beyond doubts about his accuracy, was that he struggled to read defenses and process what was in front of him at warp speed the way top NFL QBs need to.

House dismissed that skepticism. "He's already proved it," he told me. "He couldn't throw accurately, and he still won in the NFL.

"It's going to take someone who understands that kids can get better and understands that the entourage that comes with Tim Tebow, if managed properly by the front office, is not an issue at all. Belichick proved that already. There'll be a perfect spot for Tim. I just hope it happens sooner rather than later.

"I'd like to call some of my contacts in football to say he's ready."

These were uncharted waters for House. His other famous football protégés were more established in their NFL careers. Tebow, to many people, had become a punch line, and that made House play the advocate's role.

"He's a pretty special kid," House said. "I'm not gonna lie. I was looking for holes in the program, but he's everything he appears to be."

One month later—and about a week after ESPN announced that Tebow was joining the company for its SEC Network as a college-football analyst—Trent Dilfer flew to Los Angeles to work Tebow out for a five-minute TV segment on ESPN's *Sunday NFL Countdown*.

Dilfer introduced the piece by saying he had received a call from

Tebow asking for a "brutally honest evaluation of where he's at." Dilfer, wearing his Elite 11 baseball hat and pullover, ran Tebow through a workout similar to that of any other quarterback he trained. In the segment, Dilfer made it clear that it was House—identified as the "3DQB Performance Analyst"—who had been overhauling Tebow for the past four months. The video showed Tebow, in a red, sweat-soaked T-shirt with the words I AM SET FREE on the front, going through many of the exercises that are staples of House's regimen. There was the quarterback with his hands extended above his head, dribbling in unison two grapefruit-sized balls against a cinder-block wall, as well as Tebow snapping a towel against a football held up to mirror the top of his release point in a variation of a drill House picked up in Japan. House at one point compared Tebow to Nolan Ryan for having the "same motivational muscle."

"I don't have all the answers," Dilfer said on camera, coming out of the segment. "I do know this. If you put Tim Tebow on a football field right now with four other NFL quarterbacks, [and] you didn't know who they were, and [you] just watched the ball, you wouldn't know which one was Tim Tebow and which ones were the NFL quarterbacks.

"I want you to watch this in context. This is one of the greatest players who ever played college football, and he didn't know how to pass. I believe that now he knows how to pass. Every GM, every scout, every personnel person out there should go at least watch Tim Tebow now, because he's a different guy."

Weeks later, in Indianapolis at the NFL Combine, the reaction from coaches and personnel people to claims of a Tebow transformation was a collective shrug. "The problem isn't really his arm," said one veteran NFL defensive coach about Tebow. "It's that he's not wired to process what he's seeing once the ball is snapped, and if you don't have that, you simply can't be a quarterback in this league."

Told of the skepticism, Dilfer nodded. "I think that's fair, based on his track record in the NFL," he said. "I will always err to a fault on 'nurture' over 'nature.' My argument to that is, now that he has a better passing acumen, doesn't he deserve a chance to see if that passing acumen allows his mind to free up a little bit to process?

"Tim is very transparent. He said there were times when he knew he couldn't complete the ball and was just looking for a chance to move the chains with his legs. That's a pretty honest answer, explaining a lot of stuff that's seen on tape."

Neither the latest layer of skepticism nor his budding broadcasting career would keep Tebow from House's workouts. If the NFL had given up on Tim Tebow as a quarterback, that was its decision. It wouldn't be his or House's.

As Tebow exited the baseball field to head to a throwing workout with Dedeaux at a park in El Segundo, he pulled the import/export guy in for a hug and then moved toward House, who put up his hands. "My family doesn't hug," he said half-jokingly.

Tebow, smiling ear to ear, ignored it and engulfed House in a bear hug, as he let out a big "YEAAAAAAH!"

# 7.

# QB HEAVEN

JUNE 28, 2013.

Elite 11, once again, had tweaked its format. Trent Dilfer picked eighteen top high school QB prospects for his "campetition," rather than the twenty-five it had in 2012 or the eleven it had for its first decade in existence. The organizers overhauled the process, so that now, by week's end, a "top eleven" was determined based on quarterbacks' performance in a very, very wide variety of opportunities and situations. It was Dilfer's personal lab, a way to beta test his research and theories.

Most of the week's activities were held at the exquisitely manicured Nike campus in Beaverton, Oregon. A dozen-plus QB coaches from eight different states helped run the event. Many of them were former NFL QBs who had gone into the private-quarterback-coaching business and had come together as part of the season-long Elite 11 process that bounced all over the country trying to ID elite high school prospects. They all were working for Dilfer, who continued to build his TDFB brand, the venture he called a "holistic coaching ecosystem uniting coaches & expanding their influence." None of them was paid other than for travel expenses.

By 9:59 a.m., the room was packed with coaches, and an eight-person camera crew was documenting the week.

"I'm a big thirty-thousand-feet guy," Dilfer began by telling his staff. "We're not doing a camp anymore, guys. This is truly a culture."

Dilfer and the folks from Student Sports, Inc., who have run the Elite 11 since its inception, have been consumed by trying to find ways to give the young QBs every edge and opportunity imaginable to grow. Since Dilfer's arrival at the Elite 11, the camp's competitive nature had amped up. In 2012, he even brought in the Navy SEALs to run the high schoolers through a rigorous challenge in the ocean. He and his staff kept tallies on it all. He reminded the college-age counselors that their words were even more meaningful to the kids.

"You're their idols," he said, looking at Michigan quarterback Devin Gardner [Elite 11 Class of 2009] and Clemson QB Tajh Boyd [Elite 11 Class of 2008]. "Teach them how to learn."

Dilfer's also added to his staff a "high-performance psychology" coach, Dr. Michael Gervais, who helped coach the Seattle Seahawks and in 2012 trained six Olympic gold medalists.

"We're not looking for the top eleven quarterbacks; we're looking for the top eleven competitors," said former-USC-assistant-QB-coach-turned-Pac-12 commentator Yogi Roth, who was called up to the front along with Dr. Gervais for a quick presentation. Roth helped run the camp and was one of the voices of the ESPN TV show.

Most of the curriculum covered in Dilfer's meeting probably sounded familiar to a coaching staff that had spent its life around football, with many of the Elite 11 assistants having played the game at a high level. Two of the staffers in the room, Neil Lomax and Ken O'Brien, each spent a decade in the NFL. Dr. Gervais's messages, though, often took the football guys into uncharted waters. There were diagrams with triangles and overlapping circles of mental flow charts.

"We're going to teach confidence," said the forty-year-old surfer before asking where confidence came from. The old QBs threw out a bunch of guesses—preparation? past success?—before Dilfer, a protégé of Gervais, provided the right answer.

"It only comes from one place—self-talk," Gervais agreed. "We need to teach, as coaches, how to speak well, how to think well. This is why language matters."

Of course, here in Dilferland, it all mattered.

The players also were put on a high-tech, brain-training system, AXON, to help them, among other things, process coverages faster—and "to show how pliable their brains are," Dilfer said. Another group Dilfer had brought in was debuting a cutting-edge camera (smaller than a fingernail) built into a helmet that would give the QBs—and the coaches—a full perspective of what the quarterback was seeing, or "Ground Truth," as Dilfer put it.

"We're the product. The kid is the consumer," he said. "Everything we do. High energy. High respect for others. Let's be aware of our language. Everything we say matters."

The Super Bowl–winning QB told his staff exactly what he was looking for from them and for the kids. Dilfer was passionate, moving around, punching key points. Each of the morning's speakers he called on hit on elements to illuminate an environment that Dilfer said had the kids who won invitations there feeling like, "I get to go to QB Heaven."

Dilfer also was mindful of the perceptions of his group from the outside. "We're bringing an army up here, guys, and it just takes one weak link to ruin the whole thing," he said. "How we carry ourselves and how we interact with the hotel and the people with Nike matters. We pick up any garbage, and we leave a room better than when we found it. I want people to say, 'That is the coolest bunch of cats.' "

That week, there was another group the Elite 11 staff got warned about—the NCAA. Dilfer announced to the staff that the NCAA would have two investigators there. "They're from the gaming and compliance side of things," he said. "These are the badasses for the NCAA. They'll be disguised as Nike execs. They're looking for one slipup. One coach talking to a player about an agent or something. These high school kids are going to be pros someday.

"They [the NCAA] can't believe we can pull something off like this clean. It's our job to pull it off clean."

Brian Stumpf, a former Cal receiver who had helped run the

Elite 11 and Student Sports, Inc., camps for a decade, interjected that another concern for the NCAA investigators was college influence and people swaying recruits. The issue had become quite a headache for the NCAA with the increased visibility of recruiting—who the recruits were, where they were going to camps, and whom they were interacting with—especially with social media providing much more of a window into it all than ever before. It wasn't just concern about the college counselors doing some recruiting among the Elite 11 quarterbacks; since the event was attached that year to The Opening—another Nike-run event in which 160 of the nation's top prospects were coming to Oregon later in the week to compete in the 7-on-7 tournament and linemen drills—it was also a reminder about not trying to sway prospects to a certain program related to the Elite 11 coaches, either.

"This should be a good thing," Dilfer added, "because I want them to hear your message."

That message had been refocused from the camp's first few years under Dilfer. In the past, Dilfer said, they had tried to find ways to break the young quarterbacks or expose their weaknesses. That year would be different. "This Elite 11 is about getting them primed and ready," he said. "Our job is to create an environment [in which] they're aiming for peak performance."

Jordan Palmer was called up to the front. He spoke about a couple he had brought in from a children's foundation he'd gotten involved with. Palmer had begun working with the foundation on Tuesdays (that's the players' off-day in the NFL) by visiting hospitals and helping sick children.

"If we're going to teach them [QBs] how they should keep their elbow up or read defenses, we'd be crazy if we didn't also try to teach 'em how to become better men," Palmer told the coaches.

One thing that hadn't changed about the Elite 11 was the sense of fraternity among the QBs.

"I'm also here because I really want to help the kids get better," Devin Gardner told me after the room started to clear. "When I was at the Elite 11 in high school, [then-counselor and UTEP QB] Jordan

Palmer helped me so much." Gardner said he'd really thrown a flat ball, and Palmer had tweaked his footwork and delivery.

By early afternoon, the Elite 11's hotel was overrun with QBs, both young and not so young. The group reconvened later in the afternoon on the sprawling Nike campus in the Bo Jackson Building for the event's first official activity: Dynamic Athletic Yoga in a hot room.

Along with the high schoolers, Dilfer assigned a couple of his coaches to join in. In fact, the first one whose mat was pooling with puddles of sweat was former Green Bay Packer Craig Nall, the thirty-four-year-old Dallas-area QB coach.

At 4:45, QBs, counselors, and coaches had assembled on the football field in the middle of the Nike campus. All the participants stood up and introduced themselves and spoke about what they were hoping to get out of the week. Then the "Golden Gun" competition began, as QBs—and counselors—hustled all over the field, trying to fire a football through stationary targets in a variety of scenarios while the coaches studied virtually every move each quarterback made.

"There is no defense for a perfect thrower," Dilfer shouted out several times over two eight-minute sessions that must've felt like twenty-minute periods, as each player's shirt was soaked with sweat.

Texas A&M commit Kyle Allen, considered by many to be the top pure passer in the country, won the gold shirt for the day. Sean White, a QB from Fort Lauderdale, took second, although the uncommitted 6'1", 195-pounder might've overtaken Allen, save for an inch or two on about four or five of his throws that rattled around the metal targets but didn't go through. Other QBs who stood out in either how they handled the dynamic yoga or the field work—because Dilfer tasks his staff to keep tabs on everything: Florida commit Will Grier; Cal commit Luke Rubenzer; Texas commit Jerrod Heard; Vandy commit K. J. Carta-Samuels; Virginia Tech commit Andrew Ford; and Clemson commit DeShaun Watson, who impressed coaches with how he rallied from near the bottom of the rankings after the first round of the Golden Gun competition to finish third, battling through fatigue.

Day One of the Elite 11 ended, perhaps fittingly, with an audible.

For as much thought as had gone into scripting every hour of the week, a power outage forced Dilfer to do some adapting. Instead of meetings in the air-conditioned rooms of the hotel, the group ended up in the roundabout outside.

Shit happens, right?

No matter. Dilfer brought up Palmer, who talked in more detail about the "impact" guys in their position—star quarterbacks—can have on their communities. Then, Palmer introduced the evening's main speaker, Erik Rees, the CEO of NEGU (Never Ever Give Up), a charity inspired by his daughter, Jessie Rees, a twelve-year-old who had battled a brain tumor for ten months before passing away in 2012. Despite her ominous prognosis, she was always concerned with why some kids in the hospital didn't have visitors and wanted to focus on spreading joy to other kids fighting cancer. Her attitude and efforts inspired a movement, Rees said. His daughter knew that having cancer made people feel lonely and isolated, so she decided to spread love to them through her JoyJars, a care package of sorts.

Later, Palmer told the campers that one of the Elite 11 QBs from the 2012 group, Johnny Stanton, now a Nebraska Cornhusker, was committed to being the NEGU ambassador in Lincoln, spurring the movement to help sick kids and families there. Palmer then made a parallel that seemed to register with many of the young men looking up at him.

"Think about Jessie's stats: working with 240 hospitals and reaching 55,000 children," Palmer told the young QBs sitting with their legs crossed on the pavement in front of him. "Now think about your stats: yards, touchdown passes. Pretty insignificant, right? This isn't really just about NEGU; it's about your opportunity [to contribute something]."

Many of the campers nodded. It had been a long day. Most had flown across the country to get there. They'd met a lot of new people in the past twelve hours and had a bunch of information thrown at them. And now they had finished the night on a very emotional turn. They each were given a flashlight as they filed back into the darkened hotel. Turned out, the power wouldn't come back on for another hour.

Saturday would bring new challenges. Starting at 4:30 a.m., Dilfer had them beginning the day by climbing a mountain.

THE COLLEGE COUNSELORS WERE able to sleep in and skip the climb. But Saturday was a big day for them, too. That's when the Counselor's Challenge was scheduled.

Every year, a half dozen or so college QBs also came to the week-long camp to compete against one another in addition to their roles assisting the Elite 11 staff. The 2013 group was the most star-studded batch of college counselors the camp had ever had. There was Johnny Manziel; Devin Gardner; Tajh Boyd, the ACC's Player of the Year; San José State's David Fales; Georgia Tech's Vad Lee; and Louisville's Teddy Bridgewater, a guy many were projecting to be the first overall pick in the 2014 NFL Draft. Gardner and Boyd came to Oregon a few days early just to get in some extra work with Whitfield.

The opportunity to compete against the Heisman winner and the possible first overall draft pick had the other guys fired up. Especially Boyd. "That's all he's been talking about for two days," said Gardner.

It's doubtful Manziel would've even bothered to come halfway across the country for the event had George Whitfield not been helping coach. Manziel was there because of Whitfield. And a few of the other college QBs were there because of Manziel.

The six quarterbacks competed in a series of different passing drills, testing their footwork and accuracy. Manziel and Bridgewater were touted by most at the Elite 11 as the favorites. The other remaining Elite 11 coaches pegged Boyd, the most talkative counselor, as the winner. In the Clemson quarterback's last game, against eighth-ranked LSU on New Year's Eve in the Chick-fil-A Bowl, Boyd showed how "clutch" he could be when he converted a fourth-and-sixteen throw into tight double-coverage from near his own goal line to spark a last-minute, come-from-behind victory. Boyd was telling anyone who would listen that he was going to win the Counselor's Challenge.

David Fales, the San José State quarterback, was on the other side of the spectrum. In a camp full of alphas, Fales was the quietest quarterback on the Nike campus. In truth, none of the other counselors had ever heard of Fales till that week. Even though Fales led the nation in completion percentage (73 percent) and carried the Spartans to a Top 25 finish in 2012, it was not as if he'd arrived at college with much buzz. San José State only had to beat Indiana State to get him out of junior college. Before Fales's stint at Monterey Peninsula College, he was at Wyoming (for less than a month) and Nevada and was buried on the depth chart at both places.

Fales later admitted that he'd always wondered how he compared to the other top QBs in the country. Turned out, at least in that kind of setting, Fales was more than capable of holding his own. His pinpoint accuracy, particularly while throwing on the move, had all the Elite 11 coaches and campers hooting and hollering with every perfect pass as he jumped to a big-points lead over Boyd. Manziel, constantly trying to fire up Fales and Boyd—and himself—rallied to close the margin and put the pressure on the San José State QB. Fales, though, never cooled down and hung on to win the competition.

"It's eye-opening," Fales said later, before qualifying that the competition was not like an actual game, though.

"It really doesn't matter. It's all hype kinda, but it did help my confidence."

So, yeah, maybe it did matter.

EACH NIGHT OF THE Elite 11, Dilfer and his staff retreated to their office on the sixth floor of the hotel for a war-room session that sometimes dragged on for four hours. Dilfer had framed his rating system around four categories to rank the eighteen quarterbacks: competitive temperament, functional football intelligence, passing proficiency, and trainability on a scale of 1–5. Dilfer mandated that a grade of 5 should be rare.

"Jameis had unique competitive temperament," Dilfer said, evoking the name of the star of the 2011 Elite 11, Jameis Winston. "*That's* a 5."

Dilfer also wanted to incorporate some sort of new quarterbacking metric into the Elite 11 evaluation, which would rely on the statistical data.

Almost all the ratings in the first hour were 3s or 4s with plenty of qualifiers. After a half hour of discussions, Dilfer put the name of David Blough, a 6'1" Texan committed to Purdue, on the big screen at the front of the room. Joey Roberts, Dilfer's ESPN protégé-turned–Elite 11 general manager, made a compelling case for the week's first 5 in regard to Bough's competitive temperament.

"I talked with Kyle Allen, Jacob Park, and DeShaun Watson [three of the camp's highest-rated recruits] and said, 'Who's the alpha in this group?' Blough was the one commonality," Roberts said.

Blough was an unheralded recruit till he'd caught the eye of the Elite 11 staff at the regional camp in Texas and then made them believers in Chicago one month later. He had zero scholarship offers at the time. He learned that he'd landed a golden ticket to the Elite 11 finals while sitting in his fifth-period Technologies class. A buddy told him to check Twitter. Blough tapped at his smartphone and noticed a tweet from NFL star Drew Brees mentioning him: "On behalf of coach @TDESPN the fifth golden ticket to the @Elite11 Finals goes to fellow TX QB @David_Blough10 Welcome to the fraternity David." A few days later, Brees's old college became the first to offer Blough, who accepted one month later.

Blough studied the previous *Elite 11* shows on TV and bought in to Dilfer's message. In one of the earlier events of the week, the high schoolers had a pre-dawn, 4.4-mile run up a hill that concluded with a last-man-squatting competition. Blough outlasted everyone and remained in the squat position for six minutes just to prove a point.

"I learned it's about a lot more 'mental,' the leadership and being able to adapt and make plays work," Blough later told me. "It's a lot more than just being able to throw the ball; it's all about how you're wired, how you work. A thousand kids can throw the ball, but it's the intangibles that separate you.

"They really stress it. That was something I had to focus on if I wanted to be noticed. I was slapping people's hands when they caught a pass for me; I tried to bring high energy, and it seemed to work. So it's stuck with me."

Months later, Dilfer was told about how years of watching *Elite 11* had affected Blough; he was not only parroting Dilfer's message but said he was trying to live it. "That's why I pushed for the TV show," the former NFL QB said. "It's great that we're nominated for an Emmy. It doesn't make me more money. I've lost a lot of money on the Elite 11. A lot. The TV show is important to me because it's the way we message the next generation, because I want these kids to understand, this *is* nurture, not nature. You are not born to be a quarterback. That is the stupidest argument I've ever heard. There are kids who are born to be leaders. There are kids born with more talent than others. They are not born to be Tom Brady, to be Peyton Manning. A lot of that is nurture, and the TV show is part of the nurturing process for the next generation. They get to see what is emphasized, and they get to see it played out the year or two before they get to go through it."

Dilfer shifted into a story about another high school QB, this one a blue-chip prospect, whom he'd "loved" on tape. "I'd invite him off of tape," he said. "NFL body. NFL arm. NFL pedigree. [The prospect] had seen the shows, and he cowered [at one of the Elite 11 regionals]. He disappeared. He brought nothing. I talked to a couple of coaches who'd recruited him. They both said when they talked to him on the phone, there was nothing there. He was so soft and unsure of himself. When that happens, it is a red X. You have seen what is important to us. You have seen what we emphasize. My talk is the same. 'I don't wanna hear you. I wanna feel you. Thermostat and thermometer,' to the point people roll their eyes. There has to be a major paradigm shift for this kid to survive in a college locker room, let alone in an NFL locker room."


AFTER DAVID BLOUGH'S FIRST two days in Oregon, it sounded as if Purdue had gone into Texas for another recruiting coup, as the Boilermakers did in the '90s when they plucked out Brees after the big in-state schools passed on the Austin native.

Craig Nall mentioned that after he took a baseline test on AXON, measuring his ability to instantly deduce defensive looks, Blough approached the old ex-NFL quarterback, inquiring what his score was.

Nall said that Blough, who had the highest initial score among high schoolers, looked genuinely disappointed to find out that the onetime LSU Tiger had topped him. Nall felt compelled to point out to the kid that he did have a bit of an advantage on the test: "I reminded him, I did play in the NFL."

One of the coaches chimed in to say that Blough had approached him earlier to report, "Coach, I haven't taken the elevator yet."

A coach from the back of the room pointed out, "Everything he does is an A+. He's just locked in."

Another said, "NFL evaluators look at joint structure. With his wrists, hands, and knees, he has 6′5″ joints in a 6′1″ body."

Dilfer observed, "When we went around that circle introducing ourselves, I swear he wanted to say, 'I'm here to kick your asses. I'm not here to make friends.'"

Palmer added, "It's ironic that he's going to Drew Brees's school."

For as much as David Blough had made a glowing early impression in Oregon, a taller, much more touted QB with one of the strongest arms in the camp had turned off several of the coaches.

"He'll throw a touchdown on a ball he shouldn't have thrown," said one of the younger coaches. "He's arrogant to other people, and he turns his back to me when I know he can hear me."

One of the coaches said that the teen was "the least-liked person here."

DILFER: What scares me is, he has an "I know more" attitude, or it's like he doesn't trust that he can do what you're asking.

PALMER: You almost feel like he's asking, "Do I need this?" And that's a danger zone.

For Dilfer, the quarterback was treading into the direction of the two other blue-chip recruits who had recoiled when faced with the challenges of the Elite 11. The forty-one-year-old still cringed about how those previous situations had deteriorated, and he was determined not to let it happen again.

● ◦ ●

THERE'S A FLOOR-TO-CEILING PICTURE of one of Nike's newest break-out stars, Colin Kaepernick, in a second-floor classroom inside the Bo Jackson Building. Back when Kaepernick was a high schooler, he was off the national college football recruiting radar. He was a lanky pitcher who doubled as a quarterback in the run-heavy Wing-T offense; he threw the ball sidearm. Kaepernick tried out for the Elite 11 at two regionals, one in Vegas and one in Berkeley, in 2005. Stumpf recalls that Kaepernick was pencil-thin but showed off a powerful whip of an arm, although he was too raw to get the invite to the national camp in a class that featured Matthew Stafford, Jake Locker, and Tim Tebow.

Chris Ault, the former coach at Nevada—the only FBS program to offer Kaepernick a scholarship—said he wouldn't have offered based on film. Kaepernick competed at the Wolf Pack's summer camp, but even after that, Nevada didn't pull the trigger. It wasn't until months later, after figuring that Kaepernick could probably be a good free safety or wide receiver if he couldn't make it at quarterback, the Wolf Pack offered.

"We didn't know he was getting ready to put his cape on," said Ault, "and it's now with a big *K* right in the middle of it."

The NFL is actually full of quarterbacks fueled by skepticism and snubs. Warren Moon going undrafted and detouring to the Canadian Football League for six seasons before getting his shot at *the* League. Tom Brady lasting till the 199th pick of the draft. Aaron Rodgers having zero scholarship offers out of high school. It was a theme exercised repeatedly when the counselors were called up one by one to share their stories with the campers. Even George Whitfield stretched to bang that drum in his introduction of Johnny Manziel . . .

"He scored seventy-five touchdowns in his senior year. Seven-TEE FIVE! But TCU still said, 'Slow down. Not all dreams end with being a Division One player.'"

Whitfield's intro quickly turned into a testimonial, tracing the fiery Texan's emotional state through the recruiting process to the time he showed up during the spring break of his freshman year at Texas A&M, to each step on each rung up the Aggies' depth chart. Whitfield perked up as he got to the Thursday-night phone call he received from Johnny Manziel, while he was checking out another one of his protégés, Virginia Tech's Logan Thomas, facing tenth-ranked Florida State. At the time, the Aggies were less than forty-eight hours from a huge test at number one Alabama: "I know you're watching Logan, so I'll keep this short. This is gonna be like going into the Roman Colosseum," Manziel said, hatching a gladiator/ dragon-slayer theme that Whitfield would soon adopt for his own brand—DRGN SLYR. "We are going to shock the world on Saturday. We're gonna knock out Alabama. I can feel it. I just know it. I'll call you after."

The whole room broke into applause by the time Whitfield brought Manziel up to the front.

Unlike the other counselors who'd preceded him, Manziel didn't give a short speech but rather an offer to an open forum: "Wassup, fellas? Y'all know what I'm doing every second of every day just by turning on ESPN. I've been asked probably every question you can imagine, but I'll answer anything you like."

When he was asked what his biggest challenge had been, Manziel's response was as much a glimpse into how his life had been transformed from anonymous to the surreal as it was an answer to the question.

"I am still the same person. Me and Whit, a year later, our relationship's grown even tighter. We still talk the same," Manziel said, smiling at Whitfield.

"Keep your circle even tighter. People come in and out of my life every day wanting this or wanting that. It's hard to trust people in this situation. You learn. You adapt. It's not just meeting LeBron and saying, 'Wassup?' It's trying to pick his brain. He's played in a couple of NBA Finals. I talked to Kobe the other day. I thought he was going to stop texting me because I was wearing him out so much asking him, 'How do you handle this? Handle that?' "

Manziel's biggest motivation?

"It's essentially guys like you—the anointed Elite 11 campers. I was not even in the Top 100 in the state of Texas. I was, like, the 35th-ranked quarterback. It's different now. The shoe is on the other foot. They used to say, 'He's too short. Improvises too much. Runs around too much.' And I know there are people out there who are doubting me now. Still.

"For whatever reason it is, people always like to doubt me, but one day, down the road, in twenty or thirty years, people will stop doing it, but I won't ever stop."

Seated ten feet away from Manziel, fellow Texan—and former two-star recruit—David Blough could relate. Blough knew what it felt like to have the big Texas schools come by his school to watch him and leave without saying a word to anyone. "It felt like he was speaking right to me," Blough said later. "It was really cool to listen to how he wanted to prove all the people who passed on him wrong. He plays with a chip on his shoulder, and you can see it in everything he does, and that's exactly how I'm trying to be. I really do wish I get to play at Texas or Texas A&M someday."

Manziel later elaborated on his arrest in the summer of 2012 when his buddy reportedly directed a racial slur at a man, which prompted a scuffle after the Texas A&M freshman tried to play peacemaker and ended up all over the Internet with a shirtless mug shot and charged with three misdemeanors for disorderly conduct, failure to identify, and possession of a fictitious driver's license.

"I was so blessed to have an opportunity to get a full ride to a school in the state of Texas. I go out one night and make a bad decision, and I felt like I pressed my foot on the [lever] and flushed it all down the toilet. I didn't know if I was gonna be on the team anymore. Lowest point of my life. Teammates are not really messing with me anymore. I just continued to chop wood. Worked on the things Coach Whit told me to focus on. Just kept chopping wood.

"I'll never forget the day. I grew up the biggest Texas Longhorn fan in the world. Vince Young was the baddest man on the planet. He was the man. I always wanted to play for them. I almost didn't play football anymore so I could play baseball for the University of Texas. That's how bad I wanted to go there. I'll never forget, Coach Duane Akina called me and said they had one last scholarship, and it was between me and this one other kid from San Antonio—for DB—'and we went ahead and offered the other guy.' It crushed me. But, at the end of the day, it only made me work that much harder. I wanted to show Mack Brown and everyone else in that program that y'all really, really, really messed up."

A few hours later, the Nike store in downtown Portland was jammed with blue-chip high school football recruits. Nike had closed down the store so it could host the Elite 11 guys and the 160-plus other players who had just arrived in town for The Opening. Nike trotted out some of its most celebrated football clients for a Q&A session hosted by another Nike guy, ESPN announcer Desmond Howard, and including Ndamukong Suh and two-sport legend Bo Jackson. After a few minutes, while the store was having problems with the panel's microphones, it became apparent that the recruits couldn't care less what "Bo knows" and instead were riveted by the presence of Johnny Football hanging out with Boyd and Fales. For the rest of the day, both at the Nike store and back at the hotel, Manziel was mobbed by recruits asking to take a picture with him or just shake his hand.

"I never, ever heard of him [Bo Jackson] till today, but this is Johnny Football, man," explained one seventeen-year-old, 300-pound lineman standing in line to get a pic on his smartphone with Manziel. "He's a legend."


NIKE'S INVESTMENT IN *Elite 11* and The Opening stretched well beyond just giving a couple hundred teenage football prodigies from around the country the run of its campus and turning over the Nike store. It also meant bringing in active NFL stars to help with some on-field instruction—and motivation. The biggest celeb of the bunch was Aaron Rodgers, a former NFL MVP, who moved around through morning drills for a few hours. Rodgers mostly observed and occasionally chatted with Trent Dilfer. The Northern California–bred QBs are golf buddies who share the same mentor, Jeff Tedford, and the same agent, David Dunn.

David Blough, like most of the high schoolers, was starstruck by Rodgers. When he misfired on a route with a receiver, he figured he had a once-in-a-lifetime opportunity to pick the NFL star's brain.

"I feel I did something wrong there," Blough said to Rodgers.

"Yeah, you're over-striding on your back step, and you didn't get your full rotation through," Rodgers told him.

"Well, what do you think I need to work on the most?"

"You're staring down your target," Rodgers replied. "You're throwing one-on-ones, so, of course, you're gonna stare down your receiver, but challenge yourself. You've got all the arm talent in the world. You know you're throwing to this guy, but why not stare down the middle of the field and know what timing he's going to be on, and then, on your last step, look over at him and deliver the ball. Find a way to challenge yourself even if it's a little routine drill or routes-on-air (against no defenders)."

Blough later said it was some of the best advice he'd ever gotten. He was well-versed in Rodgers's path to stardom. Months ago, when he was ranked as a two-star recruit and had no scholarship offers, his dad would tell him different stories about the meandering routes NFL quarterbacks often had to take. Such as Kurt Warner bagging groceries and playing in the Arena Football League, or Rodgers starting out in community college after being overlooked by every major college in the country in high school. To Blough, Rodgers was an inspiration. To Craig Nall, Rodgers was a sour reminder of a star-crossed NFL career.

Nall, too, was once a blue-chip recruit. The Louisiana native picked LSU over Florida. The way the Tigers depth chart set up, Nall figured he'd develop behind an upperclassman and then have three years to start. Problem was, in 1999—his third year in the program— the Tigers brought in another, more-hyped QB, Josh Booty, a local legend who had spent the previous five years playing professional baseball after signing a million-dollar deal with the Florida Marlins. Booty had been a rival of Peyton Manning coming up in the state. In fact, in 1994, it was Booty—not Manning—who won *USA Today* and *PARADE* magazine Offensive Player of the Year honors.

Nall, though, still beat out Booty and another future NFL quarterback, Rohan Davey, to win the starting spot, but after he helped the Tigers to a 17–7 first-half lead, he was pulled. "They were just doing that to appease me," Nall says, "knowing I was only gonna start a half. 'Then we can start Booty the rest of the year,' which was what happened."

Feeling he had no shot to overtake Booty, Nall opted to transfer down to 1-AA-level Northwestern State in Natchitoches, Louisiana. The Green Bay Packers—impressed by how Nall had carried the undermanned Demons to an overtime upset win at TCU after leading a fourth-quarter, two-minute rally and by another two-minute drive he piloted in the 1-AA playoffs against eventual champion Montana—drafted him in the fifth round in 2002.

Nall entered an ideal situation. The starter was a superstar, Brett Favre. The backup was a thirty-four-year-old vet who had also played his college ball at a small school in Louisiana, Doug Pederson. "I was [Packers quarterback coach Darrell] Bevell's little pet project," said Nall, who only started twelve college games. Bevell overhauled how the former college javelin thrower gripped the ball, eventually breaking Nall's habit of pointing the ball down and toward his back foot as well as spreading his fingers out and farther down on the laces by a notch, so he stopped pushing so many of his passes.

"I threw in the net every day my whole rookie season," said Nall. "When special teams practiced, I was there throwing in the net, thirty minutes a day, with Darrell. All during training camp. All off-season, throwing in the net.

"We overhauled everything. During college, I didn't get a whole lot of instruction. It's compete, compete, compete all the time for a starting job. I came from a system with [LSU offensive coordinator] Jimbo Fisher, where you're making protection calls and sight adjusts and doing all that type of thing to Northwestern State, where you ask, 'So what happens if they bring more than we can protect?' And the answer is, 'Just go make a play.' It was one of those conversations. 'OK, let's do it.' "

Nall ended up spending years marveling at Brett Favre, the NFL's king of "Just Go Make a Play." Nall cited a short touchdown pass that Favre threw as an example. The called play was a running back screen to the right. Favre, though, signaled [wide receiver] Robert

Ferguson to run a slant on the back side of a screen, which typically doesn't mesh with the call. No matter. Favre still fired a touchdown pass to Ferguson.

"You can't really coach that," said Nall. "You don't want your QB playing outside the system like that, but he made it work. You don't want to encourage him to do that, because he'll do it more and more, but what do you say? He's got the most interceptions in the NFL, too.

"One of the things he told me in my first year there was, 'When in doubt, just throw it hard. Defensive guys are over there for a reason, because they can't catch it as well as offensive players.' The second part of that is, 'If you do throw a pick, head to the back pylon, because they can't hit you there.' That's why he played for twenty years."

Ask Nall to name the most amazing thing he ever witnessed Favre do, and he thinks for about twenty seconds before nodding and then breaking into a big smile.

"So, we're out on the practice field in the indoor facility," he said. "At the top of the uprights, there's a little box cutout for the film guy to get the end-zone copy. We're standing on the 40-yard line. Brett goes, 'You think I can throw this ball into that square up there?'

"I said, 'Nope, but I wanna see you try.'

"He rears back, [then] let's it go—*zhoooom!*—the guy had to put his hand in front of the camera or it would've broken the lens. This was up a good forty feet on top of it being about fifty yards away. So you're talking about at least a 60-yard throw into a foot square, on the first try. I swear, it's true."

And then, before Nall could take another breath, another Favre moment came to mind, this one in a game against the Jets. Favre's rolling to his left out by the numbers. He stops. Puts his feet in the ground and—*zhoooom!*—hits his receiver in the back right corner of the end zone when the DB was only five feet away. "Absolute laser," Nall says. "Fifty yards to the back corner.

"No, wait. This is the one," Nall said.

"Probably the other most amazing thing I've ever seen him do is, he gets a concussion. Pederson comes in for about a quarter. So, we're on, about, the 38-yard line, and we're going for it on fourth-and-five. Everyone's thinking, 'Should we go for it?' Favre all of a sudden gets up off the bench, kinda moves everybody out of the way. He gives [head coach Mike] Sherman the thumbs-up as he's trotting onto the field, like, 'Yeah, I got the play. I'm good.' Pederson runs off. Favre throws a touchdown—our only touchdown of the game. Afterward, [he] tackles [Javon] Walker and hits his head again. He doesn't know what down it is or what the situation is. After that, they hid his helmet. Of course, he ended up playing [the] next week."

In Nall's third season in the NFL, he got into some mop-up duty late in games. He was sharp, connecting on 70 percent of his passes while throwing 4 touchdowns and 0 INTs. That winter, Doug Pederson retired to move back to Louisiana, prompting the Packers to give Nall a unique assignment.

"Sherman pulled me aside and said, 'Look, [Brett's] best friend's gone. There's hardly anybody left from the Super Bowl team. You need to fill that role and be that voice of reason in his head and keep him grounded and give him something to do outside of football.' It was, like, part of my job description was to go hunting with Brett Favre."

Two years earlier, the Packers had Nall go to Scotland to play in NFL Europe. He led the league in touchdowns and QB rating and returned to the United States with his confidence brimming, only to find out they'd signed onetime first-rounder Akili Smith. However, the former Oregon star struggled to pick up Green Bay's system and was soon released. The next year, the Packers brought in another former first-rounder, Tim Couch. But the Packers cut him, also.

With Pederson gone and Nall feeling good about his 2004 performance, Green Bay then drafted Aaron Rodgers after the Cal star fell in the first round and the Packers snagged him with the twenty-fourth pick. It created an awkward dynamic, with the team bringing Rodgers in as the eventual successor to the franchise's beloved hero, Brett Favre, after Favre had just thrown for over 4,000 yards.

Nall had his own friction with the rookie first-rounder. Like most rookie QBs, Rodgers struggled in his first training camp. According to the *Milwaukee Journal Sentinel*, Rodgers didn't lead the Green

Bay offense to a single point until his twentieth and final series of the pre-season, when the Packers scored a touchdown on a drive that was aided by a long pass interference penalty.

"If the number two quarterback job had been awarded based on performance in training camp and games, it would have gone to Craig Nall, hands down," Packers beat man Bob McGinn later wrote.

Rodgers still was named Favre's backup, and Nall was third on the depth chart. The fourth-year vet was devastated. It reminded him of when he got passed over for Josh Booty at LSU. Nall asked to have a conversation with Sherman.

Sherman's explanation was blunt: "He's a first-round pick, and we have money in him. I can tell you, you're gonna get fucked."

"After that, me and Coach Sherman had a great relationship," Nall said. "We could talk frankly."

Nall's psyche took another hit whenever he'd be leaving the Packers' facilities and fans would ask for his autograph, thinking he was Rodgers.

"It's the eyes, I guess—even my wife agrees we have some similar features," Nall said, adding that he soon realized that the resemblance afforded him a way to get a jab at Rodgers. Whenever he'd hear someone call him "Aaron" or "Mr. Rogers," he'd laugh to himself at the thought of blowing them off and leaving fans thinking, "That Aaron Rodgers, what a dick!"

After the 2005 season, Nall opted to sign a three-year contract with a $1-million signing bonus with the Buffalo Bills. The starting job was open. On the second day of training camp, he went the entire morning practice without one of his passes hitting the ground, he said. Then, on the second to last play of practice, he tried to outrun a linebacker to the corner of the end zone and felt his hamstring give. "That hamstring was the beginning of the end for me," Nall said. "I was inactive number three the rest of the year." One year later, he was out of Buffalo and on the Texans' roster before ending back up in Green Bay in 2007. Nall lasted one more season in the NFL, with the Houston Texans, before retiring. He's proud to note that he's somewhere in the Packers' record book for having thrown the most passes (48) without an interception.

"I ended up behind two Super Bowl–winning quarterbacks," Nall said. "We know Favre is going into the Hall of Fame, and Rodgers is on his way. Had I gotten drafted someplace else, who knows? Had I gone to Florida instead of LSU, who knows? But I don't have any regrets. I try not to let myself go there, because it could be maddening, since there's nothing you can do about it."

DILFER, A GUY WHO played with, among others, Ray Lewis and Hall of Famers Warren Sapp and Walter Jones, called Aaron Rodgers the "most confident human being I've ever been around."

Observing the Elite 11 quarterbacks, Rodgers said he couldn't believe how good some of the QBs were. It didn't take much for him to recall being their age. Of course, when he was, nobody wanted him as a quarterback, which had actually turned out to be a very useful thing for him. Rodgers, now thirty, said he still had the letter a Purdue assistant once sent him that said, "Good luck with your attempt at a college football career," after he'd mailed the Boilermakers his high school tape.

"You really need to remember where you came from and have appreciation for the journey that you went on," Rodgers said. "I think a lot of kids these days, especially with the outlets we have, the exposure that we have, where a lot of these young guys are 'blue-chippers' from the time they're in high school to the time they get drafted, there's not a ton of adversity that they go through. I dealt with adversity on every level, from not getting recruited out of high school to going to junior college, to being a backup in D1, to falling farther than I thought I would in the draft. For me, it was great, because I got to sit and learn and be with the disappointment. Those experiences can either strengthen your character or make you really bitter. Thankfully for me, it really strengthened my character and gave me a good resolve."

Rodgers, like Dilfer, credited Jeff Tedford with enabling him to become a first-round pick: "Jeff's a perfectionist in nature, and that rubbed off on me a lot," he said. "He challenged me to be perfect in my footwork, in my preparation, in my reads, and in my execution.

It's that kind of mind-set that allows you to never be complacent, even in your greatest games. I owe Jeff a lot. I often felt like I had to prove to him every single day that I was mentally tough, I was physically tough, and I was good enough to be his quarterback."

The metamorphosis of Rodgers's game early in the QB's career in Green Bay that Dilfer spoke of was actually inspired by none other than Brett Favre. Not long after Rodgers arrived in Green Bay, there were numerous reports of friction between the two. Rodgers said the relationship was "mischaracterized. To be an older player like myself, ten years in now, it would have been difficult to have your successor picked before you're ready to give it up. He played three more years when I was there, and then he played three more after that." Still, fitting in on Favre's team, in his town, was challenging, but Rodgers soon realized how fortunate he was to have a firsthand, close-up look at one of the most extraordinary talents to ever play the position.

"He did things so differently than what I was used to," Rodgers said. "I had three years to really practice all those things and figure out what I liked. I've been reading Hank Haney's book about Tiger Woods. What I found interesting was when Tiger's talking about ninety percent of the things that he hears, he throws out. Five percent he works on and then throws out, and then the other five percent he incorporates into his game. For me, it was absorbing a lot of information from Brett, watching him, listening in the meetings, listening to him in the huddle, watching him in practice, and trying to figure out what I wanted to absorb into my game and what I wanted to change and do differently or do better.

"It also challenged me to play around with some things, and I had the luxury of not having been thrown in there right away to try to help the team win. I got the chance to hone my skills and incorporate some things and change some things that I wanted to in order to be successful. Those three years were crucial to me in becoming a better player. Here I was, looking at a guy who was unorthodox at times and trying to figure out why. Jeff Tedford taught us things, and when he did, he told us to ask the 'Why.' I think that is the most important question a quarterback can have, because once you figure out why you're doing it, then you can really figure out how to make it work for you in a clutch situation. I watched Brett for years . . . [and] I would figure out the Why—why he would offset one way and throw back the other way; why he would load his leg one time and not another time; why he would use a certain footwork on a certain drop. And when I was able to figure out why he was doing it, it made sense to me. Then you can really take it and make it useful in your own game."

Rodgers had three years to study up on Favre's preternatural on-field geometric wizardry. He was able to distill some of the uncanny and unconventional off-script plays that had become Favre's trademark. Even Favre's own coaches had given up trying to explain how the three-time NFL MVP ended up doing some of the remarkable—and often ill-advised—things he could pull off on a football field. Rodgers, though, not only figured out Favre's rationale, he found his own way to mimic the maneuvers.

"The one thing I really learned is, you have to have a real, innate sense about how each throw affects your body and really harness that instantaneous feeling/reaction about how each throw feels," he said. "So when you're making a throw on the run to the left, eventually you learn you have to aim a little bit inside, because your body is moving hard to the left, and then you compensate. Well, it's the same thing in the pocket, when you throw a ball off your back foot or throw a ball moving hard to your left or up in the pocket—you really want to capture that feeling. I think that is what Brett did so well. He was really able to harness that feeling in his mind about how to put the ball in a spot he wanted based on what his body was doing and disconnecting often from his upper body and his lower body. He was able to harness those feelings and then could recall them in a split second to make the proper throw. As incredible as that might've looked sometimes, to Brett, I don't think it was that difficult, because he knew what that felt like, and he had that muscle memory ingrained in his mind so he could repeat that on multiple occasions, and that's what gave him his advantages."

The depths Rodgers went to expand his game sometimes didn't

sit well with the Green Bay coaches. In his rookie season of 2005, Mike Sherman's team would have "Feel Good Friday," a no-pads practice with shorts and helmets, leading into the weekend.

"The defensive coaches wanted me to throw the ball to this certain guy every single time on the scout team," Rodgers said. "What it really meant was, they wanted me to throw an interception every single time. As a competitor, I just couldn't do that. I told our guys, 'You just run to the proper spot, and I'm gonna no-look almost every throw.' So, one, I was working on, can I no-look a throw and put it in the proper spot? Two, the competitor in me is saying, 'I am not gonna throw a pick. I don't care if Coach Duffner is coming over to tell me to, if Jim Bates is coming over to tell me to throw it, or if Speedy Washington is telling me to throw a pick. I'm too much of a competitor to throw a pick every single time, even if it is practice on a 'Feel Good Friday.' Finally, after five or six weeks of doing that and ticking off the defense, Sherman pulled my QB coach, Darrell Bevell, aside and said, 'Tell the young kid to stop doing that.' So they tried to put a stop to that (ha-ha), but it didn't really work."

Five seasons later, Rodgers earned Super Bowl MVP honors for leading the Packers to a victory over the Pittsburgh Steelers in Super Bowl XLV. A big reason for Green Bay's title and the subsequent NFL MVP trophy Rodgers won the following season stemmed from all those hours he'd spent deconstructing Brett Favre's magic, experimenting at the Packers facility, reinventing himself—and the quarterback position.

HEADING INTO THE 7-ON-7 tournament, Dilfer posted a leader board ranking the top eleven quarterbacks. To Blough's surprise, he was number one.

The dynamic of how the event unfolded, with the Elite 11 quarterbacks having the run of the Nike campus for a few days before The Opening kicked off, provided Dilfer with another window into his kids' DQ. "You had a bunch of other alphas, and other cultures came in, and now, all of a sudden, they're surrounded by 150 of the best Dudes in the country. How big were they?" Dilfer said of his QBs.

"Which ones got with their teams and just owned it? And which ones were intimidated and said, 'OK, who am I gonna follow?' I really saw those 'thermometer' leaders kick in. Half our quarterbacks become thermometers. They did it when they saw that stud [defensive back] Tony Brown or that stud receiver or that big Polynesian lineman show up. 'They have a bigger personality than me. They have more stars than me, so I'm gonna follow him.' But David Blough, who had two stars coming into this thing on his team of thirteen studs, he owned it from the second he got into the room with them. There was no doubt who the captain of that ship was."

The 7-on-7 passing competition had become a staple of off-season football. It was especially big on the high school summer scene, where traveling club teams had sprung up all over the country, much to the dismay of many high school coaches fearing it would have a similar influence to what AAU programs did in high school basketball. The "7-on"—tied in with Nike's The Opening event—were new parts to the Elite 11. Nike provided plenty of colorful uniforms, while ESPNU provided more than its share of national TV exposure.

There were six teams in the tournament. Dilfer's Elite 11 protégés, his TDFB guys, coached the teams. They had a draft to select the top eighteen quarterbacks. Even though there were no helmets or pads, the spotlight on and the trash-talking among rival blue-chippers ramped up the intensity. When one of the QBs on Blough's team, who had struggled all week in Oregon, threw a pick-six with fifteen seconds remaining in the first half to turn a 13–0 deficit into 20–0, the kid looked crushed as he slunk back to the sideline.

Dilfer, observing the action, walked over to put his arm around the young quarterback and then yelled back to Dennis Gile, the staffer coaching the losing team.

"Let's go, Dennis! Have some energy!" Dilfer called in a voice scratchy and hoarse after five days on the field. On the sideline, one of the defensive players on the team that was leading asked the kid next to him if Dilfer was "Stone Cold" Steve Austin.

Going into the final day at the Elite 11, Blough had dropped in the rankings from number one to number three. Another unheralded prospect, Sean White, one of the final two QBs selected for the

Elite 11, surged in the coaches' eyes. "He's telling the other QBs what to do; he's making these guys better," said former NFL QB Charlie Frye, White's coach on the team called the Field Generals. "Just talking about him, I'm getting goosies. He had nine incompletions and five TDs, and he also had a dropped TD."

The Field Generals began the tournament by losing their first game by almost 40 points, but that was a game White didn't play in. Led by the Fort Lauderdale native, the Field Generals rallied to win the 7-on title after White led them on a last-minute touchdown drive for a come-from-behind 21–14 win over Team Alpha Pro. The championship carried White—who ended up committing to Auburn two weeks later, a school he didn't have an offer from before coming to Oregon—to MVP honors of The Opening and the Elite 11.

Blough finished number six. "It was bittersweet," he said. "I wanted to prove to myself and prove to the coaches at Purdue that they didn't make a mistake. I was tired of being overlooked. The first two days I was killing it, and I look at that like the first half, but I slacked off toward the end, and I look at that like the fourth quarter. I'm not sure why that was. Being out in front, being the favorite, is something I had to get used to. I'd never been the favorite. My high school was always the underdog. I had to learn how to be at the front of the pack. I guess I was probably a little complacent. That won't happen again."

Dilfer's advice to Blough: "Don't you ever buy into the fact that you should live in reality. You keep living in this pretend world, because that's where you thrive."

"In his world, he's the biggest, the baddest, the toughest, the strongest, the best," Dilfer said. "I said, 'You live there. You have to be a legend in your own mind; you don't have to buy into this reality that you're six feet tall and all this other stuff.'"

The final selection of which of the eighteen quarterbacks made the actual Elite 11 was announced in front of a lake on the Nike campus. It was a made-for-TV moment, as all the campers were outfitted in matching neon yellow *Elite 11* shirts with black shorts and neon yellow socks. They all stood shoulder to shoulder in front of an elevated platform as Dilfer addressed them. He got choked up talking about what the group meant to him before he approached each QB individually to tell which to stand up on the platform, which ones had made it. That day also happened to be a very emotional one for Dilfer beyond the happenings in Oregon. It was his twentieth wedding anniversary. On top of that, his wife, Cass, was in Texas with all three of their daughters, as his two oldest girls were competing at the USA Volleyball Girls' Junior National Championship. Dilfer later said he would've loved to be with his family, but he'd already committed to the Elite 11 and that his wife understood how important that was to him.

He recalled the day at his home about five months earlier when he and his wife discussed his scheduling dilemma, "the defining moment when I knew I was in my sweet spot," he said.

"As painful as it was, it was so defining for me that I knew I was exactly where I was supposed to be. That I was doing what I was supposed to be doing. I think they know I'm better as a husband and father, and as a man, when I'm whole. Now, I think I've learned what makes me whole. They have [also] identified what makes me whole, and this is part of it, so I think they've embraced it, because they know this is part of my wholeness."

## 8.

# MANNINGLAND

JULY 11, 2013.

An hour before the eighteenth annual Manning Passing Academy began, ninety minutes north at LSU, Tommy Moffitt, with his barrel chest and Parris Island voice, was getting nostalgic. Asked about Peyton Manning, the Tigers strength coach took a big gulp of air before reaching into his desk and pulling out a bright orange folder with the name *MANNING* scribbled across the front.

Moffitt, the strength coach at Tennessee when Manning was the Vols star QB in the mid-'90s, had shown all Tiger freshmen when they reported to school this frayed old folder that contained pages of the workouts he'd prescribed for the quarterback during the summer going into his senior season. Inside, the printed sheets of paper were covered with notes Manning had jotted down, showing the player's attention to detail and indefatigable level of preparation. There were some crossed-out poundages of prescribed workout routines where Manning pushed himself to do five or ten pounds more than Moffitt had anticipated. Everything was accounted for and documented with check marks and pluses along with margin notes such as *Threw good outside 1 on 1 . . . 7x Hills Threw . . . Agilities/Sand.*

Moffitt told all his newcomers at LSU that he had never—in

twenty-five years—seen anybody as meticulous in their preparation as Peyton Manning. The weathered orange folder was Exhibit A, an artifact worthy of its place in Canton once Manning took his place in the Pro Football Hall of Fame.

"I tell them all, 'Right now, you're a better athlete than Peyton Manning ever was or Peyton Manning ever will be," Moffitt said. "But this—*THIS!*—is what makes him so special. His preparation and his attention to detail and the things he does that nobody else told him, that, 'This is what you have to do to be great.' "

Moffitt's favorite highlights of Manning's career didn't take place in Neyland Stadium. They happened around the Vols' football complex at odd hours, when almost no one else was around. Such as the time Moffitt heard a tap on the window to his office. Manning was outside. He needed help. Said he had a bunch of VHS tapes in his SUV that needed to go upstairs. Moffitt came outside to Manning's old black Oldsmobile Bravada and did a triple take when the senior quarterback opened the trunk.

It was jammed with tapes of every practice, every game, every opponent. Tight copies. Wide copies. End zone copies. Four years of film study. The ingredients to Manning's secret sauce. They ended up with two full shopping carts and kept unloading and filling.

Or the time Moffitt watched from his office window a nineteen-year-old Peyton tying a surgical cord to a goalpost and the other end around his waist so he could work on his drops from center. Back and forth. Back and forth. For what seemed like hours. Moffitt had never seen any other quarterback do that, and certainly not doing it on his own, without any coaches or teammates around.

"Nobody here told him to do that," Moffitt said. "Maybe Archie did."

Nope. It wasn't Archie's idea, either, according to the head of America's First Family of quarterbacks.

"I didn't lead him there," Archie Manning said, chuckling. Then again, he kind of did, in a roundabout, Peyton sort of way.

"Peyton told me once he wanted to be a good player," Archie said. "I told him the good players I know work at it. That's all I told him."

That was Peyton Manning, always figuring out a way on his own to get better. Moffitt said that was why the guy would be a first-ballot Hall of Famer. It was also a big reason why more than 1,200 kids and some two dozen college QBs made the trek down annually to the Manning family's week-long camp in stifling humidity in Thibodaux, Louisiana.

The camp was Peyton's idea, Archie said. Peyton, then a young quarterback at Tennessee, noticed the high school box scores in the newspaper, with teams getting blown out and their QBs going 1 for 4. Peyton wanted to have a camp to boost the level of quarterbacking in the local high schools. That first year, the Manning Passing Academy was held at Tulane University and had 180 campers. That first year, there were three college counselors helping out: Peyton, Jake Delhomme from what was then called Southwestern Louisiana, and his receiver, Brandon Stokley. Peyton's baby brother, Eli, was a high school camper. It didn't take long for the MPA to outgrow the place, shifting to Southeastern Louisiana before relocating to the Nicholls State campus in 2005.

Instruction is handled by the Mannings—Archie, Peyton, Eli, and oldest brother Cooper (a former Ole Miss wide receiver till a spinal condition ended his playing career)—and dozens of their friends who are either former college quarterbacks or coaches from all levels of the game.

"In seventeen years, the four of us have never missed a minute of the camp," Archie said. "We've bought in. That's a credibility thing. It's meaningful to us. It's the only time all year when we get four days together.

"I think it's just our passion for what the institution of high school football is, what it does for the life lessons that youngsters learn, and just the values it gives people. It's getting attacked right now, more than ever. It's our passion to try to have a good time with these kids, to help them get a little better and to understand that high school football can be a great experience for them. We really haven't changed our concept awfully much. We still try—we always try—to make it a non-recruiting thing. That wasn't its purpose. It wasn't for blue chips necessarily. We don't mind having the blue-chip players. That wasn't the concept, though. We just tried to enhance the experience of high school players, particularly quarterbacks and receivers. Just the numbers, obviously growing and growing, which means our staff gets bigger. Actually, I think, because of that, it all just gets more fun."

From sunrise to sunset at the Manning Passing Academy, there were young quarterbacks being coached in every possible element of the game at a variety of stations seemingly on every corner of the Nicholls State campus. Clearly, it was also no mere vanity project for the Mannings. They were neck-deep in it when it came to hands-on instruction and interaction.

On the evening before the camp officially kicked off, Archie and Peyton explained to their staff precisely how they wanted certain nuances of the game taught. For instance, on a 5-step drop, Peyton told his staffers, "Do drops on the yard-line, so it forces them to stay straight," or on a 3-step drop, "When you put two in the ground, it should align your hips to throw the hitch to the boundary or to the field." More than anything, for the price of $585 for three nights at the camp (it's $440 for day campers), all the budding QBs—at some point during the week—will get hands-on access to Archie and his boys. And where else can a kid be taught the little details of playing quarterback by a five-time NFL MVP?

"The Mannings really want to teach the kids, whether it's someone who has never played quarterback a day in their life and just wants to come see Peyton, or the kid who is gonna get recruited to play D1 football, and everyone in between," said thirty-year-old ex-Clemson starter Will Proctor, who first started coming to the camp as a high school junior but had since worked as a college counselor and later as a coach at the camp after finishing his playing career.

For the two dozen college QBs, the camp provided them access to a unique fraternity.

"The Mannings are football royalty," said Oliver Luck, father to Andrew and a former teammate of Archie's with the Houston Oilers, where both men were quarterbacks in the early '80s. "They are *our* football royalty. They've done it with incredible grace and class and dignity. They've set the bar for everybody who plays the position, and it's a very tough position to play. They've done it the right way.

"The Democrats have the Clintons. The Republicans have the Bushes. We have the Mannings."

The "done it the right way" is big inside the football community. Archie Manning never played in a single NFL playoff game, much less made it to a Super Bowl, but there may be no more respected man among his peers than the former two-time Pro Bowler who was once selected as the NFL's Man of the Year in 1977. Manning was often a one-man show, scrambling to extend doomed plays for the lowly New Orleans Saints, a longtime NFL punch line. Archie played more like Johnny Manziel than either Peyton or Eli. Off the field, Archie, a genuine SEC legend who married a beautiful former homecoming queen, emerged as one of the true gentlemen of the game. His legacy also was boosted by the way his boys turned out, especially Peyton, regarded as the gold standard of the cerebral quarterback and the man most identified with ushering in the NFL's era of the advanced, "Problem Solver" QB.

Florida offensive coordinator Kurt Roper was a young assistant coach at Tennessee when Peyton was the Vols' quarterback. Roper, himself the son of a coach, said the college kid taught him more about preparation than anyone he'd ever been around. "When I played at Rice, nobody watched practice right after and took notes like he did," recalled Roper. "Here, I am a [graduate assistant], and I'm asking *him* questions, thinking, 'Lemme learn from this guy.' I'd try to steal as much time with him as I could. 'How are you determining coverages? What are fronts telling you pre-snap? What are you looking at on a given play?' He was studying defense and what it was doing, so he could have a great idea what he was gonna do with the football pre-snap.

"His work ethic and his ability to be singularly focused on winning from week to week and controlling his mind and preparing for his moment was amazing. Nobody I've ever been around, coaches included, have the drive that he has to prepare. He is just different than anybody else."

* * *

OLIVER LUCK SAID HE wouldn't send his son, Andrew, to any other quarterback camp or to work with other private coaches, only the Mannings' camp. Luck, a onetime Rhodes Scholar finalist, spent five seasons in the NFL. He taught his son the proper way to throw a football when Andrew was around four or five. Just as he showed him the right way to throw a baseball or snowball, he said, adding that he was mindful of not overdoing anything, keeping football in perspective.

"Like most things in life, you have to use discretion," Luck said. "You can't do too much, because then it becomes a Marinovich sort of thing."

Any Marinovich reference when it comes to trying to develop a child super-athlete is akin to being a "Little League father" on steroids. The real Marinoviches are father Marv, a former-NFL-lineman-turned-strength-coach who studied Eastern Bloc training methods, and son Todd, aka "The Robo Quarterback," bred by his dad in a "perfect environment" free of fast foods or sweets. Todd made it to the NFL as a first-round draft pick, but he lasted less than two seasons as he battled a string of drug problems that had first come to light in his college days, when he was arrested for cocaine possession at USC.

"I've always believed that if you're a parent and you think you've got a talented kid—doesn't matter what sport—encourage the kid, make sure the kid is getting quality coaching," said Luck, "and, at some point, probably around their freshman or sophomore year of high school, the kid—boy or girl—has to have the fire in his or her belly to say, 'I'm not doing this because my parents encouraged me to or because my girlfriend likes the fact that I'm a quarterback; I'm doing it because I just really like this stuff—the 6:00 a.m. practices, the hundred-degree heat. My goal was not to raise an NFL quarterback. I'm happy as a clam that Andrew is able to do what he's doing in the NFL, but my wife and I just wanted to raise good kids with the proper values who followed whatever passion they had.'"

Years later, when Andrew was a star at Stanford, he also worked

the camp as a college counselor. The college guys say they might ben-
efit from the camp even more than the kids do, because they get to
pick Peyton's brain and know specifically what they're seeking out,
whereas the high schoolers usually don't know what they don't know
and are just giddy that Peyton or Eli said something to them.

Cody Fajardo, a quarterback at Nevada, who worked the camp
in 2013, asked Peyton Manning, "How do you watch film?"

"The thing about that is, they're full-time NFL guys, and I'm still
a college student," Fajardo later explained the rationale for his question. "My time management is a little tougher, but Peyton told me
on Mondays, he will watch all third downs. On Tuesday, he'll watch
first-and-tens and first-and-ten-plus. On Wednesdays, he'd watch all
the blitz tape. On Thursdays, he'll watch the complete game. On Fri-
days, he'll watch the complete game again. On Saturdays, he'll watch
a bunch of cut-ups and what he wants to see in situational football.
He's got it all mapped out in increments, so it's not boring. He'll take
notes. That's what I'm gonna try to implement in my film study, so
instead of watching an entire game in one sitting, you're looking at
stuff in increments and still getting good work in the film room."

The Manning camp also acted as an annual reunion for former
college-QBs-turned-coaches. For some, like Will Proctor, the former
Clemson quarterback now married to a FoxNews morning anchor
and living in Manhattan, this was the one week a year when he got to
be back on the field mingling with his old football pals.

Proctor might have been the only former Manning camper who
actually came for Buddy Teevens, the Dartmouth head football coach
who doubled as the MPA's associate director. Proctor's dad and Teevens
were teammates at Dartmouth in the '70s. In 2000, the younger Proctor was the starting quarterback at an Orlando-area program so small
that it had fewer members on its team than the school's state-champion
debate team had.

Will Proctor didn't have much sense of just where he ranked as
a college prospect. After all, Trinity Preparatory School had never
produced a Division I football player till Teevens, then the Florida
Gators' QB coach, offered Proctor a scholarship. At the Manning
camp, Proctor's confidence grew. The camp had such a different vibe

from all the other football camps Proctor had attended. Everyone just seemed so approachable, whether it was Archie or Peyton or Eli, who at the time was an Ole Miss Rebel. One night, the sixteen-year-old Proctor found himself in a lounge near his dorm room in front of a TV chatting with Major Applewhite, the starting QB at Texas; Ben Leard, the starting QB at Auburn; and Tyler Watts, the starting QB at Alabama.

"We're talking about our favorite college uniforms, and I remember just sitting there thinking, 'Wow, this is so cool! I am being treated like a peer by these guys,'" said Proctor.

"I remember asking Major Applewhite, 'What's with the helmet? Why do you pull it down so low?' Tyler and Ben were, like, 'Yeah, why do you do that?' He goes, 'I like to have some shade.' And he put his hand up like the brim of a hat."

During one of the quarterbacking stations, Watts, an option quarterback, was assigned to teach "Deep Ball."

"He'd say 'If you're ten yards apart, picture a ten-yard wall in between you guys, and you have to throw it over that wall and try to get the nose to turn over. Now the wall is twenty yards high. You gotta get it over that wall.' I remember watching him not be able to get the nose to turn over, and I'm thinking to myself, 'I throw the deep ball better than him at sixteen.' I'm thinking, 'I'll be able to make it, because this guy starts for the Crimson Tide, and he can't do the drill he's trying to teach.'"

Proctor, a onetime CFL teammate of former Texas A&M offensive coordinator Kliff Kingsbury, actually coached Johnny Manziel at the camp four years earlier, when no one knew who the undersized Texan was. Proctor himself didn't even recall that he coached Manziel during the camp's 7-on-7 tournament.

"I had this complete stud who was playing safety and getting interceptions, playing wide receiver and catching all these touchdowns. He was doing everything. He just said, 'You tell me what to do. I don't care.' He just loved to play and compete. The kid was a freak athlete.

"Then, one day, someone tells me at the camp, 'Remember that kid who was on your team last year? He's at A&M now.'"

For the dozens of other coaches working the camp, it also had become a ripe networking opportunity, said former UCLA head coach Rick Neuheisel. "I tell every aspiring coach, 'If you want to get into this business, don't send résumés. Don't try to get at guys where they're working. You need to go to their camps. That's when they're letting their hair down, and when you go there, you need to volunteer for every shit job there is, because they're always looking for people to do stuff, because everybody else wants to go have fun. If you'll be that guy, and they notice your effort, that's how you get a foot in the door.'

"I used the guys who did that in my camps, the guys who said, 'I'll do bed-check. I'll do this. I'll do that.' Those are the guys I kept my eye on, because they're the worker bees that you really want. Nepotism is alive and well in the football industry. If your dad's not one of the coaches, this is how you get in."

Neuheisel's impression from his time working the Manning camp?

"It's a factory," he said. "Some coaches work. Some don't. You get ten to fifteen kids under your wing, and it's your job to make sure they have a great experience, but it's all the luck of the draw regarding how hard your guy is gonna work. And how much does he really know? The Mannings, to their credit, are ambassadors. Cooper is classic. He's funnier than hell, and it's his chance for everybody else to see that he is still *that* brother, the one who tells the other two what the hell to do. Peyton takes over on the field, and Eli has no problem letting Peyton take over.

"It was a great experience to see it in living color. My son and I were gonna be living in the dorms. We get in our room, and it's Spartan, really Spartan. We turn off the lights, and on the ceiling of the room, there's this black-light picture of a scrotum with the words 'Ghetto Balls' in neon. I said, 'Jerry, get your stuff. We're going to a hotel.' You wouldn't have seen it till the lights went off."

Neuheisel had his own favorite story about youth football camps and Peyton Manning, but it actually came from a Bill Walsh football camp at Stanford. Peyton was a senior at the time and attended the camp in Palo Alto.

"Bill Walsh had been on the brochure saying, 'Learn the West Coast offenses from one of the best coaches in football,'" Neuheisel said. "At the end of the camp, when Walsh is asking if anyone has any suggestions, Peyton stands up and says, 'Coach, if you're saying this in the brochure, I'd suggest you be here more than one day.' Archie later made Peyton call Bill Walsh and apologize."

"MEDIA DAY" FOR THE Manning Passing Academy was on a Friday morning and was scheduled for a thirty-five-minute window, which was reminiscent of how, in *Caddyshack*, "Caddy Day" at the Bushwood pool welcomed caddies from 1:00 to 1:15. According to the camp's PR director, it was the only opportunity for the media to speak with any of the Mannings or the college quarterbacks staffing the camp. A half dozen camera crews packed into the Century Room, the tight media area inside Nicholls State's Guidry Stadium. On average, there was usually only about half as big a media turnout, but Governor Bobby Jindal had made an appearance to honor the Mannings and announce that Nicholls would receive $1.2 million in appropriations to make improvements to the twenty-acre stretch of land the Manning camp used for its twenty-five football fields.

In the back half of the room, metal folding chairs were placed against the walls. Above each was a small sheet of paper with each of the college counselors' names. Before the Mannings and Jindal were finished with their remarks, a few reporters had already staked out spots next to the chairs of Johnny Manziel and Alabama's AJ McCarron.

Asked what he was hoping to learn from being around the Mannings, McCarron pointed out that it was actually his third year of coming to the camp. "I think it's more of an off-the-field type of help than on-the-field for us in terms of how to handle yourself, how to carry yourself with everyone watching you and everything," he said. "The way the world is nowadays, social media is everything. It's really how to handle yourself off the field, and I've learned a lot about that here."

Within five minutes McCarron was asked about his relationship with Manziel, seated ten feet away behind a half dozen reporters.

"We're friends," McCarron said. In fact, they were rooming together at the camp. "He knows if he ever needs anything—advice—I'm here for him and vice versa. People try to make the football thing a competition. When we're inside the white lines, yeah, we're both playing to win the game. But football's just a game. It's not life, so us being friends is a lot better than us being enemies, because we're not gonna get anything out of us being enemies."

The relationship of the two SEC stars would take an odd, public twist while they were in Thibodaux. A little more than twenty-four hours later, word started to circulate around the camp that Johnny Football had been booted from the camp. Later that night, a blog, *Rumors and Rants,* reported that Manziel was asked to leave after he "enjoyed himself a little too much Friday night and rolled back into the camp" around noon. ESPN reported that story was "inaccurate," according to camp officials, who said he went home to Texas because he was feeling ill. Paul Manziel, Johnny's father, told the *Dallas Morning News* that his son was resting as he recovered from "dehydration." Problem was, several people had tweeted seeing the Aggies star out in bars in College Station after midnight.

Days later, *Rumors and Rants* posted another account, alleging that Manziel threw McCarron "under the bus by forcing him to answer questions about why he didn't wake him up on Saturday morning," and that Manziel was seen on Bourbon Street in New Orleans (more than an hour from the Nicholls campus) around 4:00 a.m. However, a quarterback who was out with Manziel late that night said they actually never left Thibodaux.

"That story about him being in New Orleans is 100 percent BS," the quarterback said.

In truth, it didn't seem to matter much whether Manziel was out drinking on Bourbon Street or at a bar in Thibodaux—although it did give the story more shelf life and made it sound a bit sexier. It also didn't matter much if he was hungover or got all of eight minutes of sleep, either. The only thing the Mannings would've cared about was that Manziel managed to be accountable enough to show up on time for their morning meeting, which he wasn't. That was Manziel's real offense, said an NFL friend of the Mannings.

"That's not the Manning way," said the former quarterback. "You're a quarterback, and there's a certain way you should act. And that's powerful stuff. It's not to say they're all choirboys, because they're not, and if you wanna go light up the town, that's fine. Just be ready to go to work at 8:00 a.m., because you've got a station to work, and kids are counting on you."

Manziel wasn't the first college QB to disappoint the Mannings with how he handled the late-night scene around the camp. He was just the first to make national news for it.

## 9.

# OFF SCRIPT

JULY 17, 2013.

Three weeks before Texas A&M's fall camp kicked off, Johnny Manziel had morphed into a de facto ESPN reality show. Rumors about exactly what happened at the Manning Passing Academy had become the hottest topic on the TV sports channels just as the Aggies star was about to walk into the biggest circus in college sports—SEC Media Days, a three-day event in Hoover, Alabama, at the Wynfrey Hotel—with over 1,200 reporters in tow. Making matters even messier, the story unfolded during the slowest news week of the season in sports and tied football's resident "It" dude to the First Family of football, the Mannings. Beyond that, the story took on a life of its own in a farcical way, as if there was a congressional hearing on "Did or didn't someone wake up another guy at a summer camp?"

By this point of the off-season, the hype around Manziel had surpassed the hype around Tim Tebow at the peak of his media frenzy. Before Manziel was ushered around to a dozen different media platforms and interview sessions, he was brought to the main ESPN stage, where he was grilled by host Joe Tessitore for ten minutes. Manziel, after having spent much of the previous forty-eight hours with PR coaches, did his best to downplay the story. His answers were measured. His smile was ready. He repeatedly pointed out that he was still a twenty-year-old kid who could make mistakes and who still wanted to live his life. At one point, he told Tessitore that he sometimes felt like Justin Bieber—a comment that, no doubt, made NFL personnel men wince.

"I'm not going to change who I am because of the spotlight," he said, but he added that he would "adapt."

Later, he told reporters at the print-media session, "At the end of the day, I'm not going for a Miss America pageant. I'm playing football."

The SEC had seen more than its share of larger-than-life stories in recent years, but nothing quite like Manziel's. His style and swagger had rival coaches reeling, not just trying to cope on the field but off it, as well.

"This is a scary image for coaches," one of the SEC head coaches said after asking what the scene was like around the Wynfrey for Manziel's appearance. "Players look up to Johnny, and they see he can be wild and get away with it. And he's thriving, man. So that's negative reinforcement."

Weeks earlier, when he was told he was like a guy who is fifty pounds overweight and trying to diet, only he keeps breaking down and gorging on ice cream and sweets, reasoning to himself, "I don't need abs. I already got the hot girl," Manziel smiled and nodded. He was neither embarrassed nor proud of it. He seemed simply resigned to it. As if that was just how he'd been wired. Manziel knew he didn't have it all figured out, he said. Many times he got angry at himself for how he responded to things, but it always seemed to work out. Somehow.

Three hours after Manziel and the Aggies contingent arrived at the Wynfrey, he and head coach Kevin Sumlin and two A&M PR men were whisked off by private plane to Los Angeles for ESPN's ESPY awards. At some point, while Manziel was probably flying over the Midwest, his pal rap star Drake tweeted to his ten-million-plus Twitter followers:

"You handled yourself well today. Proud of you brother! @JManziel2"

Manziel, who hadn't tweeted in a month, retweeted the message.

Manziel's roommate from the Manning Camp, Alabama QB AJ McCarron, also seemed to have Manziel on his mind, tweeting a vague dig at the Heisman winner: "You're right, I'm not at the ES-PY's! I don't have to be at an award show to know what my team did. I'm back at school working to get another #16." The "16" was a reference to the number of national titles the Crimson Tide was shooting for. McCarron promptly deleted the tweet, but the next day, when it was his turn at SEC Media Days, he repeatedly went out of his way to distance himself from Manziel.

Asked about the tweet, McCarron said, "You know, everybody is a grammar teacher when it comes to Twitter," he said, perhaps explaining his reasoning for deleting it. "I know when I step out of the door, especially in the state of Alabama, I'm always going to be watched. I feel like I've always handled myself in a first-class way. That's the way my second dad, Coach Saban, and my coaches have taught me. That's my thought process behind everything. I never want to bring any bad attention on anybody that's close to me."

After the ESPYs that night, Sumlin walked into an after-party where Snoop Dogg was performing, and Dwyane Wade, Gabrielle Union, and LeBron James were hanging out in a private room along with Manziel, who was walking around holding his ESPY trophy. The coach noticed there were two huge portraits in the background. One showing LeBron James. The other, Johnny Manziel. Asked, how does all this not mess with the head of a twenty-year-old, Sumlin laughed. "It messed with *my* head."

The day after the ESPYs, Manziel arrived back in Texas late that afternoon. His teammates were already conducting a 7-on-7 session when he arrived wearing a polo, khakis, and untied Air Jordans. He walked onto the field with the other Aggies, moved the ball back to the 10-yard line (instead of the normal 30-yard-line start) and picked apart the A&M defense to lead the offense on a touchdown drive, punctuated by a perfect pass through tight coverage. As his teammates gathered around him, one senior defensive back yelled out to Manziel: "Listen. We don't give a fuck what people are saying. We don't care about what you've done this summer. We would've all been doing the same thing if we were in your position. All we care about is that we know if we ever need you to make a play, shit like that is going to happen, and we will always love you!

" 'Family' on three . . . One. Two. Three. *Family*!"

"That was a big thing for me," Manziel told me later. "That really showed me how the guys on the team felt about me, especially at such a time when I was so criticized."

The real Manziel drama, though, was only just beginning. Later in July, ESPN posted a story, "The trouble with Johnny," on its website from the *ESPN The Magazine* college football preview issue. In the story, Manziel's dad, Paul, was quoted saying that the NCAA and A&M—including coach Kevin Sumlin—were "starting to get under our skin," because they were "so selfish."

The *ESPN The Magazine* story, which kicked off a couple more days of intense Johnny Football coverage on ESPN's various TV channels, provided a snapshot of life with the Manziels back at their home. "His parents wanted to get jffmom and jffdad on their license plates—[referencing] Johnny 'F—ing' Football, as the name was originally coined on the A&M message boards; they were so caught up in the mania that it took their seventeen-year-old daughter, Meri, to point out the bad example that might set for kids who looked up to her brother," wrote *ESPN The Magazine*'s Wright Thompson. Paul Manziel, in NFL personnel men's eyes, also basically said his son was a ticking time bomb: "It could come unraveled. And when it does, it's gonna be bad. Real bad. It's one night away from the phone ringing, and he's in jail. And you know what he's gonna say? 'It's better than all the pressure I've been under. This is better than that.' "

That colorful portrait, which also included a scene of the Manziel clan gathering for a family dinner and of Johnny Football snapping at his aunt, telling her to "Shut the hell up," framed the Aggies quarterback, at the very least, as the anti-Tebow.

In truth, Manziel's on-the-edge persona probably wasn't all that different from that of many other standout athletes or star quarterbacks, including one of his own idols, Brett Favre. What was different, though, was that Manziel came from money, had way more access to celebrity stuff, and was in a new kind of fishbowl, thanks to social media, smartphones, and round-the-clock sports channels covering—and regurgitating—"stories," whether it was the twenty-year-old's tweets or Instagram photos of his travels to big sporting events or late-night partying or his dad's distressed comments, which came together like some version of *The Real Quarterbacks of the SEC* show.

The folks at A&M already knew that at the core of Manziel's belief that what made him so special on the field and in the clutch—his reckless, brash, "loose cannon" persona—was the same thing that was causing him, his parents, and the Aggies' brass so many headaches off the field.

Less than a week later, ESPN published a more troubling story for the Manziels and Texas A&M, regarding whether the Heisman Trophy winner was paid for signing hundreds of autographs on photos and sports memorabilia in January. Two sources told ESPN's *Outside the Lines* that Manziel had agreed to sign memorabilia in exchange for a five-figure flat fee during his trip to Miami for the Discover BCS National Championship Game, but neither of the sources said they actually witnessed the exchange of money. Day after day, more details and more anonymous sources surfaced. An ESPN reporter claimed he had watched video showing Manziel signing white Texas A&M helmets and footballs laid out on a bed in a hotel room in New Haven, Connecticut, while the QB was attending the Walter Camp Football Foundation event. Manziel was allegedly paid $7,500, but the video didn't show Manziel accepting any money, and the broker and his partner originally requested money to release the videos for use on ESPN, which ESPN said it declined to pay.

Inside the A&M football offices on the third floor of the 125,000-square-foot "Bum" Bright Football Complex, Manziel prepared as if he wouldn't miss a game. On a mid-August afternoon, he sat in the office of Jake Spavital, the Aggies' new quarterbacks coach and co-offensive coordinator, watching tape of the 2012 LSU game, his worst performance of the season.

"I didn't know where I was looking last year," Manziel said, studying his actions as Tiger defensive linemen maneuvered up field, opting to hem him in rather than aggressively rush towards the QB.

Manziel got upset at himself every time he watched plays from this game, as if he was seeing it for the first time. "Oh, shit! . . . That was the stupidest fucking read ever! . . . Throw it! Throw it!" After getting sacked by an LSU defender he never saw, he banged the clicker on the desk.

The 2013 season, he believed, would be different. He knew the offense, he had a better grasp on coverages, and, thanks to his work with Whitfield and his coaches at A&M, he was more comfortable setting his feet and stepping into his throws. But heading into the Aggies' final scrimmage of fall camp, no one inside the building was sure he would get the chance to show how much he'd improved.

"HE'S FIFTY FEET UNDERWATER with chains around his ankles, but you know you just can never count out this rascal," Whitfield said of Manziel.

Six days before the Aggies kicked off the 2013 season against Rice, Manziel met with NCAA investigators for five and a half hours. Throughout the meeting, which was focused on the quarterback's financial records, Manziel told the NCAA that he did not accept money from memorabilia brokers for autographs, according to sources. Less than seventy-two hours later, the NCAA opted to suspend Manziel, but for only the first half of the Rice game. That was for an "inadvertent violation" of NCAA rules, A&M associate athletic director Jason Cook explained, and that the "NCAA found no evidence [that] Manziel received monetary reward in exchange for autographs."

Manziel's reaction to the news: "Time to play some fucking football."

Manziel entered the Rice game with the Aggies, a 27-point favorite, up just 28–21. The staff had called a play that would've turned into an easy long touchdown pass, but Manziel was so wound up, he bolted out of the pocket as soon as he felt a bit of pressure from his left, squirted through a crease, and out-sprinted three Owl defenders to the sideline for an 11-yard gain. It didn't take long for Manziel to get rolling or to give his critics more fodder—whether it was his old hand gestures with his teammates (that everyone outside the A&M team assumed was a brazen reference to making money) or trash-talking to the Rice players. After he scored his third touchdown, Manziel was flagged for unsportsmanlike conduct on the way back to the A&M sidelines. Before he made it there, he was greeted by Coach Kevin Sumlin, who let him know he wasn't happy with his QB's antics. Manziel didn't appear to say anything and kept walking, which only seemed to give his critics, who took that as an indication that he was ignoring his coach, more ammo. Sumlin didn't allow Manziel back into action for rest of the game.

Whitfield, Manziel's personal QB coach, also had seen his own platform raised with the start of the 2013 season. ESPN's *College GameDay* hired him to be an on-air analyst, which increased his visibility among potential clients about a hundredfold. His reaction to his star protégé's behavior: "He has rabbit ears. He's kicking their ass. The moment he hears, 'Man, you suck,' he gets crooked. It's the same as Twitter. I tell him, 'You're the heavyweight champ. You gotta be bigger than that.'

"I want to point out how ridiculous it is. It just looks so small-time. I have to figure out how I can say it. In a weird way, it's as if the suspension emboldened him. After all that he went through, and it was almost gone, and then he just got [suspended] a half."

ESPN's Mark May, who had ripped Manziel on Twitter several times before, said the QB's actions were indicative of "a very selfish player who doesn't care about his teammates." May's colleague, Lou Holtz, said, if he were Manziel's coach, he "would have grabbed him by the throat." Sumlin later said that a lot of folks commenting on Manziel's reaction to him had no clue what they were talking about.

"When he came off the field, basically I made two statements to him, neither one of which should he have responded to," Sumlin said. "They weren't questions. They were direct statements that I can't repeat right now. So what's amazing to me is the perception that he ignored me. The worst thing that could have happened was for him to reply, based on what I told him."

Johnny Football, thanks to the hand-wringing of some polarizing TV talking heads, had become an antihero. He'd also become the first college athlete to make the cover of *TIME* in almost forty-seven years. Manziel's picture showed him striking the famed Heisman pose next to the cover line: *It's Time to Start Paying College Athletes.* But by the end of Week One, there was another quarterback who had the sports world buzzing.

SEPTEMBER 2, 2013.

For the opening week of the season, college football takes over the Monday-night stage, instead of the NFL on Labor Day night. That meant all eyes were on number-eleven-ranked Florida State's game at Pittsburgh. They tuned in and saw the much-hyped debut of Seminole redshirt freshman "Famous" Jameis Winston, the most impressive QB prospect to come through the Elite 11 since Trent Dilfer took over. Dilfer said Winston could be "a rock star" in the NFL and the first pick of the draft someday. The Noles' former offensive coordinator James Coley, who had left FSU to coach at Miami, told me the 6'4", 230-pound Winston was the "best natural leader I've ever seen." Others inside the FSU program echoed that sentiment.

As hard as it would be to live up to all that buildup in his first college football game, in prime time on national television, on the road, against a team that returned nine starters from what had been the number seventeen defense in the country in 2012, Winston managed to exceed the hype. Winston was nearly flawless, opening the game completing his first 11 passes en route to a dazzling 25 of 27 passes with 5 touchdowns in a 41–13 romp. He set an FSU record for completion percentage in a game (92.6 percent).

At some point, while Winston was carving up the Pitt defense and sending Twitter into a frenzy, the story of the FSU QB's recruitment started to circulate. Well, specifically, that the former five-star recruit actually wanted to go to Texas, but the Longhorns never were interested in him. "I'm an OU fan, but I always wanted to go to Texas. If I'd gotten offered from Texas, I'd be going to Texas right now," Winston was quoted as saying. The quote was months old, but the late-game tweet fed into a meme about the Longhorns' decline.

Given the recent history of star QBs who either grew up dreaming of being Longhorn quarterbacks or were Texas natives bypassed by Mack Brown's staff—Andrew Luck, Robert Griffin III, Johnny Manziel—the story gained a lot of traction. And probably nauseated a lot of Longhorn fans. The next morning, a UT staffer said the school did reach out to Winston's coach but was told the QB wasn't seriously interested in Texas.

Matt Scott, Winston's head coach in high school, said that wasn't the case at all. Scott said he called the UT football staff "four or five" times and one time even spoke to a woman at UT after he tried the main line to the Longhorns football office.

"I said, 'I know you get this call every single day. But lemme tell you, I've got a guy some think is the number one quarterback in the nation. Let me help you. You're gonna want to get this message to the right folks. He's interested in your school,'" Scott recalled telling her.

"She said, 'OK, I've got it.'"

But neither Winston nor Scott ever heard from Texas. Scott said it was possible that Winston's recruitment got muddled in the transition of Texas going from Greg Davis as UT's outgoing offensive coordinator to Bryan Harsin, who was hired from Boise State in January 2011.

Told that someone at UT said the staff did reach out to Winston's coach but didn't believe the dual-threat quarterback was "seriously interested" in Texas, Scott said he'd never heard from them.

"I can tell you this: They didn't call me, and I was on the front line," Scott said. "His dad made it clear he wanted Jameis and I to handle it. I can promise you, they didn't call me, and I called them multiple times. And it's hard for me to believe that one of the nation's top programs is gonna concede, 'Well, we're not going to get this guy.'"

Scott said he and the younger Winston were very organized in their recruiting process. "He's a planner, and I'm a planner, too. We had people knocking the door down 'round the clock [to try to recruit Winston]. After his sophomore year, we sent out twenty DVDs— Ohio State, Miami. As soon as they got it, they offered."

The coach said Winston was very interested in Texas. "I'm telling you, they'd have been in the top two or three for sure," Scott said of the Longhorns. "He knew they had great programs in baseball and football. The baseball is just as important as the football. He researched it. He's not a fly-by-the-seat-of-his-pants guy. He wants to be a podiatrist, and when Miami recruited him, he'd look up and show me all this stuff about their medical program.

"How'd he end up at Florida State? They had a great program in baseball and football, and because he knew that Jimbo Fisher and Mike Martin have a great relationship, and there wouldn't be a problem playing both.

"Bottom line, [Texas] was the only school that he wanted to check out, and they weren't interested in him."

SEPTEMBER 8, 2013.

The most hyped game of the 2013 season was a Week Three matchup: Alabama visiting Texas A&M. Touted as the Tide's revenge for the Aggies upsetting them in Tuscaloosa, the real subplot was, what answers had Bama coach Nick Saban been able to conjure up after he and his vaunted defense got de-pantsed by Manziel, surrendering 20 points before the first quarter was over as the freshman QB opened the game completing 21 of his first 22 passes. Surely, with ten months of prep time, Saban should've been able to find some ways to corral Manziel, most college football analysts said.

"I gotta set the tone tomorrow and say, 'This is another game,'" Sumlin told his staff at their Sunday-afternoon meeting, six days before kickoff. "Everyone's gonna try to make it into 'The Game of the Year,' 'The Game of the Decade,' and all of that. But the reality is, whether or not we win or we lose, we still have nine games left. Just like Georgia. Georgia loses to Clemson in the first week of the season, and they can still play for the national championship. We beat them [Alabama] last year, and they still got to the national title game. It is a big game, but it's a big game because it is the next game. The more you win, the bigger the games get.

"We're gonna talk about us and not Alabama. It's about 'playing hard,' because they're gonna get it from everywhere else about how big this game is. Just know that whatever happens, we're gonna be sitting right here next Sunday, trying to figure out how to beat SMU. This is not our Super Bowl. It is our first SEC game. We're in conference play, and we're trying to win the West. It is going to be a circus out there, starting Tuesday. We can't make this a different week than the other weeks we've had, because the kids will pick up on that. It's just like we're playing Rice or Sam Houston."

Sumlin went around the table, asking each position coach to brief him on how that group's players performed in the Week Two 65–28 win over Sam Houston State, before getting to Spavital. The twenty-eight-year-old, third-generation coach, who had been a graduate assistant under Sumlin back at Houston, was one of the rising stars in the coaching business. He helped groom Brandon Weeden (Oklahoma State) and Geno Smith (WVU) at his two more recent coaching stops and came to A&M to help handle Johnny Manziel, who was, in his own way, even more of a project. It helped that Spavital came in with the highest recommendation from Kliff Kingsbury, the Aggies' former OC who left to become the new head coach at Texas Tech. The charismatic Kingsbury was probably one of the few people Manziel truly respected. The fact that Kingsbury was such a believer in Spavital, a colleague from their days at the University of Houston, was a big factor for the Aggies' combustible star.

"I thought Johnny played well," Spavital said. "It was a good game for him to get back into the rhythm of things. He was going up against a scheme that makes you throw the ball more. I was very pleased with how he was spinning it. I thought he made some mature decisions. He wasn't forcing things downfield as much. He was getting to his jet routes and 618s."

"He threw the ball out of bounds," Sumlin said with a tone of satisfaction.

"He's gotta keep his emotions down on some of the unnecessary things, 'cause he slows down the tempo of the game when he's bitching at the referee or talking shit to somebody," Spavital continued.

Manziel's frenetic nature was different from that of any of the quarterbacks Spavital had ever been around. "I asked Johnny, 'You see what they're doing?' He goes, 'Nah, I'm jus' playin' ball, man,' " Spavital told a couple of A&M assistants later Sunday night. "It's like he has to get hit to get focused."

Throughout the week, the flat-screen TV in Spavital's office was tuned to ESPN, and an episode of *SportsCenter* didn't seem to go more than ten minutes without some variation of Johnny Football's name showing up in the left-hand rundown column of the screen. All the different talking points du jour about Manziel—how he'd handle the pressure from Alabama, whether last season's game was more a case of his catching the Tide and Saban off guard, his late-night habits, his attitude—fueled expectations that Alabama–A&M might become the most-watched afternoon college football game in decades. Much of the national media contingent, which typically filtered into a college town on a Friday for a big game, was already in place seventy-two hours earlier, so they could be ready for Texas A&M's regular Tuesday press availability. Many of the questions the Aggies players and coaches got were Manziel related.

- "What about the Johnny Cam?" someone asked about the extra camera fixed on Manziel all afternoon, something CBS was touting as part of its enhanced game coverage.

- "Basically, I just heard about it maybe an hour ago," Sumlin said. "To me, it's interesting. Everything we do, everything I try to do, everything we try to do here at A&M, is about team. It's about building our team, building our program, and trying not to be an individual. I just don't understand why there's got to be one guy singled out and [have] a camera on [him] all the time. That's not what we're about, not what we're trying to promote, and certainly, from my standpoint, with all of the criticism about individualism on the football team, I don't think this helps enhance the team concept one bit."

- "How does a receiver prepare for Johnny Football's freewheeling scrambles?" someone asked.

- "Just from constant practice," said wideout Malcome Kennedy. "We came up with a drill we do that accompanies Johnny when he's running. We practice that every week, right before the games. . . . I don't remember the first time we did it. It was definitely the spring when he first got here. It was weird, because we weren't used to a quarterback who could move in one direction, make a throw across his body, and be accurate. We've incorporated that into our drills, and now we're in sync with everything he does."

The most newsworthy quote at the press conference came when Sumlin was asked why star QB Johnny Manziel wasn't meeting with the media. "Quite frankly, his family and his lawyers have advised him not to talk," Sumlin explained, "and I'll respect his wishes."

Three floors above, Manziel, wearing a gray T-shirt with WITNESS in big pink letters, black shorts with maroon socks, and orange and black Nikes, sat at Spavital's desk watching Alabama video.

"I like stuff over the middle this week," he told Spavital.

"When you tempo, they'll play zone, because they're unsure," Spavital said.

"I want this right here every time," Manziel said as he paused the video where A&M's 6′5″, 225-pound, go-to receiver Mike Evans was matched up one-on-one with Alabama cornerback John Fulton, attempting to jam the hulking wideout at the line.

"Mike gets really angry with fuckers in his face," receivers coach David Beaty said.

The Tide won't like Mike Evans when he's angry.

"If we can get this a hundred times, I'll take it all hundred," said Manziel.

On the video showing the Tide's defense, Manziel matter-of-factly pointed out the Alabama linebacker; he'd look off to the three-receiver side of the formation, "We do this, and it'll be like stealing."

Spavital told Manziel he expected Alabama to play man-up coverage against the Aggies.

"I hope so," said Manziel. "It's a bad deal. I will fuck them up. I'm excited now, fuck."

Sumlin popped in to see Spavital grinning. Manziel, seated at the desk, asked why the coach wasn't letting him speak to the media that week.

"I didn't [decide that]," Sumlin said. "That's what your people want. That was Brad's decision. That's what Brad wants."

Brad was Brad Beckworth, an attorney and longtime family friend the Manziels had hired in August to help shepherd Johnny through the NCAA mess and through his 2013 season. Beckworth had become Manziel's consigliere.

"I don't like Brad," Manziel sighed in a tone that sounded only half-serious. "He never lets me do anything."

"You just want yes-men," laughed Sumlin.

"Hey, there's nothing wrong with yes-men. Didn't you see the movie?" Manziel said, referencing the 2008 Jim Carrey comedy *Yes Man*.

"Yeah, and I saw how that movie ended, too," the forty-nine-year-old coach said, noting how Carrey's character's life went into a downward spiral after agreeing to say yes to everything.

The dialogue between star player and coach illuminated some of the reasons Sumlin emerged as one of the hottest commodities in the coaching world, with annual interest from NFL teams. No coach in the college game related to players from a wide spectrum of backgrounds and personalities better than Sumlin did. He was also equally adept at schmoozing with a seventy-year-old billionaire oilman or a seventeen-year-old inner-city football talent. The coach subtly, and sometimes not so subtly, poked at his star player, knowing which buttons to push and when. He had also allowed Manziel the flexibility to be himself, on and off the field. And, while the byproduct of that might irk some people, Sumlin didn't care. And deep down, Manziel appreciated all of that, he said.

"People, even inside the program, really don't know just how special my relationship is with Summy," Manziel told me later.

The biggest misconception about Manziel, Sumlin felt, was how the quarterback fit in with his teammates. Manziel, despite his constant *SportsCenter* presence and jet-set off-season, got along very well with his teammates. During Bama week, he would take his entire offensive line out for steak and lobster. He treated Conner McQueen, the redheaded, scout-team, walk-on QB, like his little brother, and he constantly joked with Mike Evans, his roommate on road trips, and the other receivers at practice. Manziel also communicated with fellow QB standouts Tajh Boyd from Clemson and Michigan's Devin Gardner after every game, since the trio had become tight after their week as counselors that summer in Oregon at the Elite 11 camp. (Gardner would go on to say in a few days that Manziel sent him a text to keep his head up after Michigan's bad showing against an awful Akron team the same day as the Alabama–Texas A&M game.)

Sumlin had been around a lot of future NFL stars but said he's never seen a QB with the spirit Johnny Manziel had. As if Manziel was convinced he was the baddest man on the field every time he pulled his helmet onto his head. Drew Brees, who was at Purdue when Sumlin was an assistant, had something. But Manziel's spirit was different for a QB. The one other player Sumlin had been around who had that kind of spirit: Adrian Peterson. Sumlin vividly recalled Peterson's first game for Oklahoma against archrival Texas. Peterson backed up all his bravado by breaking off a 44-yard run the first time he touched the ball. He went on to hammer the Longhorns for 225 yards, more than any freshman ever had in the ninety-nine years of the rivalry. The running joke around the A&M football office was, "Just get to Tuesday," as in, that's when the real work for the players would begin. Sundays, A&M players were off, and Monday was a light day, with an hour practice that was heavy on special teams and corrections from Saturday's game.

"I just asked him in our meeting, is he gonna watch film this week, or is he going to just go out there and wing it like last week?" Sumlin said to Spavital and David Beaty as Manziel rolled his eyes and smirked.

MANZIEL: Ask Spav what I said to him.

SPAVITAL: I said after the first series, "You see how they're playin you? He goes, 'Nah, I'm just playing ball.'

MANZIEL: I don't know what the fuck they're doing. I'm just throwing to the open guy.

SUMLIN: Monday, get to . . .

MANZIEL: Get to Tuesday.

SUMLIN: That's what we have to do every week. Get to Tuesday. Saturdays are all right. Game time is the easiest part of the week.

MANZIEL: (*breaking into a wide grin*) After the game . . .

SUMLIN: Just get to Tuesday. . . . You think I'm kidding?

BEATY: I know. I know.

SUMLIN: That's where we are. By the way, that's a nice sock-shoe combination.

MANZIEL: I came in with no shoes on. I just walked in barefoot.

SUMLIN: I'm somehow not surprised.

MANZIEL: It happens. At least I'm here.

Manziel didn't watch much film in his first season as the starting quarterback, he told me. "We mostly just watched it in the meeting room. Oklahoma [at the end of the season] was the game I probably watched the most.

"I like to see people's tendencies more than anything else." Gauging how aggressive rival players were was big for him. He could use that. He could manipulate them. Now he could influence defenders to move them out of position with his eyes, something he couldn't do or even think to do in 2012. "I was just trying to get through the games last year."

For all Manziel's frenetic ways, Spavital said the sophomore quarterback had an uncanny sense of finding holes in defenses. It was as if Manziel was some sort of geometry savant who could calculate spatial equations on a football field in milliseconds. A *Good Will Hunting* in shoulder pads. As spectacular as he was in his freshman season in Tuscaloosa, Manziel had spotted plenty of things he could've—and had—improved on. His arm was stronger. His mechanics tighter. His awareness sharper.

Each hour he spent in Spavital's office during the week, Manziel's name probably was mentioned a dozen times on the TV tuned to *SportsCenter*. The only time he seemed to notice was when there was a mention of Charles Barkley ripping him. Spavital checked Twitter and read that the NBA great, an Auburn product, said he was about to do the unthinkable and root for Alabama, because "Johnny is annoying me so much," and he compared Manziel to Miley Cyrus.

Manziel rose up out of his seat, playfully winced, and headed toward the door. "OK, I'm a bad person.

"And, on that note . . ."

• • •

"THE HARDEST THING FOR me is having a genuine love for *SportsCenter* and ESPN for so long as a kid," Manziel told me. "It was a huge part of my life. For such a long period of time over this off-season, it was hard to not watch it. But I just couldn't watch it, because I was getting bashed every day. It was hard to block out, but I got used to it.

"I've had to grow up a lot with the whole NCAA deal with all of the scrutiny. It made me realize it wasn't the best idea, posting about all the places I was going to and all the stuff I was doing. I've learned a lot from my mistakes. I'm off Twitter for now, and I just want to focus on the season. I'm not tweeting, and I don't have time for that. The biggest thing for me is, I want people to know that all the stuff that was talked about with the off-season didn't get in the way of all the work that I had put in with Coach Whitfield 'cause I worked hard to become a better passer. We talked all the time. It was nice to go out and show how much I got better. I really did work hard. Were there times I could've been out here slaving this summer? Yes, but I didn't feel like that was what I needed to do. I felt like I deserved to have a little bit of fun, and it was really blown out of proportion."

SEPTEMBER 14, 2013.

For those hoping Manziel would be exposed against the Tide, they'd be disappointed. The Aggies got the ball, and within the game's first ten minutes, A&M was up 14–0. Manziel completed four of five passes for 102 yards with 36 rushing yards on four carries. The Aggies' plan to target Mike Evans looked prescient. By the midway mark of the first quarter, Evans had a 100-yard receiving day and had scorched John Fulton so badly, the Tide cornerback had lost his starting job. However, the A&M defense was a mess and got overwhelmed. The Aggies lost, 49–42. At the midfield post-game handshake between the two head coaches, Saban told Sumlin, "You took ten years off my life."

The sixty-one-year-old Saban probably felt as if Sumlin's quarterback had taken twenty years. All that bluster about how Bama, with ten months of prep time, would contain Manziel, seemed laughable. The Aggies ripped Alabama for 31 first downs and 628 yards, the most the Crimson Tide had surrendered in more than one hundred years. Manziel showed up for the post-game press conference wearing a white Texas A&M baseball hat and a red T-shirt that said NO NEW FRIENDS. An Aggie sports information staffer handed him an A&M polo to change into. "I worked this off-season to be a better passer and be better in the pocket and get better in those areas instead of freelancing as much," he said. "I think you can look at it today and our previous games and say that goal happened."

The 6′0″, 203-pound quarterback finished with 562 yards of offense, 464 through the air and 98 on the ground. The stat sheet showed that Manziel had a record-breaking game. The tape that Spavital would study the next morning underscored just how sharp the QB was against the Tide.

"Johnny did a great job of holding the safeties in the middle of the field with his eyes, and that's why Mike kept getting so open on the sidelines," Spavital said. "We hit three or four fades on man-free [coverage]."

On a touchdown pass to Malcome Kennedy, Manziel duped "Ha Ha" Clinton-Dix out of the play to free up the Aggie receiver. Maybe more impressive was how Manziel responded when the Tide threw defensive looks at him that he hadn't seen from them before, Spavital said. Twice the Tide overloaded one side of the line of scrimmage, and twice Manziel beat it by firing quick passes to the perimeter for 16-yard and 6-yard gains. When offensive coordinator Clarence McKinney saw the crazy third-and-8 play where Manziel scrambled but got grabbed by 290-pound Jeoffrey Pagan, only to break away and evade more rushers before flinging the ball, where his body ended up facing the opposite end zone for a 12-yard completion to spindly freshman Edward Pope, the coach just shook his head. "It's like he's Houdini."

MANZIEL'S MENTOR, GEORGE WHITFIELD'S, stock had risen almost as high as the Aggies' star's had in the previous year. The ESPN *College*

*GameDay* role got him in front of hundreds of thousands of football fans every Saturday morning. In late October, he even got a call from producers of Comedy Central's *The Colbert Report*, looking to book him for a spot in which he would teach host Stephen Colbert how to throw a football. Whitfield was a huge fan of Colbert and Jon Stewart, he said, adding that he hoped he could fit it into his schedule. Things had gotten hectic for him, crisscrossing the country on the traveling road show that was *College GameDay*, while back in San Diego, he had his own daily project—training Everett Golson, the exiled Notre Dame QB who started the 2013 BCS National Title Game but was dismissed from the school for violating the honor code by cheating on an exam and called Whitfield for help.

It was Halloween. Whitfield, who in less than thirty-six hours would be in Tallahassee with the *GameDay* gang for the Miami–Florida State game, sat on a scaled-down turf soccer field across from the University of California at San Diego Medical Center. While waiting for Golson to arrive, Whitfield answered a call from his TV producer asking if they could break down why Miami's QB Stephen Morris was struggling.

"Can you put a circle on the ground below him?" Whitfield asked the producer, hoping for some kind of graphical element to represent how the strong-armed quarterback's delivery had been hampered by an ankle injury. "I know this sounds weird, but can you make it a blinking light on his leg? Imagine he's standing on a six-foot circular mat. Does that make any sense? I know this sounds nerdy, but on the good ones can we put a jet stream on it and make it orange or red, and on the bad ones, make it blue—like he doesn't have anything on it?"

Whitfield knew he was in an awkward spot on TV, often asked to comment on a client he was mentoring. "I wanna be as true-blue as a coach as possible, but out here I don't wanna look like an apologist," he said. "I got asked three or four times before I signed anything, 'Could you be objective with your guys? Can you be critical if need be?'

"I said, 'Well, I'm not gonna be Skip Bayless, but a bad throw is a bad throw. That is a tangible thing.' I said it'd be like coaching them with an audience. I wouldn't say anything to the screen that I wouldn't say with Johnny [Manziel] or Tajh [Boyd] standing right next to me. I'm not on there to be [Paul] Finebaum. I'm on there for tactical reasons. They never put me on a panel. I have five minutes to discuss and walk them through whatever I can."

Whitfield was contracted to do thirty-five TV appearances a year with ESPN, he said. His biggest challenge came whenever the subject was Virginia Tech QB Logan Thomas, who had trained with Whitfield for three years. The 6′6″, 250-pound Thomas, who after his sophomore season was touted by NFL Draft analysts as a potential first overall pick, had been an easy target for critics, as his stats had declined while he struggled with his accuracy and decision making.

Whitfield attended Thomas's Thursday-night game at Georgia Tech. His bosses at ESPN had him comment on his protégé from the sideline. Whitfield noted that Thomas, unlike most big-time college quarterbacks, didn't play the position much before college.

"He'd only played six high school games at quarterback," Whitfield said. "That's not a lot of flight hours. It doesn't really go much to skill and ability. He wanted to be a tight end in college. The coaches at Tech saw something in him. He's raw, but he's playing.

"Here's what I like most about Logan Thomas: I always make sure I send players a text after a loss, because they're gonna hear from everybody else after a win. I was shocked when they lost against Duke. I saw it on the scroll. I'm waiting for his stats to come around. And then I saw four interceptions. Then I watched the highlights and saw three balls that should've been intercepted. I asked him, 'How you doing, and what happened out there?'

"He just texted back, 'I sucked.' And that was it. You gotta run and quickly try to wean him back up. 'Listen, some pro quarterbacks are gonna have that type of day tomorrow. And they had that day already. Imagine being in Eli Manning's shoes [throwing 15 interceptions in the Giants first six games].' You always want to bring them up to the 30,000-foot view, because they almost always think it's just them. They can't see much else, because it's their fan base—the kids on their campus and their newspapers—and that's all they're talking about, so it's just like having mirrors around them. They don't have anything else. You try to pull them back up. It is the toughest position in sports."

Everett Golson, too, required some uplifting. Whitfield picked Golson up at the San Diego airport on September 1. "He looks around and says, 'This is awesome.' Then he gets quiet for a bit and says, 'You're gonna have me throw with the strings, aren't you?'" Golson had developed the unusual habit of throwing a football with his hand *not* on the laces. Whitfield said he suspected that other coaches, including the staff at Notre Dame, had tried to get Golson to change but that no one had made a compelling enough case.

Golson arrived wearing a black DRGN SLYR T-shirt (a slogan of Whitfield's), gray shorts, and navy ND socks with gold Nike cleats. He said in the past he used to shuffle the ball *not* to get the laces. But now he's using the laces.

"There's still an adjustment period with touch [passes], because you do have more grip with the laces, but it is for the better, and, mechanically, George has really helped with my footwork a lot," Golson said. "For a vast period of my career I depended on my arm—all arm. George taught me to step through and have a base, and that's where I've seen the most improvement."

Whitfield's goal was to refine a QB lacking in consistency.

"You're throwing like he's wide-ass open," he prodded Golson as he threw deep outs to a former small-school receiver. "Train like he's not."

"You know the butcher and the surgeon deal, right?" Whitfield said later. "They both have tools. They both cut. They both are dealing with blood. They're both professionals. A butcher just gets in and out, and he's done, whereas the surgeon starts up, and he's gotta have a plan, and a Plan B, a Plan C, and a fail-safe, and be particular. That's what Everett's getting now."

The two-month training camp with Whitfield in San Diego was not cheap. Whitfield usually helped quarterbacks find accommodations. For lodging, it was around $60 a day for the two months. For Whitfield's training, it was about $500 a week. So, combined, that was $7,500–$8,000. Golson's cousin Ivan helped pay the tab, Whitfield said.

"At this point, I don't know if it's politically correct to say it like this, but it's a business decision for me," Golson said. "I'm hoping that it'll pay off in the future."

HEADING INTO THANKSGIVING, THE Heisman race was in more disarray than it had been in years at such a late stage. LSU, again, got the best of Johnny Manziel, holding him to a season-low 299 yards in a 34–10 romp.

"You have to give a lot of credit to them," Manziel said of LSU, which prepared its D for him by using its best athlete, star wide receiver Odell Beckham, as the scout-team QB mimicking the A&M star. "They came out and mixed a lot of things up. They kept us guessing, and it really took us a while to figure it out.

"We got punched in the mouth today, and it wasn't fun."

During the game, CBS reported that Manziel was bothered by an injured hand. It was actually a banged-up thumb.

"It's been a factor throughout the past couple of weeks," he said after being asked how much, if at all, the thumb was a factor. He added that it wasn't the reason A&M lost.

Later that day, two other contenders, Baylor quarterback Bryce Petty (another Whitfield client) and Oregon QB Marcus Mariota, both struggled, too, as their teams each got upset. The one guy from the front of the Heisman race who didn't have a rough Saturday was Jameis Winston. His team scored 80 on a dreadful Idaho squad and was steamrolling every opponent en route to a BCS National Title bid. With Petty's struggles, the Seminoles redshirt freshman took over the national lead in QB rating at 194.50. The bigger news surrounding Jameis Winston's day: Florida State Attorney Willie Meggs told AP that he likely wouldn't make a decision on whether the FSU QB would be charged until after Thanksgiving in a sexual-assault investigation that had surfaced first via *TMZ* in the previous ten days but stemmed from a complaint filed with the Tallahassee Police Department back in December 2012.

The matter of the timing with Winston's case became an awkward subplot to his investigation: Should Heisman electors vote for

Winston with the possibility he could get charged days later? Some Heisman voters had said in recent years that "character" is considered in their ballot, even though they don't really know these guys all that well, if at all. In 2012, Notre Dame linebacker Manti Te'o was touted by many as the ultimate "character" guy, but a little more than a month after the Heisman ceremony, a ton of questions emerged about his character after the well-chronicled story of his commitment to the deceased love of his life took a bizarre turn when it came to light that his late girlfriend had never actually existed—Te'o had been the victim of an elaborate hoax, a revelation he did not promptly disclose.

Winston, Manziel, and McCarron were among the six finalists invited to New York for the Heisman presentation. Winston got some good news leading up to the trip north: Florida State Attorney Willie Meggs concluded that "no charges will be filed" after an investigation of the case, explaining in a press conference that the "timing [of the case] has not been driven by Heisman demands or a football schedule."

At each of the Heisman media-availability sessions—one on Friday and two more on Saturday—the Alabama native adeptly handled questions, including a few that touched on the investigation and the magnitude of it.

"I knew I did nothing wrong," Winston said. "That's why I knew I could respect the process, and I'd eventually be vindicated. It was more about me being silent for my family, because I didn't want to put my family in that situation."

The young QB actually managed the weekend's media sessions much better than the adults in the FSU PR department did. When faced with any seemingly tough question, Winston was poised, polite, and kept eye contact. He never looked flustered or put-off or agitated. You couldn't say the same for the Seminole Sports Information Director who stood a few feet behind him. (At the Friday-afternoon session, a Noles SID person pulled Winston away from reporters after a rather innocuous question, and the FSU contingent cut short the scheduled availability before being brought back to the media area about twenty minutes later.)

Winston had a curious dynamic that often got skewed under the magnifying lens of a TV camera. In less formal media windows, he came across as engaging, playful, and more comfortable in his own skin than anyone in the room. However, when those moments became prime-time TV moments, he seemed to lose control, drifting toward playing to the lowest common denominator, acting like a goof, which often rubbed people the wrong way and created its own challenges for the FSU staff.

Winston called the month leading up to the Heisman his "humbling moment." He said he'd learned he couldn't go out anymore, and that his coach Jimbo Fisher had told him, "For you to be a man, the kid in you must die."

Manziel suddenly wasn't the biggest deal in the room—at least not that weekend. He was still getting A-list offers. Two weeks earlier, A&M turned down a chance for him to be a guest again on *The Tonight Show with Jay Leno*.

"They tried to entice him by saying Jennifer Aniston was going to be on the show with him," said an A&M PR staffer. "I don't think they know, she's probably a bit out of his demo." Manziel looked perfectly comfortable being in the background in New York. He conceded that he felt like "an old sophomore. I feel like I've been in college forever." Observing the media swarm around Winston, Manziel said he was impressed by how the kid had handled the situation.

Four months earlier, Winston had caused a bit of a stir when he was asked a question at FSU's pre-season media day about "Manziel disease," and he replied:

"If I ever get Manziel disease, I want all of you to smack me in the head with your microphones." The comment—even with the context that it was in response to how the question had been framed—didn't sit well with the Manziel camp, but the A&M star appeared to have no trouble embracing Winston.

"I had to go through some controversy. I had to go through some things," Manziel said. "To see him at such a young age be able to put his head down and focus on his teammates and where they are and where they're headed, I do give him a lot of credit for that. With all the scrutiny and everything that he's under, I feel like he's done a tremendous job of focusing on his team and his family and what matters most."

Winston ended up running away with the Heisman voting, winning by the seventh-biggest margin in the award's seventy-nine-year history. He received 668 first-place votes, even though he didn't appear at all on 115 Heisman ballots. Manziel got fifth place—behind Winston, McCarron, Northern Illinois QB Jordan Lynch, and Boston College running back Andre Williams.

"I can't explain and say enough how truly intelligent he is, how instinctive he is," Florida State coach Jimbo Fisher replied upon being asked what quality impressed him most about Winston. "The game makes sense to him. He always wants to know why he's having success. If he throws a touchdown, he has to understand it, so he can repeat it."

Winston wasted little time trying to get a better understanding of how winning the Heisman could change his life. He'd been picking Manziel's brain for a few days already.

"We had a really good talk Thursday night at dinner," Manziel said. "I wasn't prepared for it. I don't know if you really can be.

"It's going to be a whirlwind for a little bit, but he'll get used to it. I didn't ever want to be a different person. There are things you have to adapt to and get used to, because this is how life is going to be. No matter how bad you want things to be back to the way they were before and live a normal life, those days went out the window a long time ago for me. I've accepted that fact, and I'm fine with it, and life's good."

Manziel's best advice: "Continue to be yourself—just be you, and try not to let this thing change you."


MANZIEL'S COLLEGE FINALE CAME on New Year's Eve against one of the sweetest stories of 2013—a 10–3 Duke team that, after years of being a punch line, made it to the ACC Title Game. The Aggies limped into the Chick-fil-A Bowl with consecutive losses at LSU and Missouri.

"It was a taxing year physically and mentally," Kevin Sumlin said on the eve of the game. Weeks before the bowl game, Sumlin shook up his offense by promoting Spavital, making him the Aggies' new play-caller, taking over for Clarence McKinney. The move was expected to ramp up the tempo for A&M even more, with Spavital coaching from the sidelines and more in sync with Manziel. It helped that Manziel had time to heal after sustaining nagging injuries throughout the second half of the season.

"Johnny got his stinger back," proclaimed A&M defensive co-ordinator Mark Snyder a few days before the bowl. "I think he lost it after the Auburn game." That 45–41 defeat in late October ended whatever national-title hopes the Aggies had had. Manziel threw for 454 yards and 4 TDs but had to leave the fourth quarter for a few plays after a shoulder injury. In the aftermath, Manziel still produced big numbers, throwing 13 touchdowns over the next three games before facing LSU and Missouri, but Snyder noticed a different side of the play-making QB at practice: "I kept saying to him, 'Man, that's not you. You don't ever lose your confidence. C'mon, talk shit to me.'"

Manziel admitted that the Auburn loss was "really deflating. That just stung for a long time, especially offensively. We just kind of lost our confidence after that and never really could get it back."

Boarding one of the team buses for what would be his last full practice as a college player, Manziel was back to being himself. A grinning Manziel walked past Sumlin seated in the first row. The quarterback was followed by a bleary-eyed teammate with a gray hoodie draped over his face. Apparently, the young teammate, a freshman, had had a rough time keeping up with Manziel the night before.

"This is your fault," Sumlin said through a smile to his star, nodding toward the young player.

MANZIEL: What?

SUMLIN: You know.

MANZIEL: Nah, that's not me this time.

SUMLIN: C'mon, really?

MANZIEL: What? I'll take all of [another underclassman's] hungover days but not this one.

SUMLIN: Ah, only three more days.

Manziel, who earlier in the month had turned twenty-one, had a verbal rapport with his coaches that often sounded as if someone in Hollywood must've scripted it. When Sumlin reminded him to be on his best behavior, because he had to "impress thirty-two owners and head coaches."

Manziel corrected him. "Thirty-one."

SUMLIN: Huh?

MANZIEL: Jerry Jones loves me.

A few hours before kickoff, Manziel's old coach, Kliff Kingsbury, said he wished he was in Atlanta to "watch the last Johnny Football game. He's gonna put on a show for the ages. He's going to be the first pick after tonight."

Manziel's show, in a twisted way, was aided by A&M's own inept defense, which allowed Duke to jump out to a stunning 38–17 half-time lead. That provided Manziel with ample opportunity for more heroics to bail out the Aggies. He proceeded to hit on 12 of 13 passes, leading A&M on 4 consecutive touchdown drives, which, coupled with teammate Toney Hurd's pick-six, was enough to give the Aggies a 52–48 comeback win.

Manziel celebrated with teammates that night before going from coast to coast, meeting with LeBron James's marketing people in Miami and then flying out to Los Angeles to meet up with Whitfield and appear on ESPN for the BCS Title Game. The matchup: Jameis Winston's number-one-ranked Florida State Seminoles against number two Auburn. FSU was trying to end the SEC's run of seven consecutive BCS titles.

JANUARY 6, 2014.

Whitfield, Manziel, and Logan Thomas, the other QB in Southern California to start training with Whitfield to get ready for the NFL Draft, watched from the 20-yard-line on the Auburn sideline and had a great view as Jameis Winston made history. For 58 minutes and 41 seconds Winston looked rusty, sluggish, and confused. But his team, which at one point trailed 21–3, was down 31–27 when they took over possession at their own 20.

Winston had a simple message to his teammates before the first play of the biggest drive of his life: "This is what we came here for."

Seven plays later, the Noles had taken the lead after Winston found wideout Kelvin Benjamin in the back of the end zone on a 2-yard pass with 13 seconds remaining to cap the biggest comeback in BCS history. On the drive, Winston completed 6 of 7 passes.

"It's the best football game he has played all year, and I'll tell you why, because for three quarters he was up and down, and he fought," Coach Jimbo Fisher said. "And, just like any great player, some nights you don't have it.

"When you can go back like the great ones do—'It's not my night, but we've got a chance to win this ball game, it's in the fourth quarter, I've got one or two touches left, and you can take your team down the field and lead them to victory'—that's what a great player is to me. Very few can do it when it's not their night. And to pull it out in the atmosphere and environment and with what was on the line tonight, to me, if that's not a great player, then I don't know what one is."

Perhaps the craziest part of it all was that the ending played out almost exactly as Trent Dilfer had predicted it would over two years earlier at the Elite 11, when in front of ESPN's TV cameras, he told Winston:

"It's going to come down to third-and-7 in the fourth quarter, down by four, and they're going to keep you in the pocket. They're not going to let you be fast and quick and all that. And that's going to be a mistake, because you're going to beat 'em here [pointing to his head]."

Only thing Dilfer got wrong: it was actually a third-and-8.

_ _ _ _10.
# GRAD SCHOOL

JANUARY 13, 2014.

Draft camp season hadn't even started yet, and George Whitfield had already taken his first loss. Whitfield had been excited that he'd get to appear on Comedy Central's *The Colbert Report* after the producers from one of his favorite shows had contacted him months earlier for a segment during which the private quarterback coach would teach the show's star how to throw a football. Problem was, the producers wanted to tape the segment on January 10, which turned out to be the day Whitfield's most famous client, Johnny Manziel, was scheduled to arrive in San Diego. Manziel had come to Southern California for three months of intensive training with Whitfield and his staff to get ready for the NFL Combine and a Pro Day—just like two other quarterbacks, Logan Thomas of Virginia Tech and Brock Jensen of North Dakota State, were doing. Whitfield had to tell Stephen Colbert's people, thanks but no thanks.

"How could I look at these [quarterbacks] and tell them I want everybody dialed in, and then I fly out of town to appear in some comedy skit?" said Whitfield. Instead, Comedy Central brought in Steve Clarkson to help Colbert in the segment.

The first day of training started three days later, on the second Monday in January, although Whitfield had already done some coaching over the weekend with his star protégé. A few minutes after 8:00 a.m., Whitfield gathered his staff, which included two assistants, a half dozen interns, a strength and conditioning coach, and former NFL backup quarterback Kevin O'Connell, to run through the day's schedule. He also mentioned to O'Connell that he had changed Manziel's grip over the weekend.

"I wanted to do it the last year, but, honestly, I was too nervous about messing with him, because we did so much other stuff with him," Whitfield said, noting that previously Manziel's fingers weren't on the strings, so when he finished throws, his hand wrapped up so he could get the spin. Whitfield changed the spacing between Manziel's fingers to give them something to come off of upon release, which he said the Texas A&M star quickly took to when they got some throwing in over the weekend.

"Halfway through the first drill, he goes, 'Man, this is some good stuff right here,'" Whitfield said proudly.

Much of the training for the next three months would take place in Carlsbad, a half hour north of San Diego at Prolific Athletics, a modest, 15,000-square-foot training center owned by thirty-two-year-old former-Utah State-receiver-turned-speed-coach Ryan Flaherty.

By 10:00 a.m., Whitfield had his entire crew on the field at Aviara Park, a mile down the road. Two of Whitfield's interns maneuvered flip cams and tripods to get into position while another was filming on an iPad. Whitfield tried to script every segment of the day for his quarterbacks to save their arms and legs. Best known as the "Broom Guy," Whitfield wasn't shy about using anything in his drills. One of his favorites was having his interns wave a tennis racket above their head as a receiver ran a corner route just past them to better hone his quarterback's touch on "bucket" throws. It was the same reason he'd sometimes use soccer goals and have his receiver stand just on the edge with the net to his back, forcing a pass to be lofted over it. Manziel's touch, as NFL scouts could attest, had already proven to be feathery soft. For the rocket-armed Logan Thomas, though, it was a much bigger point of emphasis.

At 1:35 p.m., back at Prolific on the opposite side of the weight room, Whitfield had four air mattresses brought in and spaced five yards apart for nap time. He'd gotten the idea, from a Stanford professor two years earlier while training Andrew Luck there, that athletes were noticeably sharper and more energized if you could mix in an hour of sleep for their bodies and minds to recuperate. The players: Manziel, Thomas, Jensen, and Texas A&M star Mike Evans—the first wide receiver Whitfield had ever included in a draft camp—looked skeptical when Whitfield had an intern pass around sleep masks. Whitfield also walked around with a tray to collect their cell phones, just in case they were tempted to text friends or take to Twitter rather than sleep. Jokes aside, within ten minutes, all four players were zonked out on their mattresses.

One of the offices in the Prolific building had been turned into a makeshift quarterback room or, more specifically, Kevin O'Connell's classroom for the QBs to get a crash course in NFL schemes and terminology. There was a wooden table with enough room for two chairs on each of the four sides. Whiteboards had been fastened to two of the walls, with a projector in the middle of the table aimed at a third wall. The room felt cramped once the 6'6", 250-pound Thomas settled into a chair fifteen minutes after being awoken from the hour-long nap. A pair of his size-seventeen shoes sat beside his chair, looking as if they weighed twenty pounds apiece. Thomas dwarfed Jensen, the quarterback seated to his left, a guy who was listed at 6'3", 225 pounds by North Dakota State. They were up first with O'Connell, while Flaherty had Manziel lifting weights. In a week the Virginia Tech quarterback would be down in Mobile, Alabama, for the Senior Bowl, where NFL personnel men studied his every move.

"Best thing I can tell you is, for the next three months I'm somebody who's been through this," said O'Connell, standing in front of a whiteboard. The twenty-eight-year-old O'Connell's main job with the camp was to help get the QBs prepared mentally from a scheme and film review standpoint, so they could handle the team interviews with NFL coaches and GMs and aid in prep for the Wonderlic, a twelve-minute, fifty-question cognitive test used by some corporations and the NFL.

"I know the important parts, and I know the not-so-important parts. We don't need to teach you to play a game on March 1. Just so you can explain next-level thinking to a GM or quarterbacks coach."

O'Connell, a former star QB at San Diego State and the son of a former FBI agent, spent five seasons in the NFL with five teams. For the 2013 season, O'Connell worked with ESPN as a commentator. In his pro career, he backed up Tom Brady in New England after being selected by the Patriots in the third round of the 2008 draft. At about that same time six years earlier, O'Connell was being viewed as a seventh-round guy, but through strong performances at the Combine and in his individual workouts and meetings, his draft stock soared. The affable former QB was hoping his new protégés could make a similar rise.

"You can take a perceived weakness and turn it into a strength in reality in a ten-minute conversation with a GM," O'Connell said, sounding a little like a self-help guru. "I walked into the Combine, and I'm meeting with the head coach of a team, and I see San Diego State film up on the screen. Great. 'What are we gonna watch?' Film starts playing. I see it's the New Mexico game. I think back to that game: 'I think I threw three picks in the first quarter.' Every single INT was shown on that film. No touchdowns. No third-down conversions. No NFL throws. Two of them I threw right to the defender, and I had to talk through what [had] happened without throwing anybody under the bus; not about the play call or the O-line or a receiver running a wrong route. And they just sit there and watch you.

"I'm gonna be constantly watching you. Your body language while I get you up on the board answering questions really matters. The thing about the Combine and this whole process is, it's pretty uniform. Tom Brady went through it. Andrew Luck went through it. They try to put everybody through it the same way. Shorts. T-shirt. Mentally, it's all the same. How you handle the stress of everything they put you through—it all matters."

While Manziel was Whitfield's headliner, Logan Thomas spurred plenty of debate in NFL circles, too.

"He's intriguing because he's got great size, is athletic, and has a very big arm, but he was just so inconsistent," one NFL scout said.

"You wonder if he can ever put it all together. But in his defense, he really didn't have much talent to work with the past two seasons."

Thomas's career at Virginia Tech—including three seasons as the Hokies' starter—seemed to have almost as many downs as ups. He wowed his coaches in his first action, which came in a tight spot the year before he took over the starting job. In 2010, forced into action on a crucial third-and-16 at Miami after Tyrod Taylor went down, the young QB displayed an advanced understanding of the position—and his powerful arm—when he connected on a 24-yard pass for a first down.

Thomas's first season as the starter was strong. He threw for over 3,000 yards and ran for 469 more while totaling 30 TDs and completing 60 percent of his passes, leading the Hokies to the Sugar Bowl. Some NFL Draft analysts talked about his potentially becoming the first overall pick. Not bad for a guy who came to Blacksburg as the top-ranked tight end prospect in the 2009 recruiting class or, as Tech's old QB coach Mike O'Cain put it, wasn't one of those guys "who has been to thirty-seven QB camps" since the time he could barely walk.

Logan Thomas was a rising star when he spent spring break in 2012 in San Diego training with Whitfield. That happened to be the same week Whitfield took on another new client, an unknown fourth-stringer from Texas—Johnny Manziel—who came to California looking for a confidence boost. Since the time the two QBs met, their careers went in nearly opposite directions—one from undersized unknown to football phenomenon, the other from supersized prototype to enigmatic underachiever. As odd as the juxtaposition of the two quarterbacks may have been, they cheered each other on, which fit in well with the camaraderie of the QB room O'Connell was hoping to foster.

Thomas's stock plummeted in 2012, when, not so coincidentally, the level of talent around him on Tech's offense diminished. Gone were game-breaking RB David Wilson, as well as go-to receivers Jarrett Boykin and Danny Coale, all off to the NFL. Thomas went from being a 60 percent passer to a 51 percent completion mark. His 19-10 TD-INT ratio fell to 18-16. Worse still, all the hype about draft gurus pumping him up left many ripping the Hokies QB. It was almost a given that any time Tech played on a national TV stage, Logan Thomas would end up trending on Twitter, and not because he was carving up a rival defense or his team was piling up points.

"You definitely have to have a thick skin to play quarterback," Thomas told me later. "You have to have a thick, old, leathery skin about it, and I do. I know it's the most scrutinized position in sports. That [mental toughness and focus] has gotta be a part of you. You have to be calm, cool, and collected."

In 2013, Thomas—playing in a new system with a new offensive coordinator—put up slightly better numbers. His completion percentage went up 57 percent, and it didn't help that Hokie receivers dropped 36 passes—most by a team from one of the six major college conferences. But questions about his accuracy and his decision making still remained. Some had speculated about whether Thomas had lost confidence—something that can be devastating for a QB, perhaps more than any other position in sports.

"I've never lost confidence," Thomas said. "While we struggled, it was a whole team effort, and as a quarterback you have to take the blame."

Asked how he'd respond when NFL teams questioned him about why, for all his physical tools, his performance was so inconsistent, Thomas said, "I'm still a little bit raw. I've worked hard every single day. I'm still developing, and I know that."

Whitfield was excited by what he saw in the first week with Thomas in Southern California.

"He was throwing balls that everybody on the field stopped and watched and were wowed by," said Whitfield. "James Lofton [the Hall of Fame receiver who was training Evans as part of the same group] and Johnny [Manziel] and [speed coach] Ryan [Flaherty] on the opposite corner doing agilities all were staring. He was throwing ropes."

The private QB coach also made some mechanical tweaks with Thomas, who had a tendency to keep the ball by his ribs. "We're working on bringing his hands up higher—'thumbs to collarbone.' So he has leverage on the ball, and we're just trying to make sure he's fluid. This is a huge guy with size-seventeen feet. There's a lot of moving parts.

"We've told him, 'You have to have more awareness of your mechanics, more so than smaller QBs. Your machine's too big to be nonchalant.'"

In Mobile, Thomas would be coached by the Atlanta Falcons' staff, so O'Connell had a friend get him the foundation of the team's playbook so they could focus on some of the nuances of that system. O'Connell tutored Thomas not only on the Falcons' scheme, but also on the verbiage the young QB should be versed in when he spoke with NFL personnel folks. When he had Thomas go up to the board to draw up his favorite plays on third downs or red zone situations, it wasn't just what the quarterback was saying, but how he said it.

"Don't picture us sitting here. Picture Andy Reid," O'Connell told Thomas. "You live it. You love it. You're a 'grinder'! You're Russell Wilson! They said that he was the most prepared, charismatic leader they've been around. Talk big. Stand big. Sound big."

Another O'Connell classroom tip for Senior Bowl week: "Think players, not plays.

"On day one, play catch with the guys. See which guy runs good stop-routes. Who's got the jets? Who is the big physical guy? Who is your X [receiver]? Can he win on a three-step slant?

"Rule number one for Quick Game [three-step drops]: 'Pick-and-Stick.' As simplified as you can make this. Check down every time. Do not wheel back around. These defensive ends are trying to get paid, too. Also, a shot called does not equal a shot taken if it's all locked up. [Translation: Just because there's a deep pass called, that doesn't mean the quarterback should try to show off his arm and force the ball if the coverage is tight.] Check it down!"

O'Connell wrapped up his first session with Thomas and Jensen with a few words about his own knowledge. It was similar to what he began telling Manziel when he walked in ten minutes later to start his class, only with Manziel it was more tailored.

Manziel looked as if he had just finished running a marathon as he plopped down in a chair next to O'Connell. It was probably the first extended weight workout he'd done in about a year. He'd managed to steer clear of weight lifting sessions since winning the Heisman at A&M, but with so much concern about his physical size, Whitfield wanted Manziel looking as if he could take a pounding, and the hope was that he could pack on about ten pounds and be a solid 210 pounds within six weeks, in time for his trip to Indianapolis for the Combine.

"Looking swole," O'Connell said.

"Man, I don't wanna think about it," said Manziel. "I can't even feel my arms."

"In my personal opinion, there ain't no reason in the world why you can't be the number one pick in the draft," O'Connell told Manziel. "The team that has that pick—I think you fit there better than anybody. But it's gonna take you learning that offense, so that day one you prove to them that you can be 'The Guy.' They got a new coach, new coaches, and they don't have a guy.

"It took me ten minutes of watching you throw today to realize that you can be their guy. The ball comes out. You look the part. Now it's time for you to write it, read it, dream it, and speak it. I'll give you my phone number day and night—if you have a coach call to fly in to work you out, I'm there for you. I'll give you ten trigger words for that offense that will have those coaches feeling right about you. Today, I just wanna talk about the overall of what lies ahead. In a second I want you to get up and teach me about your offense at A&M. You and I need to speak the same language when it comes to A&M as fast as we can. I'm gonna take notes. You're gonna have to take what's on tape and be able to explain it on the board and for teams to be able to project you in their offense.

"This Patriots offense [the one O'Connell played in, where new Texans coach Bill O'Brien was the offensive coordinator] is what the team with the number one pick will be running, and the good thing about the Jets' offense [where he spent parts of three seasons] is, there are about a half dozen teams in the NFL that are now running it."

O'Connell drew a diagram of the four components to the NFL Draft process: the all-star games, which Manziel, as an underclassman, wasn't allowed to play in; the Combine; Pro Day; and the team workouts/visits.

"We're gonna get you right on the field. We're gonna get you right in here," O'Connell said. "You're gonna have to be ready, more so than anybody at that Combine, for those meetings. We're gonna do a ton of X's and O's stuff.

"Ever heard the story about Russell Wilson? After meeting with the Seahawks at the Combine, the team just knew he was their guy. You have the ability to do that, to leave that type of impression, and it's gonna be almost like a walk-off, where you drop the mic and leave. But obviously you do it in a way from the time you walk in to the time you walk out. You have to be everything and more than what they're expecting."

Before O'Connell invited Manziel up to the board, he asked the Heisman Trophy winner what he thought the perceived strengths of his game were.

"I felt like last year after working with Whit, teams thought, 'Hey, we're gonna man up, pressure, and have spies. We don't feel like he's a good enough passer to throw the ball downfield and beat us.' I felt like, this year, I made teams get out of that. I know against Alabama, they came out in man-coverage, and by halfway through the first quarter, they were like, 'Fuck that, we're done.' I felt like, whenever we did see man-coverage, with the exception of one game, against LSU, I felt like we did a good job of putting the ball where it needed to be.

"My interceptions were up a little bit. I had some tipped balls, so I know I gotta make better decisions, and seeing coverages is something I'd like to improve on. I see the defense well as things are going and I was good this year at manipulating defenses, whether it was using my hands to give them a stem early or seeing the soft corner to a one-high look. I felt like I got better at doing that. There are some weaknesses in being able to pick apart some zone defenses on a more consistent basis."

Manziel was already in the exclusive Heisman fraternity, but O'Connell was hoping to help him into a different kind of fraternity. One with Peyton Manning, Brees, Brady, and a select few others who had the answers to the test before the ball ever reached their palms. "What you're seeing nowadays is, everybody in the NFL is going to this system where the quarterback has a package of plays that he can get to depending on what the defense is in," O'Connell told Manziel. "You're not just gonna call 'four-verts.' The quarterback will check to it when he sees the appropriate look from the defense. Basically, nobody's wasting plays anymore. And all of that is predicated on what you do watching tape and your preparation."

Manziel had a similar story from his own days in College Station, jousting with Aggies defensive coordinator Mark Snyder, whose go-to defense was often "Tampa 2," according to the QB. "If we had a run play, and they're gonna crowd the box, I check," Manziel said. "Then he checks. I didn't even have to look over at him. I know what his go-to check is. The first thing we're going to is all-curls to high-low with a hook over the middle replacing the MIK [linebacker] every time."

> O'CONNELL: Draw it up. Perfect segue. OK, every time you go up to that board, I want you to act as if Bill O'Brien is sitting where I'm sitting. Presence. Voice. Hold that thing [the marker] like you're holding the keys to the franchise.

Manziel quickly ran through some A&M offensive staples. He explained a couple of details of "93," which is "all-curls" run at 13 yards deep, pointing out the general idea behind the play: "He [pointing to a receiver] has this whole area from hash to hash to work. Obviously, MIK [middle linebacker] is gone. Replace." With each bit of information Manziel offered, O'Connell peppered him with questions, asking for more specifics.

> O'CONNELL: Where are the Z and X [receivers] alignments? Are they touching paint [the numbers on the field]?
> MANZIEL: They're on top of the numbers every time.
> O'CONNELL: So top of the numbers, college, would be bottom of the numbers, pro. Perfect.

O'Connell wanted Manziel to get used to the altered geometry of the college game compared to the NFL due to the pro league's narrower hash marks, which meant, for quarterbacks, landmarks and angles and typical dead spots against coverages were different. He was also big on getting Manziel familiar with some key buzzwords, such as PSLs (pre-snap looks) or Pure Progressions, so he'd be ready to talk scheme with NFL folks.

For every Manziel favorite route against a certain defense or team—such as on "95" against Duke, it was Mike Evans on a stair-step route—O'Connell translated it into Bill O'Brien's language. "That's gonna be called a Sting route backside. Or a Prick or post-read Prick."

Manziel, like all the quarterbacks, was going to be grilled by coaches and GMs about what plays he liked on third-and-5, what he liked in the red zone, and on third-and-7-to-10 yards. O'Connell told him a common mistake young quarterbacks made was, they drew up the same play for fifteen different situations.

"Then Bill O'Brien asks [Texans offensive coordinator] Josh McDaniels, 'What'd he draw up for you on third-and-2-5? Four Verts. Oh, he drew the same for me on third-and-7-10 from the plus-15 [yard-line].'"

"I had 100 percent free rein to call anything," Manziel shot back.

"You should write that on your forehead," O'Connell said.

Texas A&M's offense was an offshoot of the Air Raid scheme created by Hal Mumme and Mike Leach two decades earlier. "The Air Raid is an attitude, not a playbook," Mumme liked to say. It was a perfect fit for Manziel.

"It's all based on what matchup I like," Manziel explained. "It's all leverage. If they're gonna play zone on third-and-3, and this 'backer is trying to take away this [pointing to a short route into the flat], we did a lot of stick-draw stuff.

"Most of the time I was quick enough with my feet and accurate enough on the outside shoulder at three yards to beat that guy. From there, I could have that play called and flash something [a hand signal] out there, a completely different call. I can give [the receiver] an out-route, so if it's Cover-2, you try to give them a Hole shot. I had free rein to say, 'I think that 'backer's slow to get that.' It was all hand signals, so if Mike [Evans] is one-on-one, I could give him a three-step slant or I could give him a comeback."

O'Connell sounded impressed, telling Manziel, "You're already ten times further along than I thought you'd be."

Where Manziel was lacking was in his understanding of protections, which would be his biggest challenge in draft camp, especially if he ever sat down with a team like the Packers, whose head coach, Mike McCarthy, was an old O-line guy. "They're gonna hammer you on protections," O'Connell warned.

MANZIEL: I didn't do any of it.

O'CONNELL: That's good, because they'll know and see that on tape, and by the time you're meeting with them, you'll know Scat, Jet [protections].

FIRST, O'CONNELL HAD TO teach Manziel how to "identify the MIK"—something in the A&M offense the Aggies' center was responsible for. Many fans assume that the MIK, which typically in football parlance means the middle linebacker, would refer to the position played by Ray Lewis, Brian Urlacher, or Patrick Willis, but when it came to mapping out a protection scheme, it was not that simple. O'Connell admitted he used to do the same thing when he first got into the league, looking at an opponent's depth chart and noting that Urlacher—number 54—was listed as the Bears' middle linebacker. "So every time I'd come to the line of scrimmage, I'd say, '54 is the MIK,' but that's not gonna work for you when they start moving and disguising things," O'Connell later said. "You have to have the spots in your head. You have to know if it's an 'odd' or an 'even' defense, where your weakness in your protections may be, based on the 'backer alignment or the safety rotation.

"Some defenses, you'll call out the same guy as the MIK on virtually every play. Other teams, with more exotic pressure packages, you might have to change the MIK point two or three times before you snap the ball. If you ever watch New England, and if they're in their empty protection, Tom [Brady] will sometimes change protections several times before the snap."

For O'Connell, a 6'5", 225-pounder who ran a 4.61 40 at the Combine, grasping the mental aspect of the game wasn't the reason he bounced to five NFL teams in five years and only got to throw six passes.

"Blitz me all day," he said. "That's the NFL. The problem with me and why I struggled was, I had a smile on my face—boom, boom [read the defense, find the open receiver]—and I'd just miss the throw, but it wasn't a matter of me not knowing what was coming, and that was the most frustrating part.

"Once you get a label from a first impression, you can't change that unless you get an opportunity. Once I learned everything in New England, it was, 'You know where to go with the ball. You know how to protect everything, but can you make that throw?' And when I went to New York, it was, 'You know the offense. You can run it with your eyes closed, but can you make that throw?' By the time I got to my fourth or fifth year, I knew what was happening, but I never got a rep to prove it. I spent so much time learning, I should've spent time with a private quarterback coach doing stuff to apply it instead of constantly trying to attack it from a mental perspective."

WHITFIELD ENDED HIS FIRST week of draft camp a post pattern away from his one-bedroom home at Mission Beach in San Diego. Whitfield's place was cluttered, floor to ceiling, with boxes of Nike shoes and gear as part of a new deal he had just signed with the brand powerhouse. On the walls were framed stories about him from *Sports Illustrated* and *ESPN The Magazine*, and larger pictures of his two biggest heroes, Muhammad Ali and Michael Jordan. There were also two framed posters of the New York City skyline. "That's the culmination of the two biggest evaluation points in my life," he said. "That's where they award the Heisman Trophy and announce the first pick of the NFL Draft."

Whitfield had two special guests there checking out his draft camp, Louisville quarterback Teddy Bridgewater and his advisor, Abe Elam, a former NFL defensive back. Bridgewater knew Whitfield from the Elite 11 but was still trying to figure out whom he wanted to train with. The Miami native had already been down to the IMG facility in Bradenton, Florida, to meet with Coach Chris Weinke, a former NFL QB, and earlier in the week had visited Jordan Palmer, who was also in the area and was training another projected first-round quarterback, Blake Bortles from UCF at Athletes' Performance.

"I'm just trying to see what's the best fit for me," Bridgewater said as he observed Whitfield having Manziel and Thomas doing their drops into the 55-degree water while the waves swept in, rattling their bodies as they struggled to maintain their balance, keeping both hands around the football by their chests. After a five-minute break, Manziel wandered back to the sand to join Ryan Flaherty, who had a bunch of small cones laid out in a diamond formation. It was one of a series of grueling drills Flaherty set up for them that ranged from 40 yards of bounding through the sand to sprints. Whitfield held Thomas out of the conditioning work to save his legs, since he was headed to Mobile, Alabama, to compete in the Senior Bowl. In addition to Manziel, Mike Evans, and a former running back from Central Michigan who helped catching passes for the draft camp, Manziel's marketing guy, Maverick Carter, the lanky childhood pal of LeBron James who had become the basketball star's right-hand man, was decked out in his own workout clothes to try to keep up, trudging through the soft sand while Flaherty shouted instructions.

As Thomas prepared for his cross-country flight, O'Connell seemed more like a big brother than a coach to his protégé, triple-checking with him on certain details. Whitfield, who had worked with Thomas in the off-season since 2012, said he saw a "refreshed" Logan Thomas.

"Lots of guys, as they try to make the jump to the NFL, take a huge inhale, because they're ready for the next step," Whitfield said, noting Thomas's awareness of the opportunity in front of him. "Just a great chance to reboot. It isn't so much about team anymore. It's about you.

"Once you get past Johnny, Teddy, and Bortles, who is 4-5-6 [among the QBs in the 2014 NFL Draft]? If Logan is really cleaned up, it can be him. You're talking about bringing in a guy who is 6'6", huge arm, really smart, good athlete. EJ [Manuel] went number one last year. Nobody had EJ higher than Matt Barkley at this point, but look what happened in the draft."

Thomas knew it was going to be a long process but felt he was ready for it.

"I think this is gonna help me a great deal," he said of his draft prep. "I think it's knowing what I'm getting myself into. I've learned a lot from Coach Kevin and George, and now I get to prove myself. You play the game to compete against the very best, and I'm extremely excited for this."

O'CONNELL AND WHITFIELD, WITH the help of Twitter, monitored the buzz from Mobile like nervous parents. As expected, Thomas left jaws on the floor when NFL personnel people eyeballed him. His hand size, measured at 10¾″, dwarfed that of the other five quarterbacks playing in the game. Only Miami's Stephen Morris [10⅛″] was even bigger than 9½″.

The reactions from the week's Senior Bowl practices, which matter more to NFL scouts than the actual game, were tougher to get a handle on. CBSSports.com NFL Draft analyst Dane Brugler said of Thomas: "We'll often hear this draft season that Thomas has 'what can't be taught' when referring to his physical attributes, but can touch and accuracy be taught? It can be tweaked and improved from a mechanical standpoint, but from his performances the past two days, along with three years of game film, it's tough to see the upside with Thomas. It wouldn't surprise me if the Virginia Tech quarterback ends up hearing his name called on the second day of the draft. But a team that drafts him that high is living on a hope and a prayer—similar to many of Thomas's throws this week."

NFL.com's Bucky Brooks, a former pro scout, wrote that Thomas "delivered the ball with excellent velocity and zip in drills and looked like a confident passer from the pocket . . . [and] flashed timing and anticipation on a handful of throws in 7-on-7 that showcased his potential as a passer in a pro-style offense."

Thomas's performance in the game was underwhelming. Even though he completed four of five pass attempts, it was for just 17 yards. He also was sacked five times. Perhaps the moment O'Connell cringed the most was when he heard Thomas's response to the question, "What if I asked you to play tight end?"

Thomas's reply, according to *The MMQB:* "I would disregard y'all right off the top."

WHITFIELD LOST OUT IN the competition to train Bridgewater (he opted to work with Weinke at the IMG facility), but the coach did get a visit from his mentor in late January when Cam Cameron came down to Carlsbad while on a West Coast recruiting trip. The crop of high school junior quarterbacks—the Class of 2015—was being touted as Southern California's best group ever, and Cameron, the LSU offensive coordinator, had a few prospects he'd heard great things about. He was also curious to see what new drills Whitfield had come up with.

One of Whitfield's newer drills, he called "the Creator," where he had different defensive linemen come free, piercing the pocket, forcing the quarterback to evade pressure while keeping his eyes downfield. He'd come up with the drill a year earlier to help Oklahoma QB Landry Jones improve his pocket presence and "get used to creating operational space." The premise: Very few times will all five offensive linemen hold their blocks. Often in team practices, coaches blow the whistle whenever a defender gets close to the quarterback.

"I'm trying to train a second set of instincts," Whitfield said. "It's like when you push racehorses into a starting gate. Sometimes, they don't wanna go." It was often like that with Manziel, as the drill showed. Whitfield watched Manziel give in to his natural instincts and step in between two linemen as if he was ready to bolt.

"No, no, no," Whitfield said. "There is no escape route! Only adjustments. This is not an escape."

"I could if I wanted to," Manziel said with a mischievous grin as he scooted backward with the ball while still spying downfield.

"I know you could," Whitfield said.

Cameron chuckled as much at the ingenuity of his protégé as at Manziel's daring spirit. Whitfield viewed the fifty-three-year-old Cameron as a guest professor, often relying on him for feedback on the drills he cooked up.

"You can get lost in making up drills sometimes," Whitfield later said. "You can come up with something that looks good but then realize it can have zero correlation to the game, and if that's so, then you gotta ditch it."

Cameron's suggestion for the Creator drill: to incorporate another aspect of Whitfield drills—using numbered flash cards while standing at the middle linebacker spot to force the QBs to focus downfield and make "reads." Another Cameron idea: have the quarterbacks wear helmets and shoulder pads for drills, which would be more similar to game situations.

It also didn't take Cameron long to home in on one of Whitfield's points of emphasis for draft camp with Manziel, getting him to try to drive the ball more. "It's kind of a shotgun problem," Whitfield surmised. From all his time around the Heisman winner and studying his every move, Whitfield was convinced Manziel's penchant for getting up on his toes wasn't so much for combating his lack of height but responding to the quarterback's own supersized adrenaline reservoir.

"Tell him to put his back foot flatter on the ground," Cameron said. Playing almost exclusively from the shotgun, as Manziel has, can make a quarterback "toes-y," as Cameron put it.

Two drills into the workout and Cameron became more involved as Manziel began "routes on air." Cameron, a former quarterback under Lee Corso and a point guard for Bob Knight at Indiana, walked up to a receiver lined up in the slot and got so close, the wideout could tell whether the coach had used paste or gel to brush his teeth that morning.

CAMERON: Covered or open?

MANZIEL: Covered.

CAMERON: That's wide open. That's the world you're going to live in.

That perception is one of the biggest adjustments college quarterbacks must make if they hope to succeed in the NFL. It's something Cameron spent plenty of time preaching to his first QB at LSU, Zach Mettenberger, a 6′5″ guy with prototype size and arm strength but who had been underwhelming and unfocused till the longtime NFL coach arrived before the 2013 season. Before Cameron, Mettenberger had just a 12–7 TD-INT ratio and took 32 sacks. With him, his TD-INT ratio was improved to 22–8, and he was sacked 11 fewer times and averaged 3 full yards more per pass attempt, a significant jump. An NFL caveat his old boss Marty Schottenheimer always said: "In times of crisis, think players, not plays," which resonated with O'Connell, who said he picked up that adage from onetime Jets offensive coordinator Brian Schottenheimer, Marty's son.

"It's funny, some guys are just so blackboard-oriented," Cameron told me, pointing out how his QB had to be prodded into noticing who the players were running the routes, whether they were stars or subs. "It took Mettenberger a bit, to where I'd say, 'Zach, that's Jarvis Landry there, and you're skipping over Jarvis Landry for who?' To me, you have to be a basketball-mind-set guy. It's all about match-ups, and then the blackboard stuff."

Landry's production in crunch time certainly supported Cameron's faith. In 2013, LSU threw 35 passes on third downs in the direction of Landry; 80 percent of those passes he turned into first downs.

In his days as the Baltimore Ravens' offensive coordinator, Cameron said he had to coax Joe Flacco to throw the ball more to veteran Anquan Boldin. "Joe would say, 'Cam, there's no separation.' I said, 'There doesn't have to be. It's Anquan. Just throw it in there. If you're waiting for him to get separation, you're gonna be waiting a while, but Anquan doesn't need separation. He just needs one-on-one.'"

Cameron had gotten a peek at Johnny Manziel three months earlier, when Texas A&M visited LSU. It was rainy and cold, and the Tigers dominated on both sides of the ball, winning 34–10. Manziel completed just 39 percent of his passes, going 16 of 41. It was the only time all season he completed less than 67 percent of his passes in a game. Cameron credits head coach Les Miles for taking star wide receiver/punt returner Odell Beckham Jr., the best athlete on the team, and putting him on the scout-team offense as quarterback to mimic Manziel to ready the Tiger D. "We also held the ball for over forty minutes in the game," he said. "We were an up-tempo team but had a plan to trim nine seconds off of every play. We just did the math."

Observing Manziel in person in Carlsbad, Cameron was reminded of his former quarterback Drew Brees, whom he coached with the San Diego Chargers, noting the Texan's oversize hands, athleticism, and demeanor.

"Drew had a presence," Cameron said. "He wasn't little to me. Hand size makes you weatherproof. I watched as the season went on how certain quarterbacks changed as the weather changed. They weren't the same. And you gotta be weatherproof in that league.

"Those are the nimblest big feet I think I've seen," Cameron said, watching Manziel's size 15s dashing all over the field, shifting the coach's train of thought. "With quarterbacks, you don't take anybody's word for it. You listen, but you gotta go form your own conclusion. Now I know why [Saints coach] Sean Peyton was at our game. Drew can dunk a basketball, could've been a world class tennis player, is a scratch golfer. He doesn't have this speed, though, but he does have great escapability. They're different, but they're similar. As everybody knows, for every quarterback the NFL has hit on, they've missed on ten. Then, if everybody's in line [as in front office and the coaching staff], that's the key."

Cameron had long thought the skepticism about a quarterback's height was overblown in the NFL. As a college head coach at Indiana from 1998 to 2001, his offense was led by one of the most dynamic dual-threat quarterbacks in college football history, Antwaan Randle El, a 5'10", 185-pounder who won Big Ten MVP honors in 2001. Cameron wasn't surprised that Randle El threw a perfect pass on a 43-yard, double-reverse touchdown play to Hines Ward in Super Bowl XL to clinch the game for the Steelers. "Not many guys can come in cold, sprint, and still throw that ball right on the money," said Cameron.

"He could've been a quarterback in the NFL, but very seldom are you going to have a GM, head coach, offensive coordinator, and a QB coach who'll all be on the same page to give a guy like that an opportunity. And you all have to be on the same page if you go that route. He had tremendous accuracy and as strong an arm as I've ever been around. We were going to draft him in San Diego to be our third quarterback and as a receiver, punt returner, but then Pittsburgh took him."

What's imperative for Cameron is to find out how resourceful—and resilient—his quarterback is, something he tries to discern almost on a daily basis at practice.

"I want to blitz them every single down from the day they walk in," Cameron said. "So many people say, 'Cam, you can't do that. You'll destroy the kid.' Well, if you drafted the right guy, you want them to get in the right mind-set as quickly as you can. I remember the day Philip [Rivers] threw four interceptions in, like, six throws in the two-minute drill. Marty [Schottenheimer] said, 'What the fuck is going on?'"

"I said, 'Coach, we'll know by tomorrow whether we drafted the right guy.' Philip came out the next day and lit it up. To me, you have to get a young quarterback coming into the league to fail as quickly as possible, and hopefully in practice or in a pre-season game, so you can start digging 'em through all the stuff they need to go through. Everybody wants to see what this guy is made of. I've seen too many guys try to protect their pick. The reason Flacco had so much success is because of [former Ravens defensive coordinator] Rex [Ryan]. He came to me one day early on and said, 'If we're blitzing too much, let us know.'

"I said, 'We need you to blitz more. We gotta get this guy to grow quickly.' He couldn't believe it. He said, 'That's awesome.' We went to the AFC title game. Same thing at LSU. I want [defensive coordinator John Chavis] Chief to blitz us every single down. And I like when the QB gets hit in practice. I don't want him hurt, but I want him scuffed up, because it's not 7-on-7."

Cameron said evaluators get "fooled" by a lot of the videotape they study on quarterbacks. "You're trying to find out, who is this guy?" Cameron said. "Go get all the away games. Look at all of those ones where they're close by seven points one way or the other in the fourth quarter. Study them. You'll be amazed at how many guys come apart at the seams and the others who have the magic. That's the closest thing that translates to the NFL, because you can't hear [due to the crowd noise], and everything you do matters. Then, take all their red-zone throws and all the third-down throws, because everything other than that can fool you."

In 2007, when Cameron was the head coach of the Miami Dolphins, many draft analysts speculated that he would use the number nine pick on Notre Dame quarterback Brady Quinn, an All-American. Cameron wouldn't touch him. "When you looked at that criteria, he was awful."

Quinn fell to the number twenty-two pick of the first round. He then bounced around to six teams in seven years and was out of the NFL before he was thirty.

A FIVE-MINUTE DRIVE AWAY from Whitfield draft camp headquarters in Carlsbad was a cutting-edge training center. To enter, you went through an enormous metal and glass gravity-hinge door wide enough for an eighteen-wheeler to roll through. The door somehow was balanced in a technological way such that an eight-year-old could pull it open. This was the entrance to the EXOS training facility, where Dilfer's TDFB protégé, Jordan Palmer, the Chicago Bears' backup quarterback, ran his draft camp. EXOS, which used to be known as Athletes' Performance, has six locations around the country.

Palmer trained three draft hopeful QBs: Washington's Keith Price, Wyoming's Brett Smith, and UCF's Blake Bortles. Smith and Price actually put up gaudier stats in their college careers, but it was the 6'5", 235-pound Bortles who had the NFL scouting world buzzing.

At five minutes past 8:00 a.m. on the last Thursday in January, Palmer scribbled plays on a glass wall inside the EXOS facility. Price and Smith scarfed down eggs and sausage on the foam plates they had brought over from the Residence Inn across the street where the quarterbacks were staying. The twenty-nine-year-old Palmer harped on details, preaching to them about drawing arrows at the ends of their lines on the routes they drew for NFL personnel people or tweaking Price's verbiage. "Don't say, 'Then, I'm gonna hop back for depth.' Say, 'Then, I'm going to re-set for depth.'

"This is not the difference between right and wrong," Palmer told them. "This is the difference between, 'This guy's pretty smart,' and, 'This guy knows what the fuck he's talking about.' It's the difference between, 'Um, excuse me, I was wondering if you come here often, and maybe I could buy you a drink,' and, 'What's up? I'm Keith. Have you ever seen ESPN? S'up, girl?'"

One of Palmer's big selling points to draft clients was his grasp of teaching NFL concepts. A few days earlier, that's what he'd hoped would've resonated with Teddy Bridgewater when the Louisville star toured EXOS. He'd quizzed Bridgewater on what the safety's responsibility is in "Quarters" coverage.

"He's got the quarter of the field," Bridgewater said.

Palmer asked Bridgewater's advisor, former NFL safety Abe Elam, if he was right. Elam said yes, before Palmer asked him again: "Or, does he have inside leverage run support and eyes on number 2 [receiver]? If number 2 travels across the field or into the flat, he moves his eyes to number 1 and forms a bracket. If number 2 travels vertically, he takes him man to man. That's what we're gonna learn, because that changes the way I read Curl-Flat."

Palmer maintained that everything with quarterbacking hinged on two things: confidence in your abilities and confidence in your understanding.

"I always start by asking, 'What is the most important trait in a quarterback?'" Palmer said, before pointing to his forehead. "This is a muscle, and we can work this every single day."

Palmer is not a "quarterbacks coach," he said.

"I am a quarterback consultant. As a consultant, as in my [marketing] business, I come in and say, 'Here's where you're at. Here's where you guys tell me where you want to be. Here's some holes, and here's some holes I think we can fill. If you don't like them, you fire me at any point and terminate our contract. If you like them, I will build a model or create a campaign to help facilitate those that you're interested in. You're the CEO. You're making the decisions.'

"I think the biggest mistake guys make, and a guy on the East Coast does this all the time from what I hear—is 'Trust me. Trust me. This is the way to do it.' I think that is the worst mistake you can make. You know how many dudes played in the League? So this guy who played in Buffalo, and he did something a little different, does that mean he doesn't know what he's talking about? I've been exposed to a lot of football. I've played with some great ones and been coached by some great ones. But the difference is, I've also gotten thousands of hours of reps through the Elite 11 of how to say it and how not to message it. I look at it as a doctor."

When Bortles and Smith arrived in Carlsbad, both loaded on their back leg. Palmer explained the drawbacks of that: "You're not on balance, and the second problem is over-striding. You can't throw the ball until your left foot hits the ground. If you want a quicker release, eliminate any unnecessary movement along the way. The longer it takes for my left foot to hit the ground, the slower everything happens."

Palmer subscribed to many of the Tom House principles about quarterbacks as rotational athletes. That explained why, a few hours later, when he brought Bortles out for a throwing session on the 35-yard turf practice field in the back of the EXOS facility, he had his star protégé doing wall-sits with his arms above his head, elbows at 90 degrees, gliding up the wall, and why the QBs were firing passes to each other from 25 yards apart while on their knees. It was also one of the reasons behind a philosophical difference between Palmer and Whitfield on a teaching point when it came to making touch throws.

"What should happen is, the arm angle should change," Palmer said. "Me and George vehemently disagree on this. He teaches guys to flick and hold, like shooting 3-pointers. It couldn't make less sense to me. That's like me saying I want you to run a 40-yard dash, but I'm gonna put a wall at 41 yards. Your arm isn't making a basketball motion. Basketball players aren't rotational athletes. You're creating all this energy. Why would I stop it?"

Palmer was quick to add that he has great respect for Whitfield. The two had become friends through their work on the Elite 11: "I've told guys, 'If you don't throw with me, throw with George, because you know what you're gonna get. You won't have a guy taking money out of your pocket. He won't make you worse.' We offer different products. We're not competitors."

Earlier in the week, Palmer had brought his three quarterbacks to Laguna Beach to try one of his passions—stand-up paddle-boarding. Palmer, who grew up surfing, kind of fell into the sport. In his first race, a woman taking part for her fiftieth birthday celebration beat him. He soon realized the workout tied in quite well for a quarterback because of how much the motions and balancing on the board amid the waves tapped into your core muscles and shoulder flexibility. Palmer was delighted when ESPN producers came with him and his QBs for a trip into the water as part of a docu-series on the 2013 draft.

"I think it's gonna blow up once it gets out, because there's no better workout for a quarterback off the field, and you can't get hurt," he told me.

Palmer's own playing career had been on life support many times. Unlike his big brother, Carson, he was never a touted recruit or praised for having a huge arm. Coming out of college, he was a sixth-round pick by the Washington Redskins in the 2007 draft and was cut before the season. He sat out the year and then signed with the Arizona Rattlers of the Arena Football League, but the day before he left for camp, his brother's team, the Cincinnati Bengals, offered him a deal. He was fifth on the depth chart. He said he didn't "know anything about football" till he met the Bengals' QB coach Ken Zampese, whom he impressed enough to get kept as the third-string quarterback. "I learned how to learn," Palmer said.

The younger Palmer lasted three seasons in Cincinnati before being released. A year later, he landed with the Jacksonville Jaguars for a season and got cut again. Then, in the spring of 2013, the week Dilfer's TDFB was launching, he got a tryout with the Chicago Bears, competing that day with two other members of the 2007 QB draft class, Jamarcus Russell, the top overall pick, and Trent Edwards, a third-rounder. "That order got flipped in terms of productivity that day," Palmer said. But he was still released by the Bears on the eve of the 2013 season. However, after starter Jay Cutler tore a groin muscle at mid-season, Palmer was re-signed and spent the rest of the year living in an Extended Stay America hotel.

"I think the Elite 11 has done a lot for my playing career, because I would've never started thinking about the sports psychology side of it," he said. "I am a slightly above average thrower and a below average athlete. Experience-wise, I'm 114th out of 114 or whatever the number of quarterbacks is. But it doesn't affect my confidence. I have developed that mind-set. I used to feel like it was something I didn't have. It's not God-given. It's how you were raised and experiences you had growing up. I developed it."

In Blake Bortles, Palmer had found another late bloomer with a similar approach. Bortles was an afterthought in the recruiting process for most schools. Tulane and Purdue both offered him scholarships, but it was to play tight end. According to the former UCF recruiting coordinator, head coach George O'Leary wasn't interested in Bortles, a local product, till the Knights whiffed on four other mid-level QB recruits. Colorado State was his only other D1 offer to play quarterback. Bortles, though, started to blossom after the first month of the 2012 season. Then, as a junior, he flashed onto the national radar after sparking visiting UCF to a 38–35 upset of Bridgewater's unbeaten Louisville team, rallying the Knights from a three-touchdown hole in the second half. For those trying to make the case why Bortles could end up as the first overall pick, it didn't hurt that he threw 3 touchdown passes to defeat Penn State, the team new Houston Texans head man Bill O'Brien used to coach.

"Blake's gonna go number one to Houston," Palmer predicted. "You have a 5′10″ guy [Manziel] who was hands-down the best player in college football. He can do things no one else can do. He's probably as confident a player as anyone I've ever been around, which is why he can do some of the shit he does. He's also a liability. Can we trust Johnny? Totally scary. Teddy [Bridgewater] is unbelievably productive. Supersmart. Doesn't own the room. No presence. Two hundred pounds. Then you've got Blake. Six-five, 240, gonna run a 4.6.

Doesn't have half the experience the other two guys have. Had a drill sergeant [O'Leary] as a coach. Doesn't throw the ball as naturally as Teddy does. He's off-the-charts coachable and will be the coolest guy in the room. Coolest, meaning likable.

"It's a crapshoot. Bill O'Brien is a very smart man. He's gonna come back to one thing: Who's the most trustworthy quarterback? If I take you as a quarterback at number one, and you're a bust, everybody gets fired."

Palmer also didn't subscribe to former NFL coach Tom Rossley's notion that the number one quality a QB needs is magic, which also factored into the Manziel versus Bortles debate.

"I think you need in today's game to be more of a problem solver than a magician," Palmer said. His example is a veteran NFL QB, who he said can be as good as anybody and as bad as anybody. "He can keep you from going to the playoffs, and he can throw for 5,000 yards every single year. Every single time [he] drops back, he's thinking, 'How do I make a play?' He can't help himself. Sometimes you gotta make a play. But if you drop back with the mind-set of 'How do I make the play?' the NFL is too good and too competitive, and you are not good enough to do that every time. And Johnny Manziel drops back every time, thinking, 'I'm going to make a play.' And he makes a ton of plays, but if he goes into the NFL with that type of mind-set and that kind of confidence, I think he's gonna have some difficulties, because Robert Griffin III sure had a lot of difficulties in the NFL this year."

FEBRUARY 21, 2014.

The first real buzz from inside Lucas Oil Stadium during the NFL Combine came when word circulated on an early Friday morning in late February that Johnny Manziel had been measured officially by the League at 5'11¾". That detail only added to the intrigue surrounding Manziel—listed by Texas A&M at 6'1"—as the entire NFL brain trust—every exec, coach, assistant, scout, and media member—gathered in Indianapolis for the week. The factoid that no quarterback measuring under six feet had been selected in the first *two* rounds of the NFL Draft since 1953 must've popped up a hundred times in the skywalks and bars around a town overrun by NFL types.

By 9:30 a.m. ET, Whitfield was making the rounds in the media area of Lucas Oil Stadium, getting pulled in different directions between NFL Network, ESPN, and a host of other people with digital recorders and flip cams.

"He's already done nine interviews since we arrived here this morning," said Jeanine Juliano, an Alabama undergrad and former Miss Teen Alabama interning as an executive assistant with Whitfield's company.

Whitfield, who had in part turned his penchant for creative analogies into a cottage industry, didn't miss an opportunity to poke at the skepticism rooted in Manziel's measuring a tad below some kind of magic six-foot barometer. He held up a quarter-inch snippet of paper on the NFL Network to make his case about how silly such thinking would be for that to be a reason not to draft Manziel.

Sal Paolantonio, a veteran ESPN reporter, commended Whitfield on his little prop as he walked by en route to the bathroom.

"Man, I'm talked out," Whitfield said, before noting that the quarter-inch piece of paper was actually a tag from his dry cleaning.

"Might as well have fun, since people love making a big deal of a quarter inch," Whitfield told me. "He's the same height he was when he was '007' in the SEC. You wanna bet your franchise on a quarter of an inch?"

After hearing that Manziel was en route to the media area for his press conference, Whitfield settled into a seat in the second row in front of the podium to get a jump on what he figured to be a mob scene. A handful of other reporters noticed Whitfield positioning himself and followed suit. One writer asked Whitfield, "What have you done this week to address his height?"

"I don't know. You'd have to talk to [Manziel's parents] Paul and Michele about that one," Whitfield said.

Kevin O'Connell, who flew in with Ryan Flaherty, entered the room and sat down behind Whitfield. Their talk went from which teams were interested in speaking to their QBs before it turned to

Logan Thomas's new look. Whitfield had prodded the towering Virginia Tech quarterback to go to a barber before getting on the plane to fly to Indy.

"I told him, 'You gotta come in clean here,'" Whitfield said. "'The beard's gonna come back. Your chance to make a first impression won't.'"

One year earlier, Whitfield had offered up a similar message to another one of his QB protégés, Arizona's Matt Scott, an athletic, strong-armed quarterback many had projected to go in the third or fourth round.

"He just did not get it," Whitfield said. "He didn't think it was a serious deal."

Scott showed up in Indy with a goatee. He ended up going undrafted, before getting signed with the Jacksonville Jaguars. Would he have gotten drafted if he had come in clean-shaven? Who knows? But Whitfield wasn't about to let Thomas give anybody another reason to be skeptical.

Whitfield had gotten something of a false alarm. Manziel's press conference wouldn't start for another ninety minutes. But it was still a mob scene. Tom Coughlin, the head coach who had won two Super Bowls with the New York Giants, was holding his own press conference on the opposite side of the room with about one-fifth the crowd of media.

Ultimately, Manziel, as he always was, appeared at ease in front of the podium. "This is life now, this is a job for me, taking it very seriously, and I'm really excited about the future," he said. "I feel like I play like I'm ten feet tall . . . I'm probably one of the most competitive people on the face of the Earth."

Some media members wrote that Manziel was over-coached for the press conference. Regardless, Whitfield was pleased. So was Manziel.

The next morning the quarterbacks were on the turf for their forties and whatever other drills the NFL coaches wanted to put them through. Manziel, like Bridgewater, had opted not to throw at the Combine on the advice of his agents, preferring to hold off till his Pro Day, where he would be working with receivers he knew and had timing with. Bortles, though, was determined to show the NFL brass he just wanted a chance to compete.

Outside the media room, about twenty yards from the ESPN set, were several big flat-screen TVs showing the NFL Network's coverage from the field. In one of the metal folding chairs by the TVs sat Palmer like a nervous father, watching Bortles throwing passes. Much of the discussion among NFL analysts, though, was about Logan Thomas, who put on a dazzling display of athleticism, running the fastest 40-yard dash time among QBs (4.61), jumping the highest (35.5 inches), the farthest (9'10"), and throwing the hardest (60 mph). (Manziel's official 40-time was 4.68, while Bridgewater chose not to run. Bortles's was a disappointing 4.93. Manziel ran the fastest 20-yard shuttle time at 4.03 seconds, ahead of Thomas's 4.18.)

NFL Network draft analyst Mike Mayock said Thomas's footwork was "lazy" but observed that the ball came out of his hand "beautifully." Still, Mayock lamented that Thomas's "tape is so bad." His colleague, former NFL coach Steve Mariucci, sounded more optimistic: "I think he's smart enough to learn. He's had some big games. I think he would be fun to coach."

Whitfield, listening to the commentary, was irked, pointing out as he walked away that Mayock also once had Cam Newton ranked below Blaine Gabbert and Jake Locker in his draft class.

Four hours later, Manziel had already flown out. Whitfield felt like celebrating. He was getting good feedback from his NFL connections about Manziel, and Thomas had created more intrigue with his arm strength and his freakish athleticism. He settled into one of the couches in the lobby bar at the JW Marriott waiting for Flaherty and Thomas. In between fielding text messages, Whitfield thumbed at his smartphone to check what was being said about his protégés.

"I had three NFL coaches say, 'We wanna see [Manziel] throw with anticipation,'" Whitfield said of the feedback he got in regard to Manziel's upcoming Pro Day, which he planned to have 100 percent from under center. Flaherty arrived grinning. Thomas looked exhausted as he collapsed onto a couch. He recounted the oddest question he had gotten asked by a team in one of the fifteen-minute meetings he had in the NFL's speed-dating setup with prospects. He was asked how many things he could do with a brick. He said he came up with six, but at the moment, Thomas was too fried to name them.

"Hey, G—You'll love this," Thomas told Whitfield. "They [the NFL coaches during his workout] were telling me to slow my drops. I lit up the outs. I was 5 of 7."

Jeanine Juliano—Whitfield's assistant—seated next to Thomas, did a Twitter search for Thomas's name, which unlocked a torrent of snarky comments reacting to any praise he'd gotten for his show in Indy. Asked why the venom toward Thomas, she was told it was probably backlash from draft analysts once touting him as a potential first overall pick of the draft.

"But I didn't do any of that," Thomas said, shrugging. "That wasn't anything I said."

At that point, he was just looking forward to getting his first-class-upgrade flight back to California and taking his girlfriend to Disneyland before gearing back up for his Pro Day.

## _ _ _ _ _11.

# THE COMEBACK ROUTE

FEBRUARY 9, 2014.

A kid with shoulder-length blond hair sprawling from underneath a white baseball cap that was turned backward took a seven-step drop. His big red Nike high-tops kicked up sod as three pass-rushers waving big puffy pads gave chase.

"PUT A LOT OF PRESSURE ON THIS GUY! GO! GET UP-FIELD!" yelled Steve Clarkson from ten feet away as he did a countdown.

"SIX! . . . FIVE! . . ."

The QB darted left, evading one of the rushers.

"SEE IT! FEEL IT! . . . THREE! . . . TWO!"

The quarterback almost survived the drill, avoiding being tagged by the D-linemen for nine seconds, but with one second remaining, the kid brushed into another player. The quarterback flung the ball down in disgust.

These were the eight-year-olds.

It was a gray Sunday morning at Cathedral High in downtown Los Angeles. Legend had it that the school was haunted. Even the Cathedral's athletic teams are named the Phantoms to honor the school's rep. In the background, you could hear constant chatter from a preacher blaring through speakers via the church located just a few yards beyond the end zone. None of the quarterbacks seemed the least bit distracted, though. A few of their parents watched from the bleachers while a dozen more sat behind them at umbrella-covered picnic tables reading books, scanning tablets, and pecking at their smartphones.

Clarkson prodded both his QBs serving as ersatz defensive linemen ("Make 'em work! Make 'em panic!") and the quarterbacks dealing with the pressure ("Try to feel the rush, and keep your eyes downfield, but NO MATTER WHAT, PROTECT THE BALL!!!")

This was a typical Sunday at Cathedral. Clarkson had been conducting his workout sessions for more than two dozen QBs—ages eight to eighteen—for the previous four years. On the football field were four different drill stations.

Almost all the QBs arrived at least a half hour before the 9:00 a.m. session began. Clarkson actually had an earlier one-on-one with a high school sophomore who had been flying in from Colorado the previous couple of weeks. The fifty-two-year-old coach, wearing a gray "Dreammaker" sweat suit, looked more like a former lineman than an old quarterback. Clarkson played in college at 205 pounds but appeared north of 255 now. The lower half of his cheeky, round face was covered with gray whiskers.

Many of these quarterbacks had been with Clarkson for years. Two quarterbacks in the 9:00 a.m. group were high-level recruits. One, Travis Waller, a 6'3", 195-pounder from Anaheim's Servite High School, came in as a wide receiver and was a standout track athlete who had already been offered scholarships at Washington and Northwestern. "He's got a huge ceiling," said Clarkson. Waller had a sense of urgency, too. Unlike a lot of Clarkson's pupils, Waller came from a modest background. He was being raised by a single mother. "I'm not the richest kid, so we give up some things so I can come here and she can pay Steve," said Waller, who had been coming to Clarkson's Sunday-morning group sessions for two years. "I take every rep seriously. It costs a lot, but it's definitely worth it. I saw a dramatic change right away."

Some of the other quarterbacks drove Mercedes and BMWs.

Waller didn't even have a car, his mom, Bridgette, said. "I drive a 2008 Saturn Vue, and we live in an apartment in Fullerton. We sacrifice vacations. We don't eat out a lot. We don't go to the movies." But the Wallers looked at the Clarkson training as an investment that could be worth $200,000 in a college scholarship and even more if he developed the way his coach said he could.

"Some people may get up and go to church on Sundays; we go to Steve," Bridgette said.

The other touted QB had high, layered, dark hair and a toothy grin, resembling a younger Taylor Lautner. He was wearing a pink long-sleeve shirt and black "Dreammaker" shorts with pink tights and black socks.

"Brady looks like a young Joe Namath," said Clarkson while taking a break, as he watched seventeen-year-old Brady White do footwork drills. "He actually reminds me of Aaron Rodgers."

White, the son of a senior vice president at CBRE—the world's largest commercial real estate service—had been training with Clarkson since he was in the sixth grade.

He was ranked—depending on which scouting service you checked—as one of the nation's top five QB prospects in the 2015 recruiting class. He played at a program known for cranking out college quarterbacks, Hart High in LA suburb Newhall, California. White already had scholarship offers from Cal, Illinois, and Indiana, among others. His online recruiting profile listed him as 6′2″, 186 pounds, but his wiry frame made him appear lighter than that. The very mention of that seemingly innocuous detail prompted a defensive comment from Clarkson.

"People forget [that] John Elway was 170 [pounds] as a freshman at Stanford," Clarkson said, evoking the third Hall of Fame–caliber QB in respect to young Brady White within a thirty-second stretch.

"Brady, are you dressed this way for Valentine's [Day]?" Clarkson yelled to the high schooler as he ran over to a new station.

In a few hours, the field would be covered with hundreds of teenage football players, not just quarterbacks, as part of a high school 7-on-7 league Clarkson helped run. One of the teams was making the two-hour drive up from San Diego. Its star quarterback was a ninth-grader named Tate Martell, another Clarkson protégé. In July 2012, as a fourteen-year-old, soon-to-be eighth-grader, Martell—then a home-school student—accepted a scholarship offer to play quarterback for the University of Washington. The Huskies program at the time was run by head coach Steve Sarkisian—one of Clarkson's first protégés some twenty-plus years earlier. Martell, then around 5'11", 170-pounds, started to draw attention from college programs with his performance for the Mira Mesa Chargers in the Throwback Football League, Clarkson said. The TFL was another Clarkson creation. It was a springtime, full-contact, club football league that played its games during the months of April, May, and June. Clarkson charged each kid $300 for the season. The sixteen-team league "was created specifically to recruit, develop, and showcase the very best football talent at the sixth-, seventh-, and eighth-grade levels." In 2013, the TFL had six more kids receive major college scholarship offers, according to the league website. "I think it's the future of football," Clarkson said.

Martell was actually a year older than most of the other students in his grade. That was because his father, a former college wrestler, had held him back in seventh grade so the boy would be more physically and mentally mature as he went through high school and college. It's a move several Clarkson disciples have made. Clarkson showed Sarkisian film of Martell and had the coach hooked.

"If you could clone Fran Tarkenton and Brett Favre, you would have Tate Martell," Clarkson told Sarkisian.

The Martell commitment, which made national news, was reminiscent of the story of his buddy, David Sills V, also a Clarkson guy. In 2010, as a thirteen-year-old, Sills committed to a scholarship offer from USC and then-coach Lane Kiffin.

Brady White and Tate Martell and their parents all were featured in a December 2013 *60 Minutes* segment about Clarkson titled "Quarterback Guru." The thirteen-minute piece had aired six weeks earlier, touted as "Morley Safer talks to the 'Quarterback Guru' who says the new norm to get to the NFL as a quarterback starts with a tutor like him training kids as young as eight."

It had been a good winter for Clarkson and his Dreammaker

brand. In January, he appeared on Comedy Central's *The Colbert Report* for a spoof of him teaching Stephen Colbert how to play quarterback.

Clarkson also planned to train Oakland Raiders QB Terrelle Pryor for the next five months on Tuesdays and Thursdays, he said. Clarkson had worked with the former Buckeyes star some when he was at Ohio State, although Pryor was still a major project when he arrived in the NFL as a third-round pick in 2011. In 2013, Pryor spent his off-season in Southern California working with Tom House. Pryor even later admitted to reporters that, until he met House, "I never really knew how to throw a football before."

BRADY WHITE AND TRAVIS Waller, the alphas of Clarkson's Sunday-morning group, were part of a loaded crop of Southern California quarterbacks in the 2015 recruiting class. White was a consensus top-five QB, and there were actually three other Los Angeles area quarterbacks ranked even higher. "Five of the eight quarterbacks we liked the most are LA kids," one SEC coach said. "Usually that area's overrated for quarterbacks. This year, it seems to be the opposite."

It had been decades since the area produced a group as highly touted. The benchmark for all Southern California QB classes was the 1979 group, led by future Hall of Famer John Elway of Granada Hills. That class included, among others, two other QBs who ended up in the NFL: Tom Ramsey and Jay Schroeder. Steve Clarkson, a record-setting quarterback at Wilson High, was a part of that class, too. That group, especially given the magnitude of Elway's career, would seem tough to beat. Some analysts, including Scout.com's Greg Biggins, a guy who spent over a decade evaluating quarterbacks for the Elite 11 staff, said the 2015 class had a chance to become the best crop of quarterbacks the area had ever had. The class's emergence came on the heels of some growing skepticism about the merits of SoCal QBs.

"Since Elway, the quarterbacks from that region have been little more than a series of flops," wrote Jason Cole of Yahoo! Sports in 2013. "While Carson Palmer, Alex Smith, and Randall Cunningham have had solid careers in the pros, they are the best of an otherwise sad group."

The piece, titled "Sorry SoCal story: Abysmal run of QBs from region has NFL personnel searching for answers," detailed a run of duds taken as high draft picks that began with Todd Marinovich (Santa Ana) and Dan McGwire (Claremont) in 1991 and continued in the twenty-first century with Kyle Boller (Santa Clarita); J. P. Losman (Los Angeles); Matt Leinart (Santa Ana); Mark Sanchez (Mission Viejo); and Jimmy Clausen (Westlake Village).

Asked for his supposition on the SoCal QB struggles, Clarkson reasoned they stemmed from the myriad 7-on-7 teams that ended up taking away from a high school program's off-season continuity. "Nowadays coaches are essentially held hostage, because they don't know who is even gonna show up," Clarkson said. "And that's led to a lot of dissension and selfish actions that have caused a rippling effect. In Texas, the high school coaches have a lot more control over their players. The high school association in California is a joke. In Florida and Texas, if you go in there to try to run your own program, you'll get strung up."

The most common theories were that many of these products of the private Southern California quarterback gurus like Clarkson had been coddled, over-programmed, and over-hyped at a key time in their development, which often bred a sense of entitlement. Perhaps because of all that, there was already plenty of skepticism in the college coaching world brewing around the touted SoCal Class of 2015.

Brian Stumpf, who had been scouting talent for the Elite 11 and traveling the country while helping run the Nike football training camps for fifteen years, suspected that many touted Southern California quarterback prospects fizzled out due to a "burnout factor with guys who have been in QB training since fifth or sixth grade and going really hard, and maybe that's pushing some kids away," he said, "because at that point, you really don't even know if they truly like football."

Two of those top-three-ranked quarterbacks were once groomed by Clarkson. Ricky Town Jr., who played at St. Bonaventure in the valley, was originally from Walnut Creek, California, in the Bay Area.

A bio of Town was still up on a DeBartolo Sports website with Steve Clarkson's logo. Town's measurables were 5′4″, 110 pounds—from when he was in sixth grade. Among the info covered in the Q&A, Town said his favorite college teams were Texas and UCLA, and his favorite cereal was Fruity Pebbles.

"I got him to move to Southern California as a seventh-grader," Clarkson said. "He was a regular. He would fly in once or twice a month into Burbank, and he'd stay with me." Clarkson stopped working with Town about three years after he moved from Chaminade High to Bonaventure. "Distance was an issue," Clarkson said. Instead, Town trained with Clarkson's son, Anton, a onetime quarterback at Oregon State, and later with Donovan Dooley, another LA-area QB coach.

Town committed to play for Alabama in the summer of 2013, weeks before his junior season began. However, a few coaching moves shook up his recruitment. First, USC canned head coach Lane Kiffin early into the 2013 season and later replaced him with Washington's Steve Sarkisian. Then, Crimson Tide offensive coordinator Doug Nussmeier left Tuscaloosa for the same position at the University of Michigan. Then, Alabama replaced him with Kiffin. Two weeks later, Town de-committed from Alabama and announced he was committing to USC, which still had a commitment from another 2015 quarterback, David Sills V, who had fallen off the recruiting radar and wasn't ranked by any of the online recruiting sites among the top ten QBs.

Seventeen-year-old Blake Barnett from Santiago High in Corona, California, was actually the first quarterback invited to the 2014 Elite 11 after he won a golden ticket at the January regional held at Santa Monica College. Barnett had spent the previous week training in Arizona, where Dilfer's TDFB protégé Dennis Gile was headquartered. Barnett had been working with Gile since the past summer and considered him like an older brother, he said. Their focus: shortening his release and improving his footwork. "It was mainly in preparation for the Elite 11 camp," Barnett said. "I wanted to be on top of my game for it."

Gile, who had been connected with Dilfer for about a year, has seen his business take off. He had helped groom some standout Arizona QBs, including UCLA star Brett Hundley, Kyle Allen, and Luke Rubenzer—two Elite 11 quarterbacks in 2013—but in recent months he'd seen his profile extend beyond his own backyard. One of his newer clients, he said, was the son of a billionaire in Texas who made his fortune off some sort of pain cream. Another new pupil, who he called the "best eighth-grader I've ever seen," had a dad who "owns a gold mine" in Nevada.

Golden ticket or not, after Barnett's performance at the Elite 11 regional, Gile told the high school junior he didn't think he deserved the invite, that he was trying too hard. "I promise you, he's better than that," Gile said.

Barnett described his selection for the Elite 11 as a relief. "I was getting too nervous and tense," he admitted.

Barnett said that before the start of his junior season, his name "was nothing" and "not relevant at all" in the recruiting world. Then, in the season opener against Brady White's team, Hart High, Barnett threw for 5 touchdowns and also ran for 100 yards. Barnett's team lost, 56–49, as White completed 35 of 46 passes for 471 yards. The game was nationally televised on FOX Sports West, and soon college coaches were coming to Santiago to check out Barnett. UCLA offered him a scholarship a few weeks later, as did Notre Dame, which he said was a perfect fit for him, both academically and athletically. When news of Barnett's commitment to Notre Dame broke around Thanksgiving of his junior season, Clarkson told the *South Bend Tribune* that ND was getting "a kid that comes around once every twenty years with that skill set. He's got a huge, huge ceiling." In the story, it said that Clarkson had been working with Barnett for about three months.

Clarkson's being linked to Barnett riled up Trent Dilfer and Gile, who said Clarkson's game was "just blowing smoke up their ass."

"He's so bitter," Dilfer said of Clarkson. "Now he's going after Gile. Now he's going after George. Now he's going after [TDFB coach] Craig [Nall]. These are my guys. I've chosen these guys for a reason, and I'm gonna defend them to the end.

"Take this Blake Barnett kid. He's really talented, a good kid—

6'4", runs 4.55, he's the real deal, and it's Gile who's been training him, but Clarkson was trying to get to the dad, and now he's taking all the credit for the kid going to Notre Dame."

Asked if he'd worked with other private quarterback coaches before, Barnett's reply was, "No, not really." He said he only threw with Clarkson two or three times and did so because it was "in the middle of the season, and I just wanted to get some extra work in, and he was out here. It's local, and it's not a six-hour drive to go to Arizona."

Barnett acknowledged that "it was awkward for a little bit" that Clarkson's name was attached to him, especially given the young QB's relationship with Gile and knowing Gile and TDFB's animosity toward Clarkson.

Clarkson knew he had become a target for many rivals, especially as more and more private quarterback coaches entered the business. He cited the recent *60 Minutes* profile as validation, as if it was some form of a prime-time televised audit. "They're looking into every nook and cranny, and if they find that you're not truthful, you'll get roasted," Clarkson said of *60 Minutes*.

"You don't call *60 Minutes*. They call you, and usually it ain't good. When they called and said they wanted to do this story, I felt comfortable. I had nothing to hide. I gave them carte blanche to do what they needed to do. They started to see these younger kids, and then the question became, 'How young is too young?' Well, the market has really changed, and I saw this six or seven years ago. When I first started, I usually didn't get kids till they were sophomores and juniors in high school. But now, with all of these camps and combines and things like that, for the most part, if a kid is not good enough by his junior year, it's already too late for him. And if he is good enough by his junior year, they already spend so much time traveling on that circuit, they really don't have time to train as much. So your work is really done by that point. Nowadays, I really don't take kids who are juniors anymore, because if you gotta come to me at that point, it's probably too late."

Clarkson said the criticism and comments from rivals were laughable. "I'm probably one of the few guys who still teaches a guy at a young age and brings him up," he said. "Now we're in the 'Day of the

Instagram Coaches,' as I call 'em, where they can get a photo op with the guy, and the next thing you know, they're responsible for the guy being the first pick in the draft. That I find hysterical.

"Let's look at *Elite 11*, for example. I encourage my kids to do it if they can do it. I just try to temper their expectations. 'Look, there is some seriousness, but there is also a show element to it. At any time you can't have just eleven great guys. It's a show. There's always the guy no one else could find or no one knows. They have to be the ones who 'discover' him. That's just the way it is. And then, there's gonna be a guy who is really good, but he's gonna come out of there not as good. If you go through the Elite 11, and the top eleven are who everybody expects them to be, then how is that a show? Is it anything that we didn't know? Andy Bark is a friend of mine, and he started that a long time ago, and I'm a supporter of it. But in that process, he'll have coaches who'll coach a regional camp, and they will watch a guy take a few reps, and then they'll take a few pictures with him, and the next thing you know, they 'coach' him. I understand that.

"A lot of these guys—Dilfer and everybody else—they have platforms that were built on networks. If you put him on ESPN, and he's an analyst, then all of a sudden, he has the biggest platform of all—the four-letter network. I built a platform that essentially built their platform. When we started back in 1986, none of [those coaches] would even be here. That's the way we look at it. I'm probably the only guy who has his own platform based all on his own, not having millions of viewers to help get them started."

Not all the TDFB guys viewed Clarkson in a negative light. "I've never met him," said Jordan Palmer. "Therefore, I have nothing against him. All I know is, I heard he made $600,000 off one quarterback over a four-year period. He's helped a lot of guys have success, though. Matt Leinart won a Heisman and two national championships."

Whitfield and Clarkson had only crossed paths once, at a park where both happened to be training quarterbacks. Whitfield described the meeting as brief and cordial. Clarkson and Dilfer have actually never met, Clarkson said before adding, "But I heard he hates me. You'd have to ask him."

Dilfer and Clarkson did share a mutual friend—Perry Klein. The gymnast quarterback, who was Clarkson's first client, was also big into the volleyball scene, the same as Dilfer, who happened to be taken in the same draft Klein was.

After the NFL, Klein returned to Southern California and joined the family business, Classic Components. He still kept in touch with Clarkson. He has observed how the business that technically wasn't a business when he was the first protégé had boomed. He's also noticed how some others have "basically stolen Steve's act" and have networked better, he said. "But, to take a raw guy, turn him into a legit quarterback—I don't know if any of these other guys have done it," Klein said. "Steve's done it more than once. The problem with Steve, though, is that he's too boisterous. It's hard for him to take direction.

"Everything I know about playing quarterback I learned from Steve. The one thing I think he hampered is that he made the game very simple. Guys complicate it, so it looks like they're doing something way above. In the end, I had bypassed a lot of steps, and then I struggled to learn the basics later on—the steps that Steve skipped. I had to learn how to take a snap when I got to college.

"Steve is overselling the dream. Every dad thinks their kid is gonna be in the NFL. They all believe in it. And when that dream doesn't happen, and he moves on, people feel slighted."

To some around Los Angeles, Perry Klein was still "infamous," he said. He realized that after he took his kid to pre-season, and someone asked him 'Are you gonna transfer pre-schools?' Now, Klein got why, because no one else back then was transferring around the way he was or getting the publicity he did. He vividly recalled how a news copter flew over his house one day to report on his story and how people talked about him as "this rich white kid taking advantage of these inner-city kids. On top of that, I was cocky back then and didn't think of the ramifications. Maybe Steve even liked it: 'Any publicity is good publicity.' "

A SLEEPY-EYED, 6′4″ KID in a Vans hat and mid-calf-length socks with Lakers great James Worthy's picture on them watched the first Elite 11 regional of 2014 from the sidelines. This was the quarterback Dilfer's staff most hoped to see throw; however, Josh Rosen was nursing a shoulder injury that he'd played through while leading St. John Bosco to a 16–0 season and the California state championship weeks earlier.

Yogi Roth, the former USC-assistant-coach-turned-Pac-12 Network-announcer/Elite 11 staffer, had scouting reports made up from his own film study on all the top quarterbacks going into the event. Among his notes on Rosen: "Deals off platform . . . Textbook mechanics . . . 'SoCal Personality' . . . Franchise guy . . . Had Macklemore on his highlight tape."

However, due to Rosen's ailing shoulder, the Elite 11 staff had to wait two months to see him work in person. By the time the top prospects on the West Coast gathered for the Nike Football Training Camp at Redondo Union High in early March, Rosen had generated more buzz than any recruit in the country. One offensive coordinator at a Top 25 program who had been to one of Rosen's games said he already threw better than some NFL quarterbacks he'd seen. Rosen's pedigree was also a curiosity on the recruiting trail. Both of his parents were champion ice dancers. His mom, Liz Lippincott, a six-foot-tall Princeton grad, comes from the Wharton family—as in Wharton, the University of Pennsylvania's prestigious business school. Rosen's dad, Charles Rosen, a six-foot-two Penn grad, is a prominent spine surgeon.

Most interesting of all: Unlike nearly all the other touted QB prospects, Rosen hadn't spent hundreds of hours by the side of any personal quarterback coach. He actually hadn't spent any time with them at all. His mother had heard stories about how David Sills V made his pilgrimages from the East Coast to see Clarkson and thought it was "ridiculous." Besides, she said, Josh had ended up with perhaps an even better method of honing his skills as a quarterback.

By the time he was six, Rosen had been immersed in the world of competitive tennis. His parents took him to a weekly private lesson and for two other regular workouts. On weekends he had tournaments. At age ten, the pace of his tennis training had already escalated, and so had Rosen's profile on the youth tennis circuit. By twelve, he was the number one ranked player for his age group in Southern California and was top fifty in the country, known in the tennis community for his blazing 105-mph serve and his creative game. The USTA was pushing for him to enter its Player Development program, where many of the kids his age end up being home-schooled.

As much as the kid loved the idea of not having to go to school, he didn't like the idea that he'd be leaving his friends behind. He already had been active playing basketball and baseball on the side with his buddies. Rosen kept training in tennis, but he wanted to "stay a normal kid," his mom, Liz Lippincott, said. A friend's parent, who was a local Pop Warner coach, asked Lippincott to let him play football. Many of his other friends lobbied him to play, too. Rosen told his mom he really wanted to try football.

"I just thought he'd try it and get it out of his system," she said. "But then I saw this other person emerge. He was so into it, and after the season was over, he asked, 'Mom, can I do another season?'"

Rosen admitted he did better than he'd thought he would at football. "At that moment I felt like I should probably pursue it," he said.

On the courts, though, Rosen still excelled, but he was growing weary of the lonely tennis lifestyle. His older sister had emerged from the rigors of tennis and become a top player at Emory University, but he grew to resent the sport. "Football is a cakewalk compared to tennis," Lippincott said. "It's tough on the body, because the repetition is relentless. It's year-round [training]. We had a whole summer of flights and national tournaments, and finally he just said 'Yuck!' and quit it cold turkey."

Rosen was invigorated by football. "The misery ended" was how he described leaving tennis behind. "Tennis was a tough time for me, but then I came into my own. A lot of this [football] recognition is pretty nice. It is just a really fun sport. You're bringing all these people to a game instead of just your parents. It's just a different energy."

His arm strength turned the heads of other kids and high school coaches. He was recruited to Southern California high school St. John Bosco and was so impressive quarterbacking the Braves' JV team as a freshman that Fresno State offered him a scholarship. Rosen's mom is convinced his skill set as a quarterback was actually honed by those thousands of hours on the tennis courts.

"It immediately transferred with the accuracy, footwork, and focus," she said. "How many backhands and volleys did he have to put into the back corner? The amount of time they spent in shot-making and training for pinpoint accuracy is incredible. And I'm so thankful for that."

Tom House, the biomechanics whiz, agreed with Lippincott's take. He has his own example of a budding-tennis-star-turned-QB—his own first football protégé, Drew Brees. The New Orleans Saints star used to beat Andy Roddick when they were tykes in the Texas tennis youth scene.

"The best carryover from tennis for quarterbacks is the footwork and the durability of the shoulder capsule," House said. "The footwork for a tennis player with angles, distance, and time translates really well for a quarterback."

Rosen laughed about the irony. Every tennis coach he'd ever gone to told him he had terrible feet and how much they needed to quicken him up. Then again, that's when he was being compared to all these 5'3", 110-pound kids he towered over. "So, all of a sudden, I come to football, and everyone's going, 'Aw, you have amazing feet. You can set up. You can re-set. You can move in the pocket so well.' It definitely carried over, because tennis is all footwork."

The psychological grind from competitive tennis also can prove quite an asset, too, House said. "It's center stage, like a golfer or a pitcher or a quarterback, where the last two are team sports, but they're individually based. When you screw up, there's no place to hide, so you have to deal with it. And the kids who learn to 'fail fast forward,' they get over the fact that failing is a bad thing. Failing can actually be a good thing. You learn as much or more from failing as you do from winning."

However, growing up in the culture of such an individually based sport can create its own challenges in the transition. "In tennis you have to be extremely self-centered," Lippincott said, adding that kids like Josh get accustomed to "the lonely life of tennis and traveling on planes with his mother," whereas in football it's a culture of "bro love and so many people telling you you're great."

Those factors can create a pretty combustible mix. After a strong debut season with the Bosco varsity, Rosen, then a sophomore, was recruited by some older teammates to join the Snoop Dogg All-Stars off-season 7-on-7 team. His second tournament with the squad ended with the Snoop team getting disqualified in Vegas after a bench-clearing brawl. "Usually coaches and parents would be there to try to break up the fight," Rosen said, "but in this one, they were coming in swinging." Rosen's team won every other tournament they entered.

"It was a very interesting experience," he said. "I saw a different side of football and learned how to relate to a lot more people. I definitely gained more cockiness after I hung around all the Snoop Dogg All-Star kids. I learned how to play with their sense of swagger. I think what people may see as arrogance is really me just having fun with the game. A lot of what ruined tennis was, I took it way too seriously, and I took myself way too seriously. All my friends were my enemies [on the court]."

To some coaches, the big concern—perhaps the only real concern—surrounding Rosen was his "DQ." Before his junior year of high school, he went to football camp at Stanford, which had been his dream school. He wowed the Cardinal coaching staff with his ability to throw the deep ball. One coach thought Rosen threw it better than any high school kid he'd ever seen. They liked that he was football smart, too, but his personality rubbed them the wrong way.

Would he fit in with the rest of the team? Could he one day lead the program? Word was, Cardinal head coach David Shaw had his doubts. And, for as much as Rosen wanted a scholarship offer, it never came from Stanford.

"I'm too confident for my own good at times," Rosen said. "Sometimes I do come off as arrogant in interviews or whatever, but I feel like that's also part of what makes my play what it is."

Rosen admitted that he's learned plenty about sharpening his psyche from his tennis roots. His self-talk, which sometimes showed up in his quotes, sounded straight out of Dilfer graduate-level curriculum, only it had gone beyond the realm of such self-talk: "I am confident when I get on the field that a defense cannot beat me, that I am going to beat them with my mind. They cannot run the right play. They will not be able to stop our offense, because the second you start to doubt yourself is the second a defense starts to win. I definitely use it to my advantage. In tennis, I serve and volley every single play, because I feel like in any match that I lose, the opponent didn't win it. I always lose it, because I feel like it's my game to lose."

What exactly happened between Rosen—an A student and consensus number-one-ranked QB—and Stanford took on a life of its own in recruiting circles, as message-board fodder often does. His mom rolled her eyes at some of the wild speculation that she'd heard and read. She admitted, though, that Josh needed to be more humble and more careful with his words.

"Let's just say he has too much confidence," she said. "He has a big personality. It's overwhelming at times. He's very smart and can think real fast. Sometimes, he forgets that all these people are around. His heart is in the right place; he just gets carried away."

A few minutes before the Elite 11's second tryout in Southern California began, it sounded as if Josh Rosen had one of *those* moments: "I'd like to try to get the Elite 11 invite," he said, just as the other QBs began to stretch. "I think I'd have to mess up pretty badly for that not to happen."

Weeks later, when asked about his brash-sounding quote, Rosen didn't seem fazed by his no-filter response.

"Yeah, I probably said something dumb like that," he said with a chuckle.

His competition that day included Brady White, Ricky Town, Travis Waller, and Blake Barnett. In the stands, Rosen's mom sat next to Town's dad, watching all the action on an eighty-degree day. Rosen, like the rest of the quarterbacks, struggled early, getting his timing with the random receivers he was throwing to. However, by the middle of the workout, his arm—and his nimble footwork—had the coaches gushing.

"He throws it better than any kid we've seen in two years," Roth said.

The coaches selected him as the MVP of the event and invited him to the Elite 11—even though Trent Dilfer wasn't in attendance to give his seal of approval.

"I think his physical tools are perfect," Roth told me days after the event. "When I hear dudes skeptical of his physical tools, I think, 'God, do I know what I'm talking about?' I think his physical tools are awesome. I don't know what Troy Aikman looked like in high school, but I bet this is what he looked like. The ball rips out of his hand. He's got a frame. On tape, he's athletic.

"You are gonna have to put him in conflict situations to see who he is. We didn't do that. But what we did do is, we got to know his personality. I don't think he's trying to be 'the number one quarter-back in America.' That's why I like him. I don't think he's trying to be anything. I don't think he knows better. He's just a kid from Manhattan Beach. Really smart parents. Got some cash. Knows he's good. Likes to compete. That's all I got. I can't wait to put him through a two-minute drill and freak out on this kid. Just to see what happens when someone's breathing down on his neck. Can't wait to see how serious he takes it. If he's truly a great one, there are no other choices. You're either competing, or you're not."

The skepticism about whether Rosen really loved football surprised Roth after watching the QB work out and interact with the other players. "I liked his personality," Roth said. "I think he's got Dude Qualities to him, but I think he needs someone to develop him. But, if that's the case [that he doesn't truly love the game], then he won't make it. You have to be a football junkie. At some other positions you can get by. Maybe this goes back to that California thing, like how many of these guys *really* need it?"

Rosen's reaction to the skepticism about whether he loved football: "I think that's a weird thing to say.

"I went from a sport that I quit because I didn't love it, and I learned a lesson, because I did not like the sport, and that's what ruined it for me. Why would I go to another sport that, deep down, I also don't like? Maybe I'm not thrilled to go to practice every day, but I love the sport of football. I love winning, and I love putting massive, obnoxiously large state rings on my finger."

He said he took pride in helping put his high school, a longtime underdog in its league, over the top to win a championship. After he announced that he would be staying in Southern California to attend UCLA, he said he hoped he could do the same for the Bruins.

• • •

WHITFIELD, LIKE DILFER, MISSED seeing Rosen's showing that earned him the golden ticket. Whitfield had to stay down in San Diego, where a dozen college quarterbacks had flown in that day to spend their spring breaks training with him. Johnny Manziel and Logan Thomas, both pleased with their workouts at the NFL Combine, were also in the final stages of prepping for their individual Pro Days. Among the college guys in town were 2014 Heisman Trophy–contender Baylor QB Bryce Petty, as well as starters from the Pac-12 (Arizona State's Taylor Kelly) and the ACC (North Carolina's Marquise Williams and Virginia's David Watford), and Jerrod Heard, a member of the 2013 Elite 11 class who was expected to help resurrect the Texas program. The vibe was different than that of a typical week of Whitfield's NFL draft camp. He brought in a DJ setup ten yards from the edge of the field blasting hip-hop; had all his interns in color-coordinated matching shirts and shorts; and rented two vans, which he referred to as "Tank 1" and "Tank 2," to shuttle the players around in.

This part of the private quarterback coach business had taken off in the past two years, especially for Whitfield. He hosted groups of college QBs for week-long gatherings from spring into the start of the summer. It was a by-product of the NCAA not allowing college coaches to be hands-on with their own players in skill development in the off-season, and of QBs seeing the "extra" work other guys around the country were getting. And of Whitfield's growing celebrity in the football world. Later in the year, Whitfield had a week during which he brought in sixteen college QBs, including two from Tennessee who were competing for the Vols' starting job. Neither kid realized the other was coming out to San Diego to train with Whitfield till the first session of the week. Whitfield also lined up guest speakers ranging from NFL greats John Lynch and Marshall Faulk to veteran QB coach Dana Bible, a Bill Walsh disciple who helped develop unheralded recruits Matt Ryan and Russell Wilson into stars. Their talks circled back in one fashion or another to perseverance.

Brandon Harris, the strong-armed Louisiana kid who the Elite 11 passed over in 2013, was one of the quarterbacks to spend a week with Whitfield, just days after Anthony Jennings, the guy he's battling for the vacant starting job at LSU, trained with the QB Whisperer. Harris was using the Elite 11 snub as motivation. "It does hurt your pride," he said. "I'm not gonna lie. I'm a completely honest person. I saw guys who I knew were better than me. I saw some guys who are great quarterbacks—Kyle Allen, Jerrod Heard—but I saw some of the guys who made the cut over me. . . . Well, it's fine, I'll grow from this. It's added some fire to me; I'm gonna play with it. I am going to prove these guys wrong. Ray Lewis spoke to us at LSU when I first got there. He said Mel Kiper said he was undersized. Ray said, 'One day I'm gonna make that guy apologize to me.' Well, I think the same thing is gonna happen for me. I'm not saying it's gonna happen at the NFL Draft. It could be when we win an SEC Championship or down the road when I'm up for a Heisman Trophy, but I think [Dilfer's] going to apologize to me and say he made a mistake."

Another reflection of the growth of Whitfield's rep: the level of blowback he was receiving from competitors. On one of the days when he had the sixteen college QBs with him, former NFL quarterback Jeff Garcia, now a private coach, showed up at the same high school field in Del Mar to train a protégé. Whitfield moved his group over so Garcia had some field to work. Then one of Whitfield's interns showed him snarky comments Garcia had made about him online. Whitfield grabbed the intern's phone and took it over to Garcia, who initially backpedaled from the tweets, but then challenged Whitfield on his coaching credentials as compared to his own NFL pedigree.

"That was great," Whitfield said. "And we cheered for you, but I don't think you understand that this is a different realm. You know Andy Reid never played quarterback, and I know Coach Holmgren never played in the NFL, and those guys are celebrated as some of the best coaches in football."

Garcia brought up having to share a panel once on NFL Network, where Whitfield was IDed as a "Quarterback Guru."

"That was bullshit," Garcia said.

"Listen, you're gonna get everything you work for in this arena, but you coming at me isn't gonna help," Whitfield said before walking back to his group.

Whitfield scheduled his spring-break QB camp in two groups that started at 8:00 a.m. in two different locations on the University of California at San Diego campus. Before Manziel and Thomas's daily sessions started, Whitfield called on them to play guest lecturers.

"Come on in here, Leonidas," Whitfield yelled over to Manziel as he strolled in five minutes after Thomas arrived.

"Between the two of 'em, they've had every experience a college quarterback could possibly have," Whitfield said before introducing Logan Thomas and Johnny Manziel to the college quarterbacks seated on the ground in a semicircle like Cub Scouts around a campfire. "They've both been booed, cheered, celebrated, and written off."

David Watford, who was actually in the same recruiting class as Manziel, asked him about the biggest change he'd made during that first time visiting Whitfield almost exactly two years earlier, which helped him win the A&M starting QB job.

"I just needed confidence," Manziel said. "I just wasn't happy with how my spring went. We picked one thing that I really wanted to work on, and that was keeping my left elbow tucked in so I could drive the ball harder."

Whitfield reminded the QBs that any time they bought something—even if it was only a pack of gum—to make sure they kept the receipt to keep their school's compliance people—and potentially the NCAA—happy. He was also candid speaking about Thomas and Manziel's own challenges in front of them as their Pro Days approached.

"Logan's biggest thing is consistency," Whitfield explained, "because he was inconsistent, so it's what he left on tape. With Johnny, some people question, 'Can he drop, and can he drive the ball, and can he play in rhythm?' A lot of the stuff they work on isn't sexy enough to write cover stories on. That's why we got the hood up and we're working on the engine. These guys are now like racehorses three days before the Kentucky Derby. They're agitated."

Another one of Whitfield's guest speakers during the week for spring break was Trent Dilfer, who showed up on Tuesday after spending Monday in Carlsbad with Jordan Palmer, to check out his draft camp with Blake Bortles. Dilfer walked around observing the various stations Whitfield's staff had set up for all the college QBs.

He stood, arms folded and beaming, as he watched two sets of quarterbacks throwing the ball to each other from twenty yards apart with both knees on the ground. "If you're doing it wrong, your body's going to fall forward, and you'll have to catch yourself," Dilfer yelled. Or the quarterbacks would, literally, fall on their faces.

The drill was one Dilfer had actually come up with at the end of his career after hearing his old QB coach Jim Zorn talk so much about the rotational nature of a throwing motion. Dilfer, being as big a student as he was of the golf swing, saw the correlation with what he noticed on super slo-mo video of how elite quarterbacks' bodies moved and their "hip-shoulder disassociation."

"When people say the feet are the most important thing, I always say they are one of the most important things if they work in conjunction with the rest," he later said. "If you're only talking feet, you're ignoring what I'm seeing on film from every great passer: They have the ability to disassociate their upper half from their lower half, because you can't guarantee your offensive line's protection. You can't guarantee where you can put your feet, but you can guarantee what you can do with your upper body.

"There always has been the one-knee-down drill that people have taught forever. I saw the flaw in that. That's not how the body moves, from what I'm seeing on tape. With one knee on the ground, you still have some lower-body control. With the knee that's up, those cleats are in the ground, and you can manipulate it. If I put my right knee down and left knee up, I can activate my left hamstring and still feel my lower half moving. With both knees on the ground, my hamstrings are completely relaxed, and I have to torque my left shoulder underneath my chin. I have to rotate my core to generate any type of speed. Not only that, my right elbow has to work backward, not up, and my left arm needs to work with it, since my left thumb is tucked underneath my Dri-FIT. It was a way of simulating the proper biomechanics when the feet aren't involved."

The muscular Watford, while still on his knees, asked Dilfer's advice about a mechanical issue he'd been trying to solve for years, where his left arm—his front arm—drives down too much in his throwing motion.

"Get your shirt on," Dilfer told him.

Dilfer's response wasn't about a show of respect, but rather about providing Watford with a prop for a little trick the old quarterback had taught himself. Dilfer had learned from his old mentor Jeff Tedford about how vital the left arm was in the throwing motion. Tedford, years after coaching Dilfer at Fresno, turned an underachieving Kyle Boller into a first-round pick after coming up with a contraption tying a shoestring to the strong-armed QB's wrist up at Cal. Dilfer had developed a mechanical flaw with his own left arm. He tried Tedford's shoestring method. He also tried using a bungee cord from his garage, but with all the surgeries he'd had on his upper body, nothing seemed to work. Then, in the mid-2000s, when Dri-FIT gear became the norm, Dilfer got the idea to stick his left thumb under the collar of his Dri-FIT shirt and realized he'd found his solution, because it kept the quarterback's motion compact.

"This is the best thing I've ever done," Dilfer said. "I started experimenting with it on kids, especially when you can put them on their knees and take their feet out of it. Your feet can make up for a lot of things. So you take their feet out of it, then you take their left arm and put it in their jersey so that it feels natural and it works. We call it being 'matched up.' It matches them up with their rotation. It's the best of both worlds. I found it to be the number one of stroke mechanics—the thumb under the jersey, on their knees—because it's teaching them the proper right/left arm synergy."

After ten minutes of trying Dilfer's Dri-FIT thumb trick, Watford was sold. "Now I have to get more Dri-FIT shirts," he said.

Two hours later, Dilfer stood in front of a classroom with Whitfield to his right and each of the college quarterbacks seated in the first two rows of chairs. His speech was similar to the one he gave to his Elite 11 quarterbacks. It was about his journey and what he'd learned about quarterbacks and what each of the best ones had told him they believe is the most vital quality for success.

"The most common response I've gotten is confidence," Dilfer said. "One of the reasons I'm so passionate about quarterback development—whether it's at the grassroots level, the college level, or the NFL level—is because it's about building the confidence muscle. The 'secret sauce' really is confidence, and when people say you either have 'It' or you don't, the 'It' is really confidence."

Dilfer told the young QBs about how he used to get "claustrophobic" when he moved up in the pocket. "I'd be thinking, 'Oh, crap, I gotta get out of here!'" He credited hours and hours in the squat rack to strengthen his base, as well as hours of practicing while in traffic high in the pocket, for remedying that mind-set. But it was his entire perspective as an NFL quarterback that he said still kept him up late at night.

"The reason I invest so much time in you guys and in my coaches is because I don't want you to go to bed at night thinking, 'I could've done so much more.'

"My initials are 'T. D.' They should be 'I. N. T.,'" Dilfer said, shaking his head, eliciting laughter from a few of the quarterbacks. "I threw 129 interceptions in the NFL. That's a lot. Two things about that: Somehow, I kept my job throwing 129 interceptions, but I also set the NCAA record for most passes without throwing an interception—318 during my junior season. That record stood for almost twenty years. In college, my coach, Jeff Tedford, he was super-positive with me. We never talked about making mistakes. It was about having an attack posture with a conservative mentality. 'Make good decisions! Make perfect throws!' That's how I was spoken to, and it translated. I was a dominant college player. I went to the NFL, and I played for really negative, conservative coaches. It was always, 'Don't take a sack! Don't throw a pick! Be careful!' It was all the negative talk. So I started talking negative with myself. So, 129 interceptions later, I'm going, 'What happened to me?' Positive self-talk is huge. When you start going negative, bad stuff happens."

Before Dilfer wrapped up his forty-five-minute Q&A, he ended up talking about his mission of trying to overhaul the way quarterbacks were developed, sharing his own education about leadership that was taught to him by a much younger teammate the season after he won a Super Bowl.

"I'm pretty sure I'm the only quarterback who won a Super Bowl, was a free agent, and was not re-signed by his team," he said. Dilfer signed with the Seahawks late in training camp because he waited to scout out his best opportunity "to knife the guy who is supposed to be ahead of me."

Seattle had just traded with Green Bay for Matt Hasselbeck, who had no NFL starts but had been "anointed the guy" before Dilfer was signed. The atmosphere in the QB room when Dilfer arrived "was very uncomfortable," he said. "Matt and I had a very contentious relationship the first couple of weeks, and two weeks into it, I'm the dude. We're back in Seattle getting ready for Week One, and he said to me, 'You know what? I just spent three years with Brett Favre. That's the greatest leader I've ever seen. He's not the most-liked guy but the greatest leader. You've led this team in the two weeks that you've been here, and it's been about you. It hasn't been about anybody else. You know what Brett Favre does? He knows everybody's name in the building. Brett Favre. He's won three MVPs in a row.'

"Matt says, 'I'll follow you when you know everybody's name in this building.'

"It was pretty profound. I had to look at myself in the mirror. I thought, 'That dude is right. I've got a lot of juice. Just won the Super Bowl. I just took this guy's job. But I wasn't leading the guy who was in the room with me every day.' So I went to work. I got one of the PR books. And if there wasn't a picture of somebody, I went around and took his picture. I learned every single person's name in that building. It was a great lesson."

# 12.

# THE DRAFT

On March 19, Merril Hoge, a former-NFL-fullback-turned-football-commentator, dove face-first into the Johnny Manziel debate that was about to become Tim Tebow 2.0 for the football world.

"I see 'bust' written all over him," Hoge said on a *SportsCenter* appearance, "especially if he's drafted in the first round." Hoge's blunt comments made a splash around the Internet, and around his own network, which kept trotting out the forty-nine-year-old running back for more versions of his Manziel take that got more biting with each new visit.

"His accuracy is questionable," Hoge said on a later show appearance. That claim actually seemed questionable, given that Manziel was the third-most-accurate passer in college football in 2013, completing 70 percent of his passes. Even ESPN's own research data noted that Manziel completed 74 percent of his passes from the pocket in 2013, highest among all quarterbacks in major college football. Manziel also wasn't prone to just relying on shorter passes, as several other QBs in the 2013 draft were. One out of every four passes he attempted from the pocket traveled at least 15 yards downfield, where he completed 55 percent of such throws—which was best in the SEC and more than 15 percentage points better than the norm in college football.

"I think he has a pop-gun arm," Hoge continued. "He doesn't translate to the National Football League. He's clearly not a first-rounder. And, if somebody does draft him in the first round, their job is gonna be in jeopardy immediately, because he will not be able to withstand the expectations that are going to be put on him, because his skill set will not handle it."

Hoge's analysis of Manziel's NFL prospects was also rooted in skepticism about whether he could develop into a capable pocket passer and that he didn't understand pass protection.

The former was something Manziel had spent two seasons working to improve with his coaches at A&M and with Whitfield. Still, it was a valid concern about whether the kid could rewire his instincts to flee the pocket to go make a play. The latter—fair or not—wasn't what he'd been asked to do at A&M and was something he had been taught only in the previous three months while at Whitfield's draft camp in San Diego.

"I don't think it's fair criticism at all," said Kliff Kingsbury, a onetime former NFL quarterback who was Texas A&M's offensive coordinator in Manziel's freshman season. "And I'm pretty sure they're not going to put the protections on him as well. I know they want him to go out there and use his God-given ability, which is pretty exceptional, to make plays. And that's what we wanted to do with him, to free his mind and allow him to check us into the right play and just play the game."

The issue of Manziel's preparation became an interesting subplot in football circles about ultimately how much responsibility, if any, should be on the college coaches to get their player ready for his transition to the NFL, much as it eventually was with Tim Tebow after the former Florida Heisman winner struggled in his pro career. New University of Texas defensive coordinator Vance Bedford tried to use the opportunity to take a swipe at the Aggies' staff when he tweeted: "Manziel is a top 10 pick by the scouts. I wish him the best. He played backyard ball for 3 years. Now he will have to learn how to be a Qb"

Whitfield hopped onto *SportsCenter* to offer his own retort: "I understand [Bedford] has an opinion. I'm just surprised he has time to tweet about it, given the Longhorns' task at hand with their defense."

Kingsbury didn't buy the notion that college coaches should balance their responsibility to their players when it came to getting them ready for a potential jump to the NFL.

"You're trying to win games at that level and go from there," he said. "We're trying to win right now with what we've got by all means necessary, and as far as preparing a kid for the next level, their level of play is going to do that, and when they get to the next level, that coach there is going to mold them and shape them however he needs them to play in his system. We're just in the here and now."

Manziel's agent, Erik Burkhardt, fired back at Hoge via social media, tweeting: "I see @merrilhoge achieved his goal of being relevant this week. Same guy who said Rodgers was "a wasted draft pick" & Luck shouldn't go #1"

That reference was to a previous on-camera Hoge assertion that he was sold more on Brian Brohm, a second-round pick by Green Bay in 2008, than Aaron Rodgers. Hoge's colleague, ESPN draft analyst Todd McShay, took a similar stance, saying Brohm had more "upside" than Rodgers. (The Packers waived Brohm after one season before he spent two seasons with the Buffalo Bills, where he didn't throw a touchdown, before bouncing around to the United Football League and the CFL.)

One veteran NFL coach called the Hoge rant "so predictable. It always seems like Merril Hoge or Jaws [Ron Jaworski] doesn't like the guy who isn't the prototypical guy. There's some wild-card draft guy, and they have to be the guy to come in and shoot him down. I try not to take much of that into account, and we say that to the players, too, not to worry about that stuff."

The interest in the NFL Draft has spawned a legion of "draft experts" in the past five years. You can pretty much find someone somewhere who either loved or hated every prospect in the country. And for every time they've been proven wrong on an evaluation, they've probably turned out spot-on on several other occasions. Hoge, to his credit, also had predicted that former college greats Vince Young and Tim Tebow would be flops as NFL QBs—and both were cut within five seasons. In 2011, NFL Network's draft analyst Mike Mayock touted Missouri's Blaine Gabbert as his number one QB prospect ahead of Cam Newton, saying Gabbert is "the one quarterback in the draft who, if you've got to bang the table for a franchise quarterback, he's the guy." McShay also called Gabbert the best QB in the draft class. The number ten overall pick in the 2011 draft by Jacksonville, Gabbert lasted three seasons with the Jaguars before being traded to San Francisco for a sixth-round draft choice. Newton, taken first overall in the draft, won NFL Offensive Rookie of the Year honors and was selected to the Pro Bowl in two of his first three seasons.

Dilfer acknowledged that his own evaluation skills were sorely lacking when he first started doing TV for ESPN. He admitted to being fooled by QBs he believed would be stars. He's also proud to say that he was "the only analyst in the business who had a first-round grade on Nick Foles in 2012." (Mayock had Foles evaluated as a fifth-round pick.) The Arizona QB went to Philadelphia in the third round and became a Pro Bowler by his second season after setting a league record with a 27-2 TD-INT ratio.

"I got made fun of when I said [Foles] should be a first-round pick," Dilfer said. "I read a lot on him about the adversity he went through and how he was coached at Arizona. Talked to people about him, although I never felt totally convinced on his intangibles, but I loved what I saw on film. From his instincts, to playing in conflict, to his being a natural passer, to his stature, and for being a limited athlete, he does a really good job of creating space and time for himself. He was brilliant on the move. He also had some basketball background. All those things added up for me to say he should be a first-rounder."

Dilfer's opinion ran counter to Hoge's about Manziel, saying the Texas A&M star actually "has high-level NFL instincts."

"Johnny's überconfident on the football field," Dilfer said. "He does some really dumb stuff. He also does some of the greatest stuff I've ever seen on a football field. He makes mistakes, but it doesn't change the way he plays the next play."

Hoge's rants about Manziel came forty-eight hours after Teddy Bridgewater's Pro Day. It was expected to be an impressive performance—quarterbacks' Pro Days almost always are, since they're so scripted. Bridgewater credited his private QB coach Chris

Weinke, the former Heisman Trophy winner, for getting him to use his legs more in his delivery. "I was just an arm-thrower before," Bridgewater said.

Both NFL Network and ESPN had TV crews on site to broadcast the workout. Representatives from twenty-nine teams turned up at the Louisville indoor facility for a closer look. Scott Turner, the Vikings' new quarterbacks coach in attendance, noticed something curious as soon as Bridgewater started warming up. The QB wasn't wearing gloves, as he did during the football season. Turner and his dad, Vikings offensive coordinator Norv Turner, were both perplexed.

"I didn't understand why he didn't wear 'em," the younger Turner said later. "He played in 'em, and he's gonna play in 'em. It's not like it's illegal or anything. If you're comfortable doing something, why would you change it?"

How much, if any, impact throwing without the gloves had on Bridgewater was hard to gauge. He misfired on several throws in the 65 passes he attempted. Eight passes were incomplete. Two of those were dropped by his receivers. The juice on many of his passes left several observers underwhelmed.

Mayock, who, going into the NFL Combine, had Bridgewater as his number one QB in the 2014 draft, said—after Louisville's Pro Day—that he would not take him in the first round. "I've never seen a top-level quarterback in the last ten years have a bad Pro Day, until Teddy Bridgewater," he said. "He had no accuracy, the ball came out funny, the arm strength wasn't there, and it made me question everything I saw on tape, because this was live."

Bridgewater later elaborated on his decision to go gloveless on Pro Day to Jon Gruden on his *QB Camp* show: "When I was training leading up to the Combine, I was back home in Florida—nice weather. I went back to my high school days—no gloves.

"I learned a valuable lesson that day. I had a few balls that got away from me, and, like I said, I was able to learn walking away from there that just do what got you there. If you're comfortable with the gloves, continue to wear the gloves. So everywhere I go, I make sure I carry my gloves with me."

Bridgewater's modest frame—he weighed in at 208 pounds (6

less than he did at the Combine)—also elicited some carping from anonymous NFL personnel types questioning the twenty-one-year-old's durability. That skepticism came in spite of the fact that Bridgewater only missed one start in his college career—and in that game he came off the bench to lead the Cardinals to a victory. Or that he played through a broken wrist and a severe ankle sprain in other games. Or that he withstood a vicious, head-rattling shot from a Florida linebacker that knocked his helmet off, and Bridgewater still popped up and proceeded to carry Louisville to an upset win over the number four Gators in the 2013 Sugar Bowl.

Blake Bortles's Pro Day, orchestrated by Jordan Palmer, came two days later—a few hours after Hoge started dissecting Manziel. Nearly every NFL franchise had a rep at UCF for the show. Bortles displayed his refined mechanics, most notably the UCF star's improved balance and base and a quicker release. Gone was his propensity to load on his back leg as he maneuvered from a variety of three-, five-, and seven-step drops. Later, in his 65-throw workout, Bortles overshot a couple of receivers, which he acknowledged occurred because in season he had underthrown a few deep balls.

"It went well," Bortles said. "I thought I showed the things I wanted to. Showed movement, that I fixed the footwork that were flaws on film. Obviously, I had a couple throws I'd like to have back, but that's going to happen when you throw 65 balls."

MARCH 27, 2014.

Manziel's Pro Day had a different vibe from Bortles's and Bridgewater's—and from any other Pro Day a quarterback prospect has ever had. The night before, Whitfield was frazzled after finding out that someone had posted the script, or, at least, an early version of it, for Manziel's workout online. Whitfield figured the culprit was someone who worked at the local Office Max, where he had made copies earlier in the day.

"Luckily, we didn't have any real notes on there, and we had some real notes," a relieved Whitfield said about twelve hours before Manziel arrived at A&M's indoor practice facility.

ESPN and NFL Network both had three-man crews on sets near the field providing analysis of the Manziel show. Aaron Rodgers provided some analysis of the analysis, tweeting: "2 of the 3 guys commenting on this workout right now have opinions that shouldn't be taken very seriously"

Rodgers didn't specify which crew he meant: the NFL Network trio of Paul Burmeister, Mayock, and Super Bowl MVP Kurt Warner; or the ESPN grouping of Ed Werder, Todd McShay, and former NFL exec Bill Polian.

Whitfield had flown in many of his San Diego crew: Kyle Bolton, a short but fast former NAIA wideout; NFL-backup-QB-turned-private coach Kevin O'Connell; Hank Speights, a former Division III lineman/Whitfield protégé who acted as Manziel's snapper, since one of the points of emphasis was to show how adept the QB was with his footwork from under center—something Manziel didn't have the opportunity to show in A&M's system. Seventh-grader Chase Griffin, Manziel's little pal, also rode over with his dad to help out as a ball boy.

Asked if he took off the day from school to attend the Pro Day, the thirteen-year-old replied, "Teachers all know why. It's Texas."

Eight NFL head coaches and general managers came to A&M to see Johnny Manziel work out, as did former President (H.W.) Bush and his wife, Barbara—and their dogs, along with Secret Service agents. The Bushes arrived in a golf cart driven by one of the Aggie recruiting staffers. Manziel arrived as his pal Drake's music blared throughout the complex as a crowd of about five hundred watched from the perimeter. Decked out in camouflage shorts, a black Nike jersey with his white Number 2 (the Aggies are outfitted by Adidas), Manziel provided another wrinkle from the Pro Day norm by wearing shoulder pads and a matte black A&M helmet.

"You play the game in shoulder pads on Sundays," he explained. "Why not come out and do it? . . . For me, it was a no-brainer."

Whitfield later said the idea stemmed from a conversation he and Manziel had prior to the Combine. Manziel had asked Whitfield, "What do NFL personnel people respect?"

"People respect a challenge," Whitfield said.

"So, what more can we do?" Manziel asked.

"Make it more like an interview. If you're going to Wall Street, you wouldn't wear a T-shirt and shorts. You'd put a suit on."

The helmet and pads were Manziel's business suit. His performance on the field was sharp, too, completing 62 of 65 scripted passes. Two of the incompletions came on balls that hit receivers' hands, while Mike Evans actually caught the other incompletion, but he was out of bounds. On several occasions Whitfield chased after Manziel with his broom as the QB deftly evaded. Several scouts admitted they were wowed seeing Manziel's ability to use his entire body like a whip to generate power while throwing the ball on the move.

"Most quarterbacks struggle throwing the ball down the field when rolling to their weak side, but Manziel didn't show any issues throwing the ball on the run to his left," said NFL.com's Bucky Brooks, a former scout for the Seattle Seahawks and Carolina Panthers. "In fact, he repeatedly delivered gorgeous teardrops on vertical throws following improvised scrambles or redirections from the pocket. This is clearly one of the strengths of his game, and his quarterback coach [Whitfield] made it a point to highlight it throughout the workout."

One NFL assistant noted only one flaw—that sometimes Manziel threw a flat-line, low-trajectory ball on intermediate routes over the middle. In all, he threw 49 of the 64 passes he attempted from within the pocket, with the other 15 coming via rollouts and simulated escapes—with Whitfield's script showing a level of emphasis on the kinds of throws many were skeptical Manziel was comfortable making. Manziel threw 21 passes off a three-step drop, 18 off a five-step drop or play-action, and 10 from a seven-step drop. He concluded the workout with a long completion to Evans and yelled "Boom!" drawing applause from the crowd in attendance.

Manziel's workout left many, including Kurt Warner, raving.

"Most guys can make the short throws," Warner said. "Most guys can make the intermediate throws. How do you make those deeper throws? Do you throw them the right way, and that's the thing that impresses me—he threw the ball the right way. I don't care if you just get a completion; I want to see it thrown the right way. His deep balls, great touch, great trajectory. The deep plays he made on the run, and I know how difficult that is to keep your body balanced while you're running away from something and being able to put the ball 45 yards downfield on the money. Those things don't happen every day. Twenty of the [NFL's] starting quarterbacks can't do those things. He was doing something consistently that not very many guys do. I was very impressed."

Ron Jaworski, who a month earlier said he wouldn't draft Manziel in the first three rounds, called the workout "magnificent," saying he saw tremendous improvement in the QB's mechanics.

Whitfield was probably the most relieved guy at A&M that day. After all, his star pupil wasn't the only one in front of the football world; he himself, the "QB Whisperer" from Dime City, was, too.

"We took a lot of time trying to lay out that script," Whitfield told a group of reporters. "Every throw in that deal is part of NFL offenses and concepts—from the footwork to the reads to the eyes. The thing he's been challenged so much about is, what people aren't really willing to give him is, he can be a systematic player. Everybody thinks he has to work off script and he's a jazz artist. He can read sheet music. We tried to iron out some Mozart out here, and, hopefully, people's ears caught it."

WEEKS LATER, CHIP KELLY described Manziel's decision to wear the helmet and shoulder pads as "interesting."

"I know one thing he did it for," the coach said. "It makes him look bigger. I was surprised that no one ever said that. I thought it was a really smart idea, and, along with that, it makes a ton of sense, since he's also going to throw in pads."

Kelly, the former Oregon coach to whom Manziel was once committed, probably attended more Pro Days in 2014 than any other head coach in the NFL. Given how the NFL coaching calendar is set up by the league, where staffs aren't allowed to do anything with their players for months after the season, Chip Kelly was surprised more head coaches weren't on the Pro Day circuit.

"I don't know what everyone else does," he said. "What are you doing in your office? We had January and February to do all our self-scout stuff, and Pro Days aren't till the middle of March. I just want to know more about the guy. You can look at the film, and you see the athletic part, but you want to see the mental part. The physical differences in this league aren't very different, but the intangibles and the intelligence are the difference, I think. That's why one guy makes it and one guy doesn't."

At the collegiate level, Kelly demonstrated his keen acumen for evaluating talent, especially quarterbacks. His was the first major program to go all-in for Manziel, and that same year, his Ducks also were ahead of the curve on Hawaiian Marcus Mariota, even though he'd yet to start a game as a quarterback. In his debut season in the NFL, Kelly was a big believer in Nick Foles, an unproven second-year quarterback.

"I'd seen Nick at Oregon," Kelly said. "I don't think people realize how big Nick is. He's 6'6", 240 pounds, and he's athletic for that size. The biggest thing I marveled at when I coached against him was how tough he was. We hit the crap out of him, and he just kept getting up and making plays. Didn't matter what was going on. You never felt like they were gonna be out of the game with him throwing the ball."

The New Hampshire native said he doesn't buy that there is any one specific quality that predicts greatness at the position, other than saying the intangibles are huge. "I don't know how to quantify it. I think it's what separates good from great. Trent [Dilfer] sees it, since he's going to Elite 11 and knows that guy's pretty throwing the ball, but it's going from routes-on-air to one-on-ones to 7-on-7 to 11-on-11 to making it live. And that list of quarterbacks starts to shrink, and it comes down to the intangibles. It's like art. It's tough to describe why it's a great painting, but you just know it when you see it. That's why their paintings are worth millions of dollars and why others are sold on a street corner.

"It's so tough to really quantify exactly what sets apart Tom Brady, who was a sixth-round draft pick and became a Hall of Famer, from other guys who were top-five picks and they don't make it. There's not a hard and fast way to subjectively say, 'He has to be this or have this.' It's the one position in the NFL where the height and weight range drastically. If you're an offensive lineman and you're not over six-foot, you're not playing in the NFL. I don't care how many intangibles you have. But the quarterback position has the biggest range of physical characteristics. And it's the most important position in the NFL, and it's all over the map as to what can win. That's what makes it so interesting. How do you predict the success of Russell Wilson compared to Ryan Leaf?"

As much as Merril Hoge and many TV draft analysts harped on their doubts about whether Manziel could handle playing the game from inside the pocket at the National Football League level, veteran personnel actually sounded more concerned about whether Johnny Football could cope with life off the field, and some of those extended beyond him being just some boozing Alpha Bro.

"Manziel's greatest strength is that he truly believes that he is unstoppable and that he can find his way out of anything," said one NFL scout. "But his greatest weakness—and the thing that scares the shit out of people—is also that he truly believes that he is unstoppable and that he can find his way out of anything. All the drinking or even if he's smoking pot wouldn't scare me. It's the kid's total reckless personality and God knows what else that'll lead to. Nothing with that kid would surprise me."

The football world, in its zeal to fit Johnny Manziel in a box and find an apt comparison, kicked into overdrive after the Combine. To some, he was like Brett Favre. To others, he was Fran Tarkenton or Doug Flutie or Jeff Garcia or Russell Wilson, who one NFL coach was convinced that Johnny definitely was not. People met Russell Wilson and got blown away by his maturity. He was first-guy-in, last-guy-out. Manziel, according to some scouts, was the opposite.

"Russell had a really good understanding of what he is and what he's about," said the coach. "That's the million-dollar question with Johnny: What is he gonna be like? Are the outside distractions and the other things gonna be an issue? That's not a question with Russell."

Aside from being unconventional quarterbacks, the one thing Favre, Tarkenton, Flutie, Garcia, and Wilson had in common: none were drafted in the first round.

Manziel's habits—on-field and off—left many NFL person-nel people with scrunched-up faces, pondering exactly what they would be investing in. "There was so much stuff that you had to sort through it," said one NFL coach. "You had to find out about the kid, because—for a lack of a better term—there is his celebrity lifestyle. Is he gonna be the first guy in, last guy to leave, because in this league, at that position, you need a guy to be like that. It was pretty fair to research that, because there were some [red] flags. We were comfort-able with him. Football is important to him, but even so, you really never know. What somewhat concerns you is that football has come pretty easy to him in his life, but no matter who you are, football is not easy in this league.

"I think that Johnny's a better passer than Vince Young, but Vince was one of the best college football players who's ever played. He just tried to play in the NFL on raw ability, and that only gets you so far. The league always catches up with you, no matter who you are."

The same coach had a much less favorable opinion of other highly regarded QBs in the draft class. He was enamored with Derek Carr's ability to throw the ball but was troubled by how the Fresno State QB played his worst when pressured or when facing the stiffest competi-tion. Alabama's AJ McCarron, who had led the Crimson Tide to two national titles, set off red flags in his meetings with teams.

"He was very quick to blame other people," said one NFL QB coach. "He was very sensitive and defensive." The assistant also said that that attitude, which he saw as a potential locker-room headache, was reflected by some comments McCarron published on his Twitter feed.

The reaction to Whitfield's other client in the draft, Virginia Tech's Logan Thomas, was even harsher: "I just don't think he's a quarterback," said the coach. "He's big and a great athlete, and he can throw the hell out of the ball, but he's so inconsistent and inac-curate on film. I don't think he's good enough to play. Can you really improve his accuracy? That's the hardest thing to fix. Deep down, I don't think you can. And it takes him a while to make decisions. He has a tendency to hold the ball, even at the Senior Bowl. You can be a smart guy, but if your mind doesn't work fast on the field, then that's something that's hard to fix."

As biting as some of those comments and rumors could be, the most eye-catching quote of all in the 2014 draft cycle came in a pair of tweets from Bleacher Report's NFL Draft analyst Matt Miller:

"I present you with the greatest QB comparison ever. An AFC North coach compared Bridgewater to . . . Willie Beaman. I'm not making this up.

"Said coach re: Bridgewater, "He's a dynamic playmaker, but is he the guy you want running your offense? They're very similar."

Don't recall watching Beaman play in the NFL? Well, that's because he doesn't actually exist. Never did outside of a 1999 film directed by Oliver Stone that centered around the fictitious Miami Sharks of the Associated Football Franchises of America. Beaman is a third-string QB-turned-star played by Jamie Foxx. The Beaman comparison—as bizarre as it was—was just one of a host of comments touting Bridgewater's seemingly plummeting stock.

Two weeks before the draft, Mayock dropped Bridgewater from being his number one ranked QB to number five. "What I'm hearing is two things," Mayock said on NFL Network. "Number one, when we saw him throw live, we didn't see arm strength and didn't see accuracy. Number two, when you draft a quarterback in the first round, you expect him to be the face of your franchise; you expect him to embrace the moment. I think people had some concerns about whether or not this young man is ready to step up and be the face of a franchise."

Matt Richner believed that Mayock had it all wrong. The thirty-two-year-old Richner saw Bridgewater as the top QB prospect in the draft class and the only one worthy of a first-round grade. Richner ranked Johnny Manziel fourth, behind Georgia's Aaron Murray and Alabama's AJ McCarron. He gave Blake Bortles a fifth-round grade.

Like many around the game fishing for an apt metric or barometer, Richner was hoping to leave his fingerprints on some next-level insight into football, much like the *Moneyball* and sabermetrics crowd did with baseball and, to a lesser degree, in basketball. Richner is an analyst for the website PredictionMachine.com. According to his bio on the site, he also has produced statistical draft reports for six NFL teams, but he said a confidentiality clause prohibited him from saying which ones he worked for, adding that he was paid only "a few thousand dollars." His day job was as a financial analyst in Seattle for a 3-D printing company.

Richner worked as an intern for the Seattle Seahawks during the 2008–09 season, not in the scouting department, but rather in PR. He never played football. At 5′8″, 130 pounds, he said he wasn't built for the game. Instead, he played soccer, but he always loved football. His love for stats took root when he was nine. His parents gave him the *Sports Illustrated Almanac* as one of his Christmas presents.

When Richner joined the Seahawks, one of his assignments was to help clean up their basement, as the franchise's offices were being moved to a different suburb twenty miles away. Richner was gathering up old scouting reports and draft reports from the '90s for the garbage. He couldn't help but read some of them.

"I just kept looking through it, thinking, 'Man, this is such arbitrary stuff: 'high motor' . . . 'violent hands' . . . 'Gets up for big games.' How do you quantify that?'" Richner said. He broke down old play-by-play recaps of games to gather his data. He did a large portion of his Master's thesis on how to use the stats he compiled to help filter out future draft busts. He offered his findings to the Seahawks personnel people and to Mike Holmgren's coaching staff.

"I can show you why Ryan Leaf and Kyle Boller were draft busts," Richner told them. He had ID-ed ways to use certain stats to show what a guy is and what he isn't. And, since much of it was based on situational football, which is part of every coach's DNA, it gave the Seattle staff something to think about. Gil Haskell, the Seahawks' offensive coordinator, became a believer in Richner. "He's really good," said Haskell, who was in his late sixties when he met Richner. "His way of looking at the game is completely different. I would hire him tomorrow in my scouting department. I tried to get (NFL head coaches) Andy Reid and Mike McCoy to hire him."

It took Richner ninety minutes to catalog his play-by-play stats for one season of a college QB, he said. One of the metrics Richner emphasized was a quarterback's completion percentage on third downs.

Richner cited onetime five-star recruit Jimmy Clausen, the QB Steve Clarkson once compared to LeBron James, as a testament to his metrics. The Carolina Panthers used a second-round pick on the former Notre Dame quarterback in 2010. Richner had pegged Clausen as undraftable. His teams at Notre Dame didn't win many games. On the surface, Clausen's numbers in his final season at ND—a 68 percent completion mark and a 28–4 touchdown-to-interception ratio—were sterling, but upon closer scrutiny Richner noted just how much the QB struggled in clutch situations. He completed 74 percent of his passes on first down, 69 percent on second down, but just 52 percent on third down—a staggering drop for a guy supposed to be a top prospect.

"The best thing Carolina did was draft Jimmy Clausen, because he was so terrible that they were able to get Cam Newton the next year," Richner said.

The year Newton went number one overall, the guy many of the other draft analysts touted as the top QB, Missouri's Blaine Gabbert, got a big red flag from Richner. The reason: In Gabbert's final season at Mizzou, he completed 71 percent on first down, 68 percent on second down, but his accuracy plummeted to just 44 percent on third down. In his final two seasons, Gabbert also faced five ranked opponents and threw just 4 touchdowns and 6 interceptions in those games.

Richner red-flagged another first-rounder that year, Washington's Jake Locker, who completed 55 percent on first down, 62 percent on second down, and just 51 percent on third down in his final season for the Huskies.

As Richner broke down the numbers for 2014, Blake Bortles reminded him a lot of Gabbert.

On first down, Bortles completed 71 percent of his passes, 75 percent on second down, and 54 percent on third down. Worse still, Bortles's UCF team only played four ranked teams in the previous two seasons. In those games, he threw half of his eighteen career interceptions.

"Most of the elite quarterbacks who have been drafted in the last couple of years, (Andrew Luck, RGIII, and Russell Wilson) did not see this significant of a drop in their completion percentage on third down," Richner wrote in his draft report on PredictionMachine.com. "Russell Wilson, in his lone season at Wisconsin, completed 71.7 percent on first down, 71.8 percent on second down, and 75.3 percent on third down. The great quarterbacks don't have a significant drop in production, and none of them were anywhere close to having a 50 percent completion rate on third down.

"The inconsistent nature of Bortles's play on third down and his careless decisions against tougher competition would make me worry about drafting him. While he has the frame and stature that most traditionalists are looking for, I believe he lacks the fundamental consistency needed to be a top-level quarterback in the NFL."

Richner's top-ranked QB, Teddy Bridgewater, completed 68 percent of his passes and had a 14-to-1 touchdown-to-interception ratio on third down. "He is everything you like," Richner said.

Manziel, whom Richner had ranked fourth, was actually a shade behind Bridgewater on third-down percentage at 67.

"Johnny's the enigma of this draft class," Richner said. "He holds on to the ball too long, at over 3.5 seconds (per pass play). A good quarterback—the Peytons, the Bradys, the Rodgers—they get the ball off in about 2.5 seconds.

"After doing a lot of the research on it, I always thought it was kind of funny. We criticize all these running backs and wide receivers because they run 4.5 or 4.6, and people are like, 'Oh, my God! They're a tenth of a second too slow!' But here's Johnny Manziel, and he has to shave a full second off his decision making? I don't see that happening."

The ability to get rid of the ball quickly, which Richner defines as "Snap to Pass" or which UK-based metrics site ProFootballFocus calls "Time to Throw," is a newer barometer Richner has begun incorporating since his days in Seattle. In the NFL in 2013, according to PFF, Denver's Peyton Manning had the fastest average time to unload the ball, at 2.36 seconds. Andy Dalton was next at 2.43. Tom Brady was 2.46. For comparison's sake in 2011, the year Tim Tebow was the starting QB when the Broncos went to the playoffs, his average release time was 3.65 seconds, nearly half a second slower than the next-slowest passer, Michael Vick. That Tebow stat, after having observed his subsequent quick exit from the NFL, seems incandescent.

Then again, the risk of reading too much into the Snap to Pass stat is that among the quarterbacks who measured the slowest in the NFL for 2013 were the guys best known for their scrambling ability: Kaepernick (3.08), Newton (3.09), and Wilson (3.18), plus Foles (3.11), considered four of the best young QBs in football, with each having led their teams to the playoffs in 2013.

ONE OF THE TWO teams that didn't have any representative at Johnny Manziel's Pro Day was the Cleveland Browns, the same franchise that had trotted out twenty different starting quarterbacks since 1999 and the same one that, according to ESPN's Sal Paolantonio, outsourced a study of the quarterback position that cost $100,000.

The project began under former Browns' president Joe Banner, but wasn't actually completed till after he was let go by owner Jimmy Haslam in February. According to CBS and ESPN, the study concluded that the best quarterback prospect in the draft was Teddy Bridgewater. Cleveland had two picks in the first round, at number four and at number twenty-six.

About three weeks before the draft, the Browns' brass—first-year general manager Ray Farmer, first-year head coach Mike Pettine, offensive coordinator Kyle Shanahan, and quarterback coach Dowell Loggains, also in their first seasons—went to College Station. They met Manziel and his reps, Erik Burkhardt and Brad Beckworth, for dinner on a Friday night.

An 8:00 a.m. Saturday workout was scheduled so everyone could be home in time for Easter Sunday. Unfortunately, no receivers showed up to run routes. Mike Evans and Travis Labhart, the Aggies' two most reliable targets, were actually out of town that weekend. Worse still, the Browns didn't even have a football to throw until they were able to get one out of the back of someone's car. Instead,

Manziel was stuck throwing to Burkhardt, Beckworth, and an old high school buddy.

Asked how the Browns workout went, one member of the Manziel inner circle described it as "a shitshow."

"I guess it's why the Browns are the Browns."

MAY 8, 2014.

Draft Day came with a wave of trade rumors, as had become the norm. Only the drama had been ratcheted up even more. The NFL had squeezed out two more weeks of hype by pushing the draft back to early May. Also, there were more buzz-worthy players in the mix. The 2013 NFL Draft had been unusually low-wattage, with the top two prospects being offensive linemen—one from the Mid-American Conference, Central Michigan's Eric Fisher; the other, Texas A&M's Luke Joeckel. The 2014 group had a charismatic, freakish talent in South Carolina defensive line prodigy Jadeveon Clowney—who was also polarizing, as questions surrounding his work ethic had been swirling for the past year—and three touted quarterbacks. The *Houston Chronicle* reported that the Houston Texans, who held the first pick, would either select Clowney or Manziel. Or they might trade the pick. Longtime *Chronicle* writer John McClain, who had the Texans taking Manziel with the first overall pick in his mock draft, was so sure Houston would take a quarterback in the first round that he said he would eat the front page of his newspaper if the Texans didn't.

The 2014 draft would also feel bigger than ever, since a record thirty prospects had accepted the NFL's invite to attend. Among them were Clowney, Bortles, and Bridgewater, and three Texas A&M Aggies: offensive tackle Jake Matthews, wide receiver Mike Evans, and Manziel.

Attending the NFL Draft at Radio City Music Hall in New York City feels like equal parts game show and pro wrestling card with its hissing fans, clunky intros, and emotional families hanging on every move. Inside the greenroom, agents and business managers nervously kept checking their smartphones, hoping for any kind of intel.

Clowney was drafted first. Erik Burkhardt, Manziel's agent, had told people in their inner circle that the Rams were poised to grab Manziel, but instead St. Louis took Auburn offensive lineman Greg Robinson second. Jacksonville, with a need for a QB, went third. Manziel had felt really good about his connection with Jaguars head coach Gus Bradley. The Jags did take a quarterback—Bortles. Cleveland was up next. The Browns were in the market for a quarterback, and the team's brass really liked Redskins backup Kirk Cousins but were unable to land him. Instead of going for Manziel or Bridgewater, the Browns opted to trade the fourth pick to Buffalo, which took Clemson wide receiver Sammy Watkins. The Raiders—also rumored to be eyeing a QB—drafted Buffalo linebacker Khalil Mack. The next two picks were both Aggies, but it was Matthews and then Evans. When the Rams came back up with the thirteenth pick, Manziel thought he would be their guy. After all, he'd had arguably his best workout for them, and he knew they'd spent as much time researching him as any team had. But instead, they drafted defensive tackle Aaron Donald from Pittsburgh.

Dallas was coming up at number sixteen. Could his buddy Jerry Jones, the Cowboys' fickle owner, resist picking Manziel, especially since his starter Tony Romo's back ailments left his future in doubt? An hour earlier, as Manziel was sliding out of the top eight, it seemed as if Jones would've gnawed off one of his arms for the shot to bring Johnny Football to Cowboys Stadium. Then, when their pick came up and no other player in the greenroom reacted as the Cowboys' allotted time ticked away, it gave the Manziel camp hope that it might be him. Instead, Dallas selected Notre Dame offensive lineman Zack Martin, who wasn't in attendance.

"There's just too much dynamic here for him, for the franchise, for everybody," Jones later explained about bypassing Manziel. "That's just too much for insurance, and it's not the usual development guy behind an accomplished quarterback. He's a celebrity. He's Elvis Presley."

Manziel had unofficially become the "free-fall" guy that every NFL draft seems to have, stuck in front of the cameras, while watching as everyone else giddily springs up from their seats and embraces family and friends to escape the greenroom. Even the NFL's official Twitter feed mocked Manziel after the Cowboys became the latest team to pass on him, tweeting: "#SadManziel???"

In the buildup for each pick, ESPN's Jon Gruden stumped for Manziel, which only kept the spotlight on the QB even more. According to Deadspin, ESPN mentioned Manziel's name a total of 113 times on its telecast of the first round, which was more than that of the top five draft picks combined. All Manziel could do was guzzle yet another bottle of water while trying not to look exasperated before the national TV audience.

"Even the best poker player wouldn't have been able to play that off," said Whitfield, who watched his protégé withstand one gut-punch after another from ten feet away in the greenroom. "I felt for him. Bortles's going number three was a shot in the stomach, then the Browns traded out of the fourth spot and then up, taking a corner [Oklahoma State's Justin Gilbert] at eight. Tampa ends up taking Mike [Evans], but that makes sense, and it's his teammate, so he's happy for him. But then Minnesota is up at nine, and they take a linebacker [UCLA's Anthony Barr], and then there was Dallas."

The NFL, mindful of the awkward dynamic of sitting on camera for hours waiting for your name to be called, had set up an alternate greenroom with no cameras allowed. NFL reps eventually asked Manziel if he'd be more comfortable in there waiting out the process, but he repeatedly declined. Then, when Manziel got up from his seat, a hovering TV producer radioed back to his booth, thinking Manziel was retreating to the "dark" greenroom to escape the camera's glare.

"Hey, he's just going to the bathroom," Whitfield told the producer. Sooner or later all that water he'd been chugging had been bound to catch up to him.

Whitfield tried to spur some activity, texting Dowell Loggains, the Cleveland Browns' thirty-three-year-old QB coach: "Let's go!"

"Coach, I'm trying," replied Loggains, who had built a relationship with Whitfield over the previous few years and had even tried to have the quarterback from his previous stop with the Tennessee Titans, Jake Locker, work with the private coach.

Then, Manziel sent his own text to Loggains: "I wish you guys would come get me. Hurry up and draft me so we can wreck this league together."

Loggains forwarded the text to Mike Pettine and to Browns' owner Jimmy Haslam, adding, "This guy wants to be here. He is texting us. He wants to be part of it."

Loggains, days later, re-told Arkansas radio host Bo Mattingly that Haslam's response was: "Pull the trigger. We're trading up to get this guy."

The Browns, set to pick at number twenty-six, traded a third-round pick for the chance to swap picks with the Philadelphia Eagles, slotted at number twenty-two, so Cleveland could slide in front of the Kansas City Chiefs as chants of "JAH-nee, CLEVE-land . . . JAH-nee, CLEVE-land" swirled around Radio City Music Hall. The move was made so they could select Manziel, who finally ended up hearing his name announced two hours and forty-three minutes into the draft. He walked across the Radio City stage to greet NFL Commissioner Roger Goodell, saluting the cheering crowd with his two-handed, finger-rubbing gesture that most have come to know as the "cashin' out" move. Manziel became the first sub-6' quarterback selected in the first round (or even second round) by an NFL team in sixty-one seasons since 5'10" Ted Marchibroda was taken number five by the Pittsburgh Steelers in 1953.

The behind-the-scenes action by the Browns to draft Manziel was almost as compelling as the story ESPN reporter Sal Paolantonio told. Jimmy Haslam, according to Paolantonio, said, "I was out to dinner recently, and a homeless person out on the street looked up at me and said, 'Draft Manziel.' "

Evidently, the homeless man or Manziel's text message had more of an impact on the Browns' draft decisions than did the $100,000 advanced-metrics study they had outsourced.

"This is a great day for me, something I've thought about since I was a kid, since I was twelve years old watching the NFL Draft, and I dreamed I would be in that room, on that stage, one day," Manziel said near midnight. "My dream came true. For me, there is no disappointment."

As for his home-state Dallas Cowboys passing on him, Manziel joked, "I don't know if the world could have handled that, honestly."

Johnny Manziel wasn't the only prominent quarterback who had a prolonged wait in the greenroom. Teddy Bridgewater looked as if he might fall out of the first round, but Minnesota traded up to the number thirty-two pick to get him. "You know the thing I like the most about him? He wins," Vikings coach Mike Zimmer said of Bridgewater. "Everywhere he's ever been, he wins. Starts as a freshman in high school, wins. Starts as a freshman in college and wins. This guy—he's got something about him."

The day before the draft, the Vikings had watched the tape of Bridgewater's so-called disappointing Pro Day and came away thinking the criticism was overblown. "He throws such a catchable ball, and he makes such good decisions on film, and that was such a big thing for us," said Scott Turner, Minnesota's QB coach, who noted that Bridgewater's issues surfaced whenever he slowed down his drop from center and whenever he didn't follow through on his throws, which caused balls to either sail on him or dip.

Whitfield's other QB, Logan Thomas, ended up being chosen by the Arizona Cardinals in the fourth round, ahead of AJ McCarron, Georgia's Aaron Murray, LSU's Zach Mettenberger, and Clemson's Tajh Boyd. Whitfield was elated.

"Perfect spot for Logan," Whitfield said.

The Cardinals' coach, Bruce Arians, loves big QBs and had helped develop Ben Roethlisberger in Pittsburgh and Peyton Manning and Andrew Luck in Indianapolis. Arians, himself a onetime Virginia Tech quarterback, said Thomas has "probably the best arm I've worked out in ten years." Arians also admitted to putting up a "smoke screen" the day before picking Thomas, when he said Arizona had no interest in taking a quarterback.

"I lie pretty good," Arians said. "I didn't want anybody jumping in front of us."

AROUND CLEVELAND, THE BROWNS were dealing with being the talk of the NFL. Season-ticket sales were flooding in. The morning after

Johnny Manziel was drafted, a billboard went up in midtown Manhattan of a close-up shot of the former Texas A&M quarterback in a Browns jersey. The caption: FOR ONCE, DEFENSES KNOW WHERE HE'S GOING.

But a bigger question still remained: How well would Johnny Manziel's magic work in the NFL?

JULY 11, 2014.

Much changed in the few months after Trent Dilfer, George Whitfield, and Johnny Manziel were together on the same turf: the *Elite 11* TV show landed an Emmy nomination in the Edited Special category. TDFB became a part of Dilfer and Steve Stenstrom's latest vision, a "forward-facing platform" called QB Centric that touted itself as "The Forum for All Things Quarterback." There was also a new darling of the Elite 11 staff: Baylor's hulking QB Bryce Petty, who wowed everyone—including the Army Rangers and Navy SEALs who Dilfer brought in to administer his first big challenge to his young QBs—with his grit and resolve up in Oregon. In fact, Petty so impressed Command Sgt. Maj. Todd Burnett, the leader of a grueling six-and-a-half-hour training session, that Burnett approached the 6′3″, 235-pound Texan and said, "I don't get easily impressed, but I'd go to war with you," before handing the quarterback his own hat as a sign of respect.

Dilfer's staff had hoped former Elite 11 MVP Jameis Winston would return as a counselor, in part so they could counsel him after the FSU star's latest off-field incident—being cited for shoplifting $32 worth of crab legs from a Publix supermarket. Winston, however, was busy back home in Alabama, where two cities were honoring him with "Jameis Winston Day."

Perhaps the biggest sign of just how big this QB "cult," as Dilfer called it, had become came on the third day of the 2014 Elite 11. ESPN.com ran a two-thousand-word story about little Chase Griffin, its thirteen-year-old ball boy. NFL.com had its own feature on Griffin one day later. "*That* proves my point about how big this thing is," Dilfer said.

On the same day ESPN ran its feature on Griffin, the Internet buzzed about a picture of Manziel tightly rolling up a dollar bill in a bathroom. The photo—and the accompanying speculation about Manziel's party lifestyle—was picked up by bloggers and mainstream media in the Charlie Sheen–like coverage of the Cleveland Browns rookie QB. The picture even jolted many Manziel defenders who had shrugged their shoulders at shots of him partying poolside in Vegas with Rob Gronkowski and chugging booze from the bottle while sprawled out on an inflatable swan weeks after the draft.

A few hours after the bathroom photo surfaced, Manziel showed up back in Oregon, wearing a Chicago Bulls hat turned backward, to check out the Elite 11 QBs and to take part in a Q&A in front of the 160 blue-chip football prospects at the opening ceremony of "The Opening." He was the new face of Nike Football. The subject of the bathroom picture never came up, but it was discussed plenty around the Nike campus.

Dilfer faced his own challenge at the 2014 Elite 11. A college coach told him that one of the eighteen invited high school QBs, Josh Rosen, might be the most talented quarterback he'd seen in the last ten years but predicted that within three days the kid would drive Dilfer crazy.

Rosen's display of skills on the Nike campus was as advertised. The recruiting reporters along the sidelines gushed about his arm. Dilfer, though, wasn't as effusive. "He's big, strong, and supersmart," Dilfer said of the former tennis prodigy who listed his off-the-field hobbies on his Elite 11 profile as guitar, beach volleyball, cars, and astrophysics. "Josh makes the very difficult look so easy, but he also makes the easy stuff very hard."

Rosen barely made it into Dilfer's final Elite 11, ranking eleventh, which raised the ire of UCLA fans—Rosen had verbally committed to the Bruins in March 2014—and a few of the online recruiting analysts as well. Before the camp wrapped up, Dilfer told reporters that, "what Josh has to learn before he takes the keys over to a major college program is that it's not about knowing more than the coach; it's about doing it the coach's way."

"His issue is that he's so freaking smart, and he's been told that the right way to play quarterback is defense-centric, and you react off defenses. That's just not true," Dilfer told me after the Elite 11. "He just didn't buy into the Axon or the playbook, but in the end, he played so bad doing it his way that he finally just admitted he wished he would've done it differently. He probably got as much long-term out of it as anybody."

Yogi Roth, who was part of Rosen's five-man group the first night of the Elite 11's military challenge, was Rosen's biggest advocate in the war room. Roth asked the five-star quarterback the question he posed to all the young QBs at the end of the week: "What's the biggest thing you learned?" Rosen answered, "I need to listen better."

"This dude was the man in our group," said Roth. "He led when he was asked to lead. He followed when he was asked to follow, and when our leader wasn't leading, that's when he stepped in. I think he's got DQs for days."

Roth's prognosis of the biggest thing that Rosen must overcome as a QB? "I think it's called being seventeen," Roth said. "I don't think he even understands what self-awareness is. I think [most of these young quarterbacks] are just trying their best to be 'awesome.' It's our job to grow their strengths and identify areas that need to be developed. In Josh's eyes, he's been through a lot in terms of competitive settings and being the lone wolf. That's what he's going to naturally gravitate to, 'I gotta figure it out because I'm by myself.' His team was him, his parents, his (tennis) coach, and his trainer, and that's it."

Blake Barnett, the former Notre Dame–committed QB who had switched to Alabama, won the Elite 11's MVP honors, leading his team to the 7-on-7 title at The Opening. He and Rosen were two of the five Southern California products to make the top 11, along with Travis Waller (third), Brady White (fifth), and Ricky Town (eighth).

Town, the kid who Steve Clarkson got to move, with his family, from Northern California down to the Los Angeles area in seventh grade so he wouldn't have to fly down a few times a month for his training sessions, struggled mightily early in the week. Nearly every pass he threw looked like it was being thrown into a stiff wind. Town's 7-on-7 team in The Opening's tournament lost all four of its games in pool play, but the next day something changed. His team went 4–0. Both Dilfer and Roth were stunned to see such a turnaround, not just in the way Town threw the ball, but in how the dour guy who had arrived in Oregon had become so upbeat. "I'm finally having fun," Town told Roth.

Dilfer broke down into tears when he looked Town in the eye and told him he had made the final Elite 11.

"You are the reason we do this. In my years of doing this, I've never been more proud of one guy," Dilfer said.

Town, despite his lofty recruiting status, had actually been one of the last quarterbacks awarded a golden ticket to Oregon. "His regional workout sucked," Dilfer said. "But his high school game film was really good."

Set to play at USC, Town had initially committed to Alabama, which didn't hurt his stock with online recruiting analysts. One site, 247Sports, touted him as the nation's number one overall prospect, a fact that only opened Town to more criticism when he struggled—a dynamic that made him press even more.

"Ricky had the greatest week an Elite 11 kid has ever had," Dilfer said. "He told me, 'Thanks, coach. This week has changed my life. The breathing [exercises he learned from high performance psychologist Dr. Michael Gervais]. The perspective. This is the best thing that has ever happened to me.'

"Ricky is everything we stand for. It's helping kids reach their potential, and unlocking something in them. At the beginning of the week in Oregon, there was just no juice in his soul. No juice in his arm. It seemed like the ball weighed thirty pounds. Like he had a thousand pounds on his shoulders. Burdened. This was a kid who was suffocated by the blue-chip recruiting attention, and it wasn't his fault. The day after the Elite 11 was over, I ran into some old USC alum, and he's telling me about Josh Rosen and Ricky Town as if he knows anything. He just regurgitated a bunch of bullshit that he had heard from the recruiting sites. I just looked at him and said, 'You know, *this* is what's wrong. What you're saying right now is exactly what's killing these kids.' A bunch of pencil-jockey ex-lawyers who know nothing about quarterbacks are defining who these kids are to the general public, and these poor kids, their parents, and their coaches don't have any choice but to listen to it. And some of the colleges recruit off of it. I'm as sick as I've ever been after seeing what it's actually done to some of these kids. I just think it's really toxic that they're being labeled at such an early age and their identity is wrapped up in it. It's really sad."

Rick Town Sr., admitted he'd been concerned about the emotional pounding his boy was taking leading up to Oregon.

The kid had come back too soon from getting his knee scoped. "Ricky was about 60 percent," his dad said. "He couldn't use his lower half to push off. He said, 'I feel like I'm not living up to expectations,' and that worried me.

"He came back from the Elite 11 and told me, 'this has changed my life,' and it has. All of his coaches at St. Bonaventure said, 'this kid has drastically changed.' His leadership has gone to a whole new level. Before, he really didn't talk much except when he was on the field. The Elite 11 unlocked something in him for sure. They gave him new tools to separate himself as a person from what he does."

Town wasn't the only one whose life has been turned upside-down by what had been happening with the Elite 11. Dilfer, in his forties with a net worth well into eight figures from his long NFL career, had actually experienced quite a metamorphosis, too.

"Having watched how Trent has changed with the Elite 11, in terms of how these athletes are growing up emotionally and intellectually, I truly believe that he is evolving the same way," said Roth. "Our job is to find out how each young man learns, through auditory, visual, or kinesthetic elements, and then tailor our teaching that way. Where we have all evolved at Elite 11 is in also tapping in to their emotional intelligence. To do that, we have to learn about our own. The Elite 11 has allowed Trent to process a lot in his own life, whether it's his son Trevin's death, being a father to a Division I athlete, or being a father figure to a thousand seventeen-year-old quarterbacks each year."

Dilfer, though, left Oregon with as many questions as answers, he admitted. Was he bringing in the right kids? Did the perspective need a little more tilting? Each year brought another downpour of reminders that the times the QBs—his QBs—were living in were changing as fast as the game they were trying to master. He believed, now more than ever, that success in the position he loved so deeply was more about nurture than nature. Still, the latter kept finding ways to torment him as he trudged through his own journey, surrounded by escalating amounts of positive and negative reinforcement and driven by his passion for finding the ideal balance of talent and training— one, he hopes, that will mold the QBs who shape football's future, and their world beyond the game.

# Acknowledgments

I must begin by thanking the entire Elite 11 crew for letting me be a fly on the wall and being patient to answer my every question. That group starts with Trent Dilfer, George Whitfield, Joey Roberts, Yogi Roth, Andy Bark, Brian Stumpf, Kevin O'Connell, Jordan Palmer, Craig Nall, Matt James, Paul Troth, Sione Ta'ufo'ou, Dennis Gile, Charlie Frye, and Quincy Avery as well as Dr. Michael Gervais, Steve Stenstrom, Bucky Brooks, and Joe Germaine.

As for getting the idea off the ground, I am grateful to Nick Khan, who, as always, provided excellent guidance. Nick also connected me with David Vigliano, who, along with Matt Carlini, helped breathe life into the book. Thanks to Dominick Anfuso for believing in it and in me, to Matt Inman for keeping things on track, and to Luke Cyphers for his time, perspective, and wisdom.

Special thanks to Tom House, Adam Dedeaux, Kevin Sumlin, Jake Spavital, June Jones, Hal Mumme, Chip Kelly, Aaron Rodgers, Tommy Moffitt, Brandon Harris, Blake Barrett, Brady White, Travis Waller, Josh Rosen, Rick Town, Cam Cameron, Steve Clarkson, Perry Klein, Gary Klein, Tom Rossley, Billy Liucci, Scott Turner, Norv Turner, Johnny Manziel, Logan Thomas, Ryan Flaherty, Jonathan Niednagel, the Griffins, Archie Manning, Will Proctor, Jeff

Faris, Amish Patel, Greg Biggins, Chris Mortensen, Peter King, Eric Adelson, Ryan Abraham, T. C. Badalato, Dennis Dodd, Pat Forde, Spencer Hall, Stewart Mandel, Tony Moss, Teddy Mitrosilis, Danny O'Neil, Jim Rome, Robert Smith, Andy Staples, Joe Tessitore, Pete Thamel, Ande Wall, Seth Wickersham, and Dan Woike.

Most of all, I want to thank my family for always being there for me.

# Index

Aaron, Hank, 116
Abbott, Jim, 105
Aikman, Troy, 47, 74, 87, 258
Ainge, Danny, 85
Akina, Duane, 158
Allen, Drew, 112, 113, 115
Allen, Kyle, 25, 27, 149, 153, 249, 260
Andrews, James, 122
Applewhite, Major, 179
Arians, Bruce, 287
Ariel, Gideon, 127
Aspay, Cade, 27
Ault, Chris, 156

Banks, Tony, 73
Banner, Joe, 282
Bark, Andy, 4, 5, 53, 58–60, 68, 75, 251
Barker, Drew, 25
Barkley, Charles, 199
Barkley, Matt, 60, 66, 226
Barnett, Blake, 248, 249–50, 257, 291–92
Barr, Anthony, 285
Bartkowski, Steve, 61
Beane, Billy, 108
Beathard, Bobby, 83
Beaty, David, 196, 198, 199
Beck, John, 139, 140

Beckham, Odell, Jr., 205, 229–30
Beckworth, Brad, 196–97, 282, 283
Bedford, Vance, 267
Belichick, Bill, 89, 142
Benjamin, Kelvin, 211
Bernstein, J. B., 129–30
Berra, Yogi, 119
Bevell, Darrell, 34, 49, 161, 168
Bicknell, Jack, Sr., 40
Biggins, Greg, 57, 246
Blough, David, 153–55, 158, 159–60, 168, 169, 170
Boldin, Anquan, 229
Boller, Kyle, 247, 263, 279
Bolton, Kyle, 272
Booty, John David, 48
Booty, Josh, 160, 161, 164
Bortles, Blake, 91, 225, 232, 234, 240, 262, 271, 278, 285
    2014 NFL Draft and, 236–37, 280–81, 283, 284
Boyd, Tajh, 146, 151, 152, 159, 197–98, 203, 287
Braden, Vic, 127
Bradley, Gus, 284
Bradshaw, Terry, 31, 87
Brady, Tom, 5, 12, 42, 47, 69, 88–89, 112, 122, 123, 136, 138, 141, 154, 215, 220, 223, 275, 281

Brees, Drew, xiii, 14, 15, 37, 47, 57, 89,
112, 121–22, 123, 125, 129, 133,
141, 153, 154, 155, 198, 220, 230,
255
Brennan, Colt, 60
Bridgewater, Teddy, 151, 224–25, 227,
233, 236, 237, 239, 240, 283, 284,
287
    NFL Draft prospects of, 151, 278,
    281, 282
    Pro Day of, 269–71, 287
Brohm, Brian, 268
Brooks, Bucky, 226, 273
Brown, Mack, 37–38, 159, 192
Brown, Malcolm, 35
Brown, Tony, 169
Brugler, Dane, 226
Burcham, Neal, 82–83, 92, 93
Burkhardt, Erik, 268, 282, 283, 284
Burnett, Todd, 289

Cameron, Cam, 7, 8, 20, 104, 105,
120–21, 227, 228–32
Cameron, Danny, 8
Cantwell, Hunter, 5–6, 106
Carr, Derek, 277
Carroll, Brennan, 79
Carroll, Pete, 48–50, 79–80
Carter, Maverick, 225
Carter, Virgil, 31
Cassel, Kolney, 92–93
Chang, Timmy, 91
Chavis, John, 231
Chmura, Mark, 89, 90
Clarkson, Anton, 248
Clarkson, Steve, x, 51–57, 58, 59–60,
61–66, 98, 104, 123, 137, 212,
242–43, 244, 246, 248, 249–52,
253, 280, 292
    celebrity of, 61, 245–46, 250
    college playing career of, 51–52
    in creating private QB coaching
        industry, xiii, 56–57, 251, 252
    critics of, 249–51
    Dreammaker brand of, 64, 66,
        243, 244, 245–46
    financial earnings of, 56–57,
        61–62, 66, 245, 251
    marketing savvy of, 53, 54, 56, 62,
        63–64, 65, 252
    P. Klein coached by, 53–56
    7-on-7 league run by, 244–45
    on SoCal QB struggles, 247
Clausen, Casey, 62–63

Clausen, Jim, Sr. (father), 62, 63–64
Clausen, Jimmy (son), 62, 63, 64, 65,
66, 247, 280
Clausen, Rick, 62–63
Clowney, Jadeveon, 283, 284
Cluck, Bob, 126
Colbert, Stephen, 202, 212, 246
Cole, Jason, 246–47
Coley, James, 191
Collier, Stephen, 23–24
Cook, Connor, 100
Cook, Greg, 29, 30–31
Cook, Jason, 189
Corso, Lee, 120, 228
Couch, Tim, 163
Coughlin, Tom, 239
Cousins, Kirk, 284
Cross, Garrett, 72
Cunningham, Randall, 91, 246
Cutler, Jay, 236

Dalton, Andy, 25, 281
Danielson, Gary, 45
Davey, Rohan, 160
Davis, Greg, 192
Dedeaux, Adam, 123, 130–31, 138,
139, 140, 141–42, 144
Dedeaux, Rod, 130, 139
Delhomme, Jake, 174
DeRenne, Coop, 127
DeRuyter, Tim, 42
Devine, Dan, 92
Dilfer, Cass, 171
Dilfer, Maddie, 17
Dilfer, Trent, x–xii, 4, 5, 6, 8, 9, 10,
12–17, 19, 20, 21, 56, 67–78, 81–83,
87, 93–97, 109, 111, 123, 137,
143–44, 145–46, 147, 148, 149, 150,
151, 155, 159, 165, 166, 168–69,
191, 211, 232, 248, 249, 251–52,
253, 256, 257, 259, 260, 275, 289,
290, 291, 292–94
    analytical mind of, 73–74, 170–71
    bonds with players forged by,
        93–94, 96–97, 294
    as critical of Clarkson, 249–50,
        251
    on difficulties and flaws in QB
        evaluations, ix, 11–12, 77, 78,
        79, 81–83, 269
    "Dude Qualities" sought by, 18,
        23, 25, 69, 76, 77–78, 80, 168
    at Elite 11 super Regional event, 2,
        3–4, 5–6, 9, 11–12, 15–17

in Elite 11 "war room" sessions, 21, 22, 23–24, 25–26, 27–28, 79, 152–53
golf played by, 75, 94, 111, 159, 262
as guest speaker at Whitfield's spring-break camp, 261–65
House on, 124–25
injuries of, 70–71, 73
on "nature vs. nurture" in QB development, 12, 77, 143, 154, 294
playing career of, 3, 10–11, 69–71, 72–73, 74, 76, 94–95, 263, 264–65
on QBs "being on balance," 13–15
and son's illness and death, 95–96, 294
"soul-building" exercises endorsed by, 75–78
TDFB and, x–xi, 6, 9–10, 12, 17–20, 22, 23, 25, 26, 27, 96, 145, 169, 235, 250
TV reality show of, x, 4–5, 8, 153–54
as TV sports analyst, 3, 73, 74, 75, 77, 78, 79, 142–43, 251, 269
Twitter account of, 26, 27, 80, 83
Dilfer, Trevin, 95–96, 294
Dodd, Dennis, 64
Donald, Aaron, 284
Drake, 46, 185, 272
Dungy, Tony, 72, 135
Dykes, Sonny, 38

Edwards, Trent, 235–36
Elam, Abe, 224, 233
Elway, Jack, 51, 52
Elway, John, 2, 13, 51, 52, 54, 87, 88, 90, 101, 244, 246
Epstein, Jack, 55
Erickson, Dennis, 54
Evans, Mike, 196, 197, 200, 201, 214, 222, 225, 273, 282, 283, 284, 285

Fajardo, Cody, 178
Fales, David, 151–52, 159
Farmer, Ray, 282
Favre, Brett, 6, 10, 17, 31, 32–34, 42, 48, 49, 87, 161–63, 164, 165, 166, 187, 245, 265, 276
    big hands of, 36–37
    college playing career of, 31–32

"gunslinger" playing style of, 33, 44, 161–62
improvised plays of, 89–90, 161–62, 167
Rodgers as backup QB to, 166–67, 168
Super Bowl audible play of, 89–90
Ferentz, Kirk, 102
Ferguson, Robert, 161–62
Feterik, Kevin, 57
Fisher, Eric, 283
Fisher, Jimbo, 161, 193, 207, 208, 211
Fitch, Nathan "Turtle," 99, 114
Flacco, Joe, 10, 122, 229, 231
Flaherty, Ryan, 213, 214, 217, 225, 238, 240
Flutie, Doug, 40, 42, 276
Flynn, Matt, 49
Foles, Nick, 38, 269, 275, 282
Forcier, Jason, 130
Franco, Julio, 119–20
Frye, Charlie, 170
Fulton, John, 196, 200

Gabbert, Blaine, 240, 268–69, 280
Garcia, Jeff, 61, 110, 260–61, 276
Gardner, Devin, 146, 148–49, 151, 197–98
Germaine, Joe, 6, 10
Gervais, Michael, 146–47, 292
Giavondo, Mike, 137
Gilbert, Justin, 285
Gilbride, Kevin, 83–84
Gile, Dennis, 27, 137, 169, 248–49, 250
Gladwell, Malcolm, 10, 74, 141
Glanville, Jerry, 32
Goldberg, Bernard, 62
Golson, Everett, 202, 204–5
Goodell, Roger, 286
Grbac, Elvis, 73
Gretzky, Wayne, 61, 65
Grier, Will, 23, 149
Griffin, Chase, 98, 99, 112, 272, 290
Griffin, Robert, III, 8–9, 38, 42, 91, 110, 192, 237, 281
Gronkowski, Rob, 290
Gruden, Jon, 135, 270, 285

Haden, Pat, 59
Harris, Brandon, 7–8, 20–21, 25–26, 113, 259–60
Harrison, Jarvis, 37
Harsin, Bryan, 192
Haskell, Gil, 33, 90, 279

Haslam, Jimmy, 282, 286
Hasselbeck, Matt, 33, 73, 265
Hayes, Woody, 1
Heard, Jerrod, 149, 259, 260
Hempel, Rick, 9
Herman, Tom, 7
Hinkley, Mike, 104
Hoge, Merril, 266–67, 268, 269, 271,
    276
Hohensee, Mike, 103
Holiday, Taylor, 9, 26
Holmgren, Mike, 74, 78, 89, 260, 279
Holtz, Lou, 190
House, Tom, xiii, 15, 116–29, 130,
    134, 136, 234, 246, 255
    biomechanics as specialty of, 15,
        121, 122, 123–24, 125, 128–29
    as pitching coach, 118, 120, 121,
        126–27
    pitching lecture of, 116–18,
        119–20, 130, 131–34
    player diets examined by, 121,
        137–38
    playing career of, 116, 126, 127,
        132–33
    scientific research of, 124, 125,
        127–28
    STATT process of, 121–22
    Tebow's training with, 136,
        137–38, 140–42, 143, 144
    3DQB business of, xiii, 138–40,
        143
Howard, Desmond, 159
Hundley, Brett, 36, 249
Hurd, Toney, 210

Irvin, Richie, 62

Jackson, Bo, 159
Jackson, Tavaris, 49
James, LeBron, 46, 63, 64, 157, 186,
    210, 225, 280
James, Matt, 22, 24, 25
Jaworski, Ron, 74, 268, 274
Jennings, Anthony, 260
Jensen, Brock, 212, 214, 218
Joeckel, Luke, 37, 283
Johnson, Bob (father), 4, 58, 59–60, 61,
    68, 104
Johnson, Bret, 58
Johnson, Jerrod, 36
Johnson, Jimmy, 135
Johnson, Magic, 33
Johnson, Patrick, 94, 95

Johnson, Randy, 118, 125
Johnson, Rob (son), 4, 58
Jones, Jerry, 210, 284
Jones, June, 83–88, 90–93
Jones, Landry, 227
Jones, Walter, 17, 165
Juliano, Jeanine, 238, 241

Kaaya, Brad, 25
Kaepernick, Colin, 8–9, 91, 156,
    282
Karam, Jacob, 112, 113, 115
Kelly, Chip, 39–40, 274–76
Kelly, Jim, 51, 87, 90, 92–93
Kiel, Gunner, 82
Kiffin, Lane, 66, 248
King, Peter, 47, 48
Kingsbury, Kliff, 42, 43–44, 46, 47,
    179, 194, 210, 267–68
Kiper, Mel, 260
Kiser, Tom, 101, 102
Kizer, DeShone, 20, 21
Klein, Danny, 52, 55–56
Klein, Perry, 52–56, 252
Knight, Bob, 120, 228

Landry, Jarvis, 229
Leach, Mike, 44, 222
Leaf, Ryan, 83–84, 276, 279
Leard, Ben, 179
LeBeau, Dick, 74
Leftwich, Byron, 33
Leinart, Matt, 60, 130, 247, 251
Lewis, Michael, 108
Lewis, Ray, 165, 223, 260
Lippincott, Liz, 253, 254–55, 257
Locker, Jake, 156, 240, 280, 285
Lofton, James, 217
Loggains, Dowell, 282, 285–86
Lomax, Neil, 146
Loomis, Mickey, 47
Luck, Andrew, 1, 2, 6, 38, 91, 109,
    110, 175, 177–78, 192, 214, 215,
    268, 281, 287
Luck, Oliver, 175–76, 177
Lynch, Jim, 30

McCarron, AJ, 181–82, 186, 206, 208,
    277, 278, 287
McCarthy, Mike, 223
McClain, John, 283
McCoy, Mike, 78, 279
McDaniels, Josh, 222
McGinn, Bob, 164

Mack, Khalil, 284
McKay, J. K., 59
McKay, John, 59
McKinney, Clarence, 201, 209
McQueen, Conner, 197
McShay, Todd, 268, 269, 272
Mangum, Tanner, 82
Manning, Archie, xi, 83, 89, 173,
    174–76, 179, 181
Manning, Cooper, 174, 180
Manning, Eli, 10, 88, 136–37, 174,
    176, 178, 179, 180, 203
Manning, Peyton, xi, 10, 14, 15, 17, 47,
    83, 154, 160, 176, 220, 281, 287
    college playing career of, 172–73,
        176
    "ESTP" personality type of, 87,
        88, 89
    as instructor at Manning Passing
        Academy, 174, 175, 178, 179,
        180
    meticulous preparation of, 172–74,
        176, 178
    at Walsh football camp, 180–81
Manning family, 173, 174, 175–76,
    177, 180, 181, 182–83, 184
Manuel, EJ, 226
Manziel, Johnny, xii, 6, 8–9, 21, 26,
    27, 35–47, 50, 156–57, 176, 192,
    200–201, 203, 207–8, 215, 217, 271,
    282–83, 288, 289
    celebrity and media coverage of,
        45, 46, 112–13, 157, 159, 182,
        183, 184–85, 186, 187–88,
        190–91, 195–96, 197, 199, 200,
        207, 216, 238, 272, 277, 284,
        290
    in Chick-fil-A bowl, 208–9, 210
    college scouting and recruitment
        of, 36, 37, 38, 39–41
    critics and skeptics of, 157–58,
        186, 187, 190, 199, 200, 219,
        238, 261, 266–67, 269, 273,
        274, 276, 277
    in draft camp, 210, 212, 213, 214,
        218–24, 225, 227–28, 230, 259,
        267
    edgy, antihero persona of, 38, 185,
        187, 188, 190–91, 276
    in Elite 11 Counselor's Challenge,
        151, 152
    Elite 11 open forum held by,
        157–59
    Elite 11 tryout of, 8–9, 77

    "gunslinger" and free-wheeling
        playing style of, 44, 46, 195–96,
        222
    high-school playing career of, 35,
        38–39, 43, 156
    injuries of, 205, 209
    late-night partying of, 46, 112,
        182–83, 186, 188, 195, 200,
        209, 210, 276, 277, 290
    legal troubles of, 43–44, 46, 158
    at Manning Passing Academy, 179,
        181, 182–83, 184, 186
    at NFL Combine, 238, 239–40,
        259
    in O'Connell's QB class, 218–24
    off-field distractions of, 98–99,
        112–15, 182–83, 186
    personality type of, 88, 91
    physical build and size of, 35–37,
        38, 39–40, 42, 157, 219, 228,
        230, 237–38
    Pro Day of, 239–40, 259, 271–74,
        282
    signed memorabilia scandal of,
        188, 189, 197
    team camaraderie with, 186–87,
        197
    at Texas A&M, 41–42, 43–47, 88,
        156–57, 186–87, 188–90, 193,
        194, 195–99, 200–201, 205,
        208–10, 220, 221, 229–30, 266,
        267
    Twitter account of, 45, 46, 186,
        188, 200
    in 2013 Heisman race, 205, 206,
        208
    2014 NFL Draft and, xii, 236,
        237, 238, 266, 267–68, 269,
        274, 276, 277, 278, 281, 283,
        284–87
    Whitfield's private coaching of,
        42–43, 98–101, 110, 112–15,
        157, 158, 200, 210, 212, 213,
        214, 216, 219, 220, 225,
        227–28, 259, 261, 267
Manziel, Meri, 187
Manziel, Michelle, 41, 42, 43, 115,
    187, 238
Manziel, Paul, 44, 182, 187, 188, 238
Marchibroda, Ted, 286
Marino, Dan, 13, 51, 63, 90
Marinovich, Marv, 177
Marinovich, Todd, 177, 247
Mariota, Marcus, 40, 205, 275

Mariucci, Steve, 240
Martell, Tate, 244–45
Martin, Mike, 193
Martin, Zack, 284
Martinez, Robert, 38, 39
Matthews, Jake, 37, 45, 283, 284
Mattingly, Bo, 286
Maui'a, Reagan, 85
May, Mark, 190
Mayock, Mike, 240, 268–69, 270, 272,
    278
Mazzone, Noel, 136
Mazzone, Taylor, 136
Means, Natrone, 84
Meggs, Willie, 205, 206
Mettenberger, Zach, 36, 229, 287
Meyer, Urban, 1, 7–8
Miles, Les, 8, 20, 229–30
Miles, Manny, 8
Miller, Chris, 90
Miller, Matt, 278
Milliner, Dee, 46
Mirer, Rick, 34
Moffitt, Tommy, 172–74
Montana, Joe, 62, 64, 69,
    87–88, 92
Montana, Nate, 62, 64–65
Montana, Nick, 65
Moon, Warren, 156
Morris, David, 136–37
Morris, Stephen, 202, 226
Morrison, Dan, 92
Mumme, Hal, 222
Murray, Aaron, 278, 287

Nall, Craig, 6, 19, 26–27, 149, 154–55,
    249
    as backup QB for Packers, 161–65
    college playing career of, 160–61,
        164
Namath, Joe, 13, 52, 69, 87, 244
Neuheisel, Jerry, 180
Neuheisel, Rick, x, xi, 57, 65, 180–81
Newton, Cam, 6, 43, 107, 109, 110,
    240, 269, 280, 282
Newton, Cecil, 107
Niednagel, Jonathan, 83, 84, 85–87,
    88, 89, 90–92, 93
Norton, Kenny, 79
Nussmeier, Doug, 248

O'Brien, Bill, 219, 221, 222, 236, 237
O'Brien, Ken, 146
O'Cain, Mike, 216

O'Connell, Kevin, 213, 225, 227, 229,
    238, 272
    QB class taught by, 214–15, 216,
        218–24
Ogbuehi, Cedric, 37
O'Leary, George, 236, 237
Orsini, Steve, 86
Orton, Kyle, 136

Palmer, Bill, 59
Palmer, Carson, 4, 19–20, 59–60, 138,
    235, 246
Palmer, Jordan, 4, 18–20, 22–23, 24,
    26, 27, 38, 148–49, 155, 225,
    232–37, 240, 251, 271
    charitable work of, 148, 150
    EXOS draft camp run by, 232–35,
        262
    playing career of, 235–36
Paolantonio, Sal, 238, 282, 286
Parcells, Bill, 89, 138
Park, Jacob, 26, 153
Patel, Dinesh, 129–30
Payton, Sean, 47
Pedersen, Jake, 48
Pederson, Doug, 161, 162, 163
Peterson, Adrian, 198
Pettine, Mike, 282, 286
Petty, Bryce, 205, 259, 289
Peyton, Sean, 230
Phenix, Perry, 94
Plunkett, Jim, 61
Pope, Edward, 201
Price, Keith, 232
Proctor, Will, 175, 178–79
Prukop, Dakota, 112, 113, 115
Pryor, Terrelle, 246

Quinn, Brady, 105, 232

Ramsdell, John, 105
Ramsey, Tom, 246
Randall, Jerrard, 40
Randle El, Antwaan, 230–31
Rees, Erik, 150
Rees, Jessie, 150
Reeves, Dan, 88
Reid, Andy, 218, 260, 279
Reynolds, Gary, 40
Rhoden, Rick, 94
Richner, Matt, 278–82
Rivers, Philip, 12, 104, 231
Roberts, Joey, 22, 24, 27, 67–68, 76,
    153

Robinson, Greg, 284
Rodgers, Aaron, 10, 12, 14, 15, 16–17, 91, 164, 165–68, 244, 268, 272, 281
  as Elite 11 instructor, 159–60, 165
  Favre studied by, 17, 166–67, 168
  first NFL preseason of, 163–64
  as ignored by college recruiters, xi, 16, 72, 112, 156, 160, 165
Roethlisberger, Ben, 6, 10, 25, 43, 47, 106–7, 287
Rollinson, Bruce, 60
Romo, Tony, 36–37, 284
Roper, Kurt, 176
Rose, Greg, 124
Rosen, Charles, 253
Rosen, Josh, 252–58, 259, 290–92, 293
Rossley, Tom, 29–30, 31, 32–37, 40, 41–42, 49, 237
Roth, Yogi, 49, 60, 79–81, 96–97, 146, 253, 257–58, 292, 293–94
  in Elite 11 "war room" evaluations, 22, 25, 79, 291
Rubenzer, Luke, 24, 27–28, 149, 249
Russell, Jamarcus, 235–36
Ryan, Matt, 15, 259
Ryan, Nolan, 118, 125, 133, 143
Ryan, Rex, 231

Saban, Nick, 45, 47, 186, 193, 200–201
Sada, Jason, 9–10
Salisbury, Sean, 110
Sanchez, Mark, 4, 247
Sarkisian, Steve, 245, 248
Schneider, John, 48, 50
Schottenheimer, Brian, 121, 229
Schottenheimer, Marty, 229, 231
Schroeder, Jay, 246
Scott, Matt, 192–93, 239
Shanahan, Kyle, 282
Sharpe, Shannon, 94–95
Shaw, David, 256
Sherman, Mike, 32, 35, 36, 37, 40, 41, 42, 163, 164, 168
Sills, David, V, 65–66, 245, 248, 253
Simms, Phil, 74, 87, 109
Singh, Rinku, 129–30
Singletary, Mike, 51
Smith, Akili, 163
Smith, Brett, 232, 234
Smith, Geno, 47, 194
Smith, Mark, 39
Smith, Will, 61, 65

Snoop Dogg, 61, 186
Snyder, Mark, 209, 221
Spahn, Warren, 119
Spavital, Jake, 47, 188, 194–95, 196, 198, 199, 201, 209
Speights, Hank, 272
Stafford, Matthew, 1, 156
Stanton, Drew, 19
Stanton, Johnny, 150
Stenstrom, Steve, 1–3, 4, 9, 58, 75, 289
Stevens, Gary, 59
Stokley, Brandon, 174
Stumpf, Brian, 22, 23, 25, 147–48, 156, 247
Suh, Ndamukong, 159
Sumlin, Kevin, 42, 43–44, 45, 46–47, 185, 186, 187, 190, 193–94, 195, 196, 197, 198–99, 200, 208–10, 226

Tannehill, Ryan, 35–36, 38, 41
Tarkenton, Fran, 87, 245, 276
Tebow, Tim, xiii, 1, 46, 91, 106, 134–38, 142–44, 156, 184, 187, 267, 268, 281–82
  debate over QB merits of, 135–36, 142, 143, 144
  House's training of, 136, 137–38, 140–42, 143, 144
  throwing mechanics of, 135, 136, 137, 138, 140
Tedford, Jeff, 69–72, 74, 159, 263, 264
  as mentor to Rodgers, 165–67
Teevens, Buddy, 178
Te'o, Manti, 206
Tessitore, Joe, 184, 185
Theder, Roger, 60–61
Thomas, Logan, 157, 210, 215–18, 261, 287
  college playing career of, 203, 216–17
  in draft camp, 212, 213, 214, 217–18, 225, 226, 259
  inconsistant performance of, 216–17, 226–27, 261, 277
  at NFL Combine, 239, 240–41, 259
  NFL debate over merits of, 215–17, 226, 241
  NFL Draft prospects of, 43, 203, 216, 225–26, 277–78
  in Senior Bowl, 214, 218, 225, 226–27, 278
  Whitfield's training of, 203, 213, 214, 216, 217–18, 225, 226, 259

Thomas, Pete, 105, 106, 107–8
Town, Rick, Jr., 247–48, 257, 292–93
Tressel, Jim, 102
Troth, Paul, 23
Turner, Norv, 6, 13, 78, 270
Turner, Scott, 6, 270, 287

Vick, Michael, 52, 282
Vollnogle, Gene, 55

Wade, Darius, 26–27
Waller, Bridgette, 244
Waller, Travis, 243–44, 246, 257, 292
Walsh, Bill, 2, 30–31, 180–81, 259
Ward, Hines, 230
Warner, Kurt, 160, 272, 273–74
Watford, David, 259, 261, 263
Watkins, Sammy, 284
Watson, DeShaun, 149, 153
Watson, Shawn, 107
Watts, Tyler, 179
Weeden, Brandon, 47, 194
Weinke, Chris, 136, 225, 227, 269–70
Weis, Charlie, 64
White, Brady, 244, 245, 246, 249, 257, 292
White, Sean, 24–25, 27, 149, 169–70
Whitfield, David, 101
Whitfield, George, Jr., xii–xiii, 6, 18, 21, 26, 101–15, 139, 151, 156–57, 189, 201–5, 210, 215, 225–26, 234–35, 238, 251, 259, 277, 289
    accessible metaphors used by, 99–100, 111, 238
    Chargers internship of, 104–5
    college coaching career of, 102–3
    critics of, 110–11, 249, 260–61
    draft camps of, xiii, 210, 212–15, 217–18, 219, 224–25, 227–28, 259, 267
    as ESPN on-air analyst, xiii, 190, 201–3
    Golson trained by, 204–5
    growing reputation and celebrity of, 107, 109–10, 190, 201–2, 224, 259, 260
    Manziel coached by, 42–43, 98–101, 110, 112–15, 157, 158, 200, 210, 212, 213, 214, 216, 219, 220, 225, 227–28, 259, 261, 267
    Manziel's Pro Day and, 271–73, 274
    at NFL Combine, 238–39, 240–41
    NFL Draft Day (2014) and, 285, 287
    playing career of, 101–2, 103
    Pop Warner QBs coached by, 103–4
    QB drills created by, 99, 100, 107–9, 213, 225, 227–28
    Roethlisberger coached by, 106–7
    spring-break QB camp hosted by, 259–60, 261–65
    on "superhero quality" of great QBs, 111–12
    Thomas coached by, 203, 213, 214, 216, 217–18, 225, 226
Whitfield, George, Sr., 99, 101
Wilkins, Manny, 24, 26
Wilson, Russell, xii, 14–15, 27, 37, 47–49, 52, 69, 91, 218, 220, 259, 276, 281, 282
Winston, Jameis, xii, 82, 96, 152, 191, 205–8, 289–90
    in BCS Title Game, 210–11
    recruitment of, 191–93
    in 2013 Heisman race, 205–6, 207, 208
Wolf, Ron, 48
Woods, Tiger, 166

Young, Vince, 158, 268, 277

Zampese, Ken, 235
Zimmer, Mike, 287
Zorn, Jim, 262